TRAIL RIDING

A Complete Guide

Audrey Pavia

HBH **Howell**
Book House™

This book is printed on acid-free paper. ⊗

Howell Book House
Published by Wiley Publishing, Inc., Hoboken, New Jersey

For general information on our other products and services or to obtain technical support please contact our Customer Care Department within the U.S. at (800) 762-2974, outside the U.S. at (317) 572-3993 or fax (317) 572-4002.

Wiley also publishes its books in a variety of electronic formats. Some content that appears in print may not be available in electronic books. For more information about Wiley products, please visit our Website at www.wiley.com.

Library of Congress Cataloging-in-Publication Data:

Pavia, Audrey.
  Trail riding : a complete guide / Audrey Pavia.
    p. cm.
  Includes bibliographical references (p.   ).
  ISBN-13: 978-0-7645-7913-4
  ISBN-10: 0-7645-7913-4 (pbk.)
  1. Trail riding. I. Title.
  SF309.28.P38 2005
  798.2'3—dc222   005003955

Printed in the United States of America

10 9 8 7 6 5 4 3 2 1

Book design by Melissa Auciello-Brogan, with Beth Brooks
Cover design by Wendy Mount
Book production by Wiley Publishing, Inc. Composition Services

To Snickers,
for showing me how great a good trail horse can be

CONTENTS

ACKNOWLEDGMENTS

For making this book happen: Grace Freedson, Roxane Cerda, and Lynn Northrup. For teaching me: Shannon Sand of Sand Bar Training in Wildomar, California; Sue Kellogg of Kellogg Equestrian Academy in Costa Mesa, California; Marc Hedgpeth and Lisa Smith of Equestrian Services in Lake Forest, California; and Jennifer Nice, friend and trail rider extraordinaire. For inspiration: Randy Mastronicola, Karen Keb Acevedo, Carrie Garufis, Dee Monkhouse, Stephanie Vrabel and her boy Flash, Terri Tuccillo, and the wonderful Oash. For help with the manuscript and for making me a healthy trail rider: Ann Boroch, N.D., CHt. For giving me a wonderful trail horse: Nicole Rivera. For being a haven for trail riders: the City of Norco, California; and for protecting the trails, the Norco Horsemen's Association. For all their help: Carol Ruprecht of the Ride and Tie Association, Kate Riorden of the American Endurance Ride Conference, Candace Brown of Sapelo Appaloosas, Becky Siler, Heidi Pavia-Watkins, and Rod Watkins.

INTRODUCTION

There is something about the outside of a horse that is good for the inside of a man. Winston Churchill wrote those words in the last century, and he knew what he was talking about. Horses enchant us, move us, and heal us. We are awed by their beauty, their power, and most of all, their willingness to be our partners, no matter what we ask of them.

Never is this truer than when it comes to trail riding. Experiencing nature on the back of horse can be a spiritual experience, and when that horse is your own, the feeling is downright magical.

Trail riding has become the most popular equine activity in North America, and it's not hard to see why. With today's stressful world and overwhelming technology, people are seeking more ways to get back to our roots, which lie in nature. Horses are the perfect companions for this journey. They are our link to the Earth.

Although trail riding these days is a leisure activity, there was a time when *everyone* rode the trail. Before engine-driven vehicles took us to our destinations, it was the horse that carried us, taking us wherever we needed to go.

Horses dutifully carried the Europeans through the New World from the moment of Columbus's discovery. The explorers blazed trails with their hardy mounts, traveling through forests and deserts that had not seen the mark of hoof prints since the Ice Age, when horses became extinct in the Americas. Years later, the West was settled by men and women who rode horses on new trails, often to their peril. Long before this, Native Americans were experts on the trail, transporting their families and searching for game from the backs of well-trained trail horses.

In today's world, recreational trail riders carry on the time-honored tradition of traveling on horseback. And although we now have trains, planes, and automobiles to take us from place to place, no feeling is more wonderful than journeying through life on the back of a horse.

Part I

GETTING STARTED

Chapter 1

LAYING A GOOD FOUNDATION

The sight of riders mounted on quiet horses enjoying the beauty of nature is one that appeals to just about everyone who enjoys the outdoors. When most people see others riding along on the trail, they get the urge to do it themselves.

Just as with any sport, horseback riding takes knowledge and skill. Most people wouldn't think of putting on a pair of skis and going down a monster slope without learning how to ski first. The same is true of horseback riding. If you know what you are doing before you embark on that first ride through the woods, both you and your horse will have a safer and more enjoyable time.

Unlike basic skiing, however, horseback riding can take longer to learn. Horses are not skis—they have personalities all their own, and learning to get on just about any horse and ride it can take years of training.

Of course, you don't need to devote the rest of your life to riding lessons in order to enjoy casual trail riding. But you will need basic instruction on how to ride a horse if you plan to enjoy your time in the saddle. You'll find advice on getting good instruction in the pages that follow.

Horse Looks

Before you actually get on a horse for the first time—or, if you've already ridden, before you embark on your new hobby of trail riding—you need to learn the basics when it comes to horses. The best place to start is with the parts of the horse. While it may seem silly at first—after all, you know where the head and tail are—you'll soon discover that the horse world has its own language. If you want to understand what horse people are talking about and have any hope of keeping up with the conversation, you'll need to know some of the lingo. (appendix A, "Glossary," can help with this, too.)

Take a look at the following diagram and do your best to memorize the various parts of the horse. It will help you a lot when you people say things like "His hocks are sore" or "She has mud on her fetlocks."

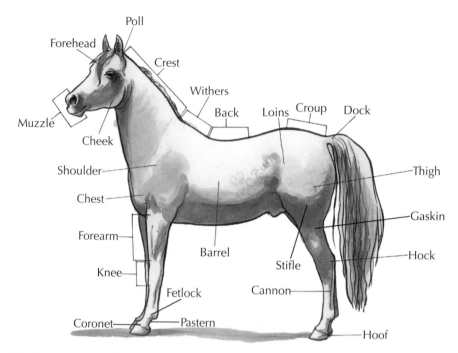

Getting to know the horse.

Once you know the names for the different parts of the horse, you are ready for a brief lesson in *conformation*. The conformation, or build of a horse, affects the animal's ability to move and maintain soundness throughout his life. This is especially important in a trail horse, particularly if you plan to do a lot of riding. A horse that is well put together and sound will be able to go longer without any leg, back, or other problems.

The best way to tell the difference between good conformation and poor conformation is to look at a lot of horses. Horses whom the average person perceives as beautiful, such as Cass Ole, the horse that played the Black Stallion in the movie of the same name, or Roy Rogers's horse Trigger, are pleasant to look at in large part because they have good conformation. Looking at well-built, well-bred horses such as these will help you develop an eye for good conformation.

Horses with good conformation not only have balance, but legs with all the correct angles. Their croups are properly sloped, and their heads are well shaped. It takes time, experience, and study to learn the finer points of equine conformation, and is something you can develop as you get more involved in the sport of trail riding.

When looking at horses, you'll eventually learn to tell the differences in their heights. Horse heights are measured in *hands*, with each hand equaling four inches. The measurement starts from the ground and stops at the top of the horse's withers. The average horse is about 15 hands high (that's about 60 inches, or 5 feet).

COLORS

One of the qualities all horses share is a distinct coat coloration. Horses come in many different colors, and each of these colors has a name. It helps to be able to identify horses when you know the names of their colors, so learning horse colors is a must when delving into any equine sport.

Six horse colors are the most common in the horse world. If you know these six, you'll be in good shape:

1. *Bay.* Brown with a black mane and tail. The brown can be anything from a deep red to a chocolate color. The famous racehorse Seabiscuit was a bay.

2. *Chestnut.* Any shade of red with a similarly colored mane and tail. The great Secretariat was a chestnut.

3. *Gray.* Any shade of white with gray points on the legs and/or muzzle, to a dark, steel gray. The Lone Ranger's horse Silver was a gray.

4. *Buckskin or dun.* A tan coloring, usually with a black mane and tail. Dun horses have a dark stripe down their backs with this coloration, while buckskins do not. Dale Evans, partner to Roy Rogers, had a horse named Buttermilk who was a buckskin.

5. *Palomino.* A light to medium yellowish coloring with a white mane and tail. Roy Rogers's horse Trigger was a palomino.

6. *Black.* Just like it sounds: a black coloration, like that of the horse in the movie *The Black Stallion.*

PATTERNS AND MARKINGS

Two distinct coat patterns can also be seen in some horses, and are specific to certain breeds. The first is the pinto pattern, which consists of dark patches against a white background or white patches against a dark background. This pattern is found in the Paint breed, the Saddlebred, the Tennessee Walking Horse, and certain pony breeds, among others.

The other common coat pattern is found in the Appaloosa and Pony of the America breeds in the United States. This Appaloosa pattern comes in a variety of subpatterns, most of which feature egg-shaped spots in a variety of configurations.

Markings are another important part of horse identification. The most common facial markings are the blaze, star, bald, snip, and stripe. On the legs, the sock and stocking are most often seen. The following drawings show various facial markings.

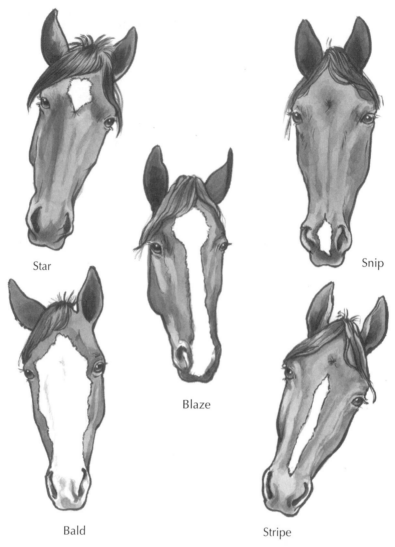

Common horse facial markings.

Breeds

Horses have been among humans for thousands of years, giving us plenty of time to develop hundreds of breeds. When it comes to trail riding in the United States, however, only a handful of breeds are commonly used. This doesn't mean that other breeds don't make good trail horses. It just means that when you are riding American trails, these are the breeds you are most likely to see:

- *American Quarter Horse.* The most popular horse breed in the world, the American Quarter Horse is famous for its ability as a trail mount. Quarter Horses are known for being sturdy, gentle, and quiet, and often make good horses for beginning riders.

- *American Paint Horse.* The pinto version of the Quarter Horse, the Paint is descended from the Quarter Horse breed and shares many of the same qualities, along with a colorful coat.

- *Arabian.* Originally bred by the Boudins of the Arabian Desert, this ancient breed was developed for its stamina as a long-distance mount. Arabians are popular trail horses, especially for competition.

- *Appaloosa.* Developed in the Pacific Northwest, the colorful Appaloosa is renowned for its abilities as a trail horse.

- *Tennessee Walking Horse.* Once bred to carry plantation owners in the deep South, the Tennessee Walking Horse features a smooth four-beat gait that is comfortable to ride for hours on end.

- *Thoroughbred.* Though most Thoroughbreds are bred to race or jump, many also make good trail horses.

- *Morgan.* Known for its versatility, this compact American breed is hardy and great on the trail.

All the breeds mentioned here are full-sized horses averaging anywhere from 14.2 to 16 hands high or more, but ponies—small horses that measure less than 14.2 hands high—can make great trail mounts too. A number of the larger pony breeds make excellent trail mounts for lightweight adult riders or older children, and smaller ponies can be good trail companions for smaller kids.

Equine Personalities

When learning about the psychology of horses, one aspect of these beautiful creatures is most important to keep in mind: Horses are prey animals. Before domestication, their ancestors were hunted by both humans and four-legged predators on a constant basis. Nature gave the horse incredible skills when it comes to self-preservation, the greatest being the ability to escape danger with considerable speed. Despite thousands of years of domestication, the horse still maintains its vigilant ways. Consequently, most horses will flee first and ask questions later.

The horse's tendency to bolt and run when faced with something it perceives as scary is probably more relevant to trail riders than to riders in other disciplines. Trail horses are asked to face all kinds of potentially terrifying objects as they traverse the roads and trails we have created. Something as benign to us as a plastic grocery bag floating in the breeze can be perceived as

Spending time around horses is a good way to learn about their behavior and personalities.

a horse-eating monster by many equines. The key to dealing with this reality is to find a relatively calm horse to ride (some horses are more fearful than others), help teach the horse you have that he can trust you and shouldn't be afraid of much, and learn to deal with situations where the horse is scared and there isn't much you can do to change his perception at the moment.

A horse's breed will also affect his qualities as a trail horse—some breeds tend to be spookier than others. But the most important aspect of any trail horse is his personality. Just like people, horses are individuals with distinct likes and dislikes. Some horses love trail riding; others loathe it. Some are indifferent, and will just plod along until it's time to head back to the barn. Horses who love trail riding are the most fun to ride because they are enthusiastic and willing. Those who could take it or leave it will get you where you want to go but you might have to do a bit more work to get them there. Horses who hate trail riding will make your life unpleasant by doing things like spooking, refusing to cross obstacles, and being generally difficult. (See chapter 3, "Finding a Horse to Ride," for details on choosing a good trail horse.)

The work that horses are asked to do in a riding arena varies considerably from what they are expected to deal with on the trail. Some horses only feel comfortable within the security of an arena and find trail riding to be a terrifying ordeal. Others dislike the arena because they get bored and much prefer a trail ride where they can see different things and not have to work so hard.

Teamwork

Every form of riding requires that the horse and rider function as a team, but in trail riding, this is even more important than in other disciplines. Trail riding means many hours spent in the saddle on the same horse, often in challenging situations and new environments.

Horses are amazing animals in that they are capable of forming close bonds with humans, including the ones they carry on their backs. People who love horses often have a profound love of trail riding because it enables them to spend many hours in close contact with a horse, enjoying nature and building mutual trust.

The love and closeness that can develop between a horse and rider who spend many hours on the trail is hard to describe. You almost have to experience it to understand what it means. Something about the horse's nature makes him open to this tremendous bond. In essense, he is the perfect wilderness companion.

When it comes to work in general, horses are a lot like people. Some like to have a job and some don't. A horse's attitude toward work depends on the horse's innate personality, the kind of training he's had in the past, the way he is treated when he works, and his physical capabilities. Most horses, if asked, would prefer to stand out in a pasture all day with their buddies munching on grass. Most are willing to work when asked, though, which is what makes them such endearing creatures.

The bottom line is that the more you know about horses and the more training and experience you have received both on and off the ground, the better you will get along with most horses. If you are a good rider, you will be able to convince most horses that they should listen to you and do as they are told. Horses respect authority, and if they sense that you know what you are doing, they will often do as you ask.

Horses Are Like Kids

It's easy to understand horses if you think in terms of children. Along with personality, age, training, and experience play a big part in what makes up a horse's demeanor and attitude.

Horses, like kids, are immature when they are young. They tend to have short attention spans, can be a bit bratty, and often resist authority. Although past experiences play a big factor in determining a horse's attitude and behavior (horses with extensive training and exposure to different situations from a young age are often the easiest to work with), age is crucial. In general, young horses—that is, those under the age of 4 or 5—tend to be immature and lacking in experience. Middle-aged horses ranging from 6 to 12 years can be either mature or immature, depending on their level of training and experience. Older horses aged 13 to 30 tend to be easygoing and laid back. Of course, these are generalizations, and individual horses may not fit into these descriptions. But these age guidelines can serve as good general rules when thinking about horses.

Training is a crucial part of any horse's makeup. Horses should be handled shortly after birth to get used them to humans. They should be trained to wear a halter and eventually to lead alongside their dams. Horses should be taught a good work ethic from a young age, meaning they learn from the time they are young that they have a job to do. Horses with this kind of training often do best when asked to do new kinds of work and handle new situations.

Regardless of a horse's age, it's important that the horse respect your authority and obey you, both on the ground and in the saddle. This doesn't mean you have to be a brute who beats up on horses; doing so will only earn you fear and distrust. You simply have to be firm and confident when you handle them. If you are unsure of yourself, most horses will pick up on this quickly and take advantage of the situation. Horses are herd animals, and they respect authority since every herd has a leader. If you don't assume the position of authority, the horse will assume it for you.

How does all this relate to trail riding? Knowing how horses think and how to relate to them is your first step to learning to enjoy the wonders of riding the trail. Before you embark on your new hobby, learn as much as you can about horses in general. Watch horses when they are being ridden and when they are in their stalls or hanging out in a pasture. Studying their behaviors and attitudes will give you a leg up when it comes time to climb into the saddle yourself.

Chapter 2

GETTING EXPERIENCE IN THE SADDLE

W hen you see people riding in the movies or on TV, it looks pretty easy. The actors just seem to leap onto the horse and take off at a gallop. What you may not realize is that these actors—or stunt people, in many cases—had to take riding lessons before they could just hop on and take off. In fact, many of them have been riding for years, which is why it looks easy when they ride.

If you want to enjoy your time in the saddle and get the most out of trail riding, you must learn how to ride. Much of that learning should be formal instruction, but time in the saddle is also key. The trick is to make sure the time you spend riding is quality time—that is, in situations where you will learn and gain valuable experience on horseback.

To Rent or Not to Rent?

Thanks to the proliferation of rental stables that provide horses for rent by the hour, many people who want to trail ride use this outlet for their first experience. And why not? The temptation is great to just hand over $15 or $20, hop on a horse, and go for a ride.

While renting a horse by the hour might seem like a good way to enjoy the trail and get some experience on horseback, for many people, this way of trail riding often proves to be an unpleasant experience.

Take Larry, for example. He had always wanted to go on a trail ride, and when his girlfriend suggested that they rent some horses at a stable while on vacation and go for a ride through the mountains, it sounded like a great idea.

Larry paid his money and was hoisted up on top of a large horse who appeared to be half asleep as he stood tied to a fence. The trail guide, a 16-year-old girl on her summer vacation, took Larry and his girlfriend out onto the trail. Larry was given minimal instruction on how to control the horse (pull back on the reins to stop and kick to go was all he was told) before the trio left for their ride, and no one bothered to notice that Larry's saddle was way too small for him.

Once out on the trail, the guide decided it would be fun to gallop. She spurred her horse into a run, and Larry's and his girlfriend's horses took off in turn. Larry, whose balance was poor because he'd never been taught to ride, bounced around in the saddle and gripped the horn for dear life. He felt like the horse was out of control, and tried to pull back on the reins as he'd been told to do, but the horse ignored him. By the time the guide slowed her horse to a walk, Larry was hanging half out of the saddle and wishing he'd never gotten on a horse in his life.

Cathy had a similar experience. On a lark, a few of her girlfriends decided it would fun to go on a trail ride. They rented horses at a local stable and a man on horseback served as their guide. Ten minutes into the ride, the horse Cathy was riding (if you could call it riding since she had no idea how to control the horse) sidled up to a tree and tried to rub her off on the trunk. Cathy screamed in terror as the horse scraped her back and forth in an attempt to get her off his back. Cathy had to be rescued by the guide, who ended up leading the horse through the entire ride to keep him from dislodging Cathy from the saddle.

Chances are, if you are reading this book, you have never had one of these unpleasant riding experiences. If you had, you more than likely would not be interested in taking up trail riding as a hobby.

The kind of problems Larry and Cathy experienced are, unfortunately, very common in situations where horses are rented by the hour. The reasons are many. First off, when you rent a horse by the hour, you are not paying for a riding lesson. You are simply paying to sit on a horse for an hour. Consequently, you are not shown how to sit correctly in the saddle, how to properly control the horse, or how to manage should a problem arise. On top of this, you are often dealing with horses who are poorly trained, or have learned bad habits from having inexperienced riders on them day in and day out. Horses aren't stupid, and many of them will find a way to take advantage of the situation to make their lives easier, if they can. These horses have also been given the wrong cues by inexperienced riders so many times, they no long pay any attention to the rider.

The point here is that you should avoid getting your riding experience from rental stables. Not all of them are inappropriate for novice riders, but most of them are. Instead, you should learn to ride and garner experience on horseback in a formal lesson situation. Good riding instructors are experienced at teaching beginning riders, and will have the know-how to help you learn to balance on the horse and give the proper cues. They will provide you with a horse for learning who is gentle, easy to ride, and devoid of dangerous habits.

A formal lesson program with a good instructor will provide you with a safe opportunity to learn to ride. You will enjoy yourself a lot more if you learn to ride on a nice horse in a controlled environment. And just think—you won't have to worry about getting scraped off on a tree!

Riding Basics

Before you begin riding lessons, it's a good idea to get a general idea of what horseback riding entails. A bit of academic knowledge can go a long way in helping you understand what your instructor is trying to communicate when you are actually up on the horse.

Let's start with the different disciplines available to equestrians. Since you'll be doing mostly trail riding, you will probably end up in a Western saddle. Western saddles, first developed by the Mexican *charros* in the nineteenth century and later adapted by American cowboys, were designed for working riders who were herding and tending cattle for many hours at a time. Western riding, done in a Western saddle, calls for a relatively long stirrup (meaning your legs will hang down with minimal bend in the knee) and both reins generally to be held in one hand. Some riders hold the reins in their left hand, while others hold the reins in their right. In traditional Western riding, the left hand is used to hold the reins so the right hand will be free to throw a lasso over a cow's head. Holding the reins in the right hand is a relatively newer trend.

Western saddles are designed to keep the rider securely in the seat, which is why they are so popular with many trail riders, particularly novices. The horn on the Western saddle provides something to grab on to if need be, and the deeper seat helps holds the rider in when the horse is moving.

English riding is the other option in a learning discipline. English riding came from Europe, primarily England, hence the name. English saddles are smaller and flatter than Western saddles, and call for a shorter stirrup and more bend in the knee. In English riding, the rider holds a rein in each hand.

Within the category of English riding are three other subdisciplines: hunt seat, dressage, and saddle seat. Hunt seat saddles are used for jumping, and are the most popular type of English saddle. Dressage saddles are used for the dressage discipline, which involves riding the horse in a way that utilizes both precision and obedience. Saddle seat saddles are primarily used in the show ring and are associated with a certain type of very animated movement on the part of the horse, although some people do trail ride in saddle seat saddles.

For many people, it takes more experience to stay secure in an English saddle. You have less saddle to hold you in, and so you must compensate with good balance.

(For more information on Western and English saddles, see chapter 4, "Tacking Up.")

Whether you are in a Western or English saddle, the basics of equitation, or how you sit in the saddle, are the same. You should be sitting up straight, with your shoulders back and not rounded. The two seat bones in the lower part of your pelvis should make contact with the saddle. Your leg should be directly below you so that you could draw an imaginary vertical line from the point of your ear through your shoulders and hips and down to your ankle, as shown in the following figure.

Proper equitation.

The position of your hands and the way you hold the reins will vary depending on your chosen discipline.

The basic cues for the horse are virtually the same in Western riding as they are in English. To ask the horse to go forward, the rider squeezes the horse with the calf of the leg. To stop, the rider gently pulls back on the reins and says, "Ho." To turn a horse in Western riding where the reins are held in one hand, the rider moves his or her hand in the direction he or she wants the horse to go. This causes the rein on the opposite side to make contact with the horse's neck. This is called "neck reining."

In English riding, turning the horse requires pulling slightly on the rein that is on the side that you want her to go, while using the opposite leg to apply pressure.

As you can probably see from reading these descriptions, it's best to learn these basics while you are actually on the horse, being guided by a qualified instructor. So much of riding is *feeling*. You can read about how to ride a horse all day long, but you won't really know how to do it until you get up there and learn how to feel it.

Taking Lessons

Hopefully, you are convinced that formal lessons are the best way to learn how to ride. In a formal riding program, you'll learn everything you need to know to control the horse so you can enjoy trail riding.

Your first task is to decide which discipline you prefer to learn. Western is the most popular discipline for trail riding. If you only wish to trail ride, consider learning Western. If you think you might like to branch out into jumping in an arena environment, then English is the way to go. Whichever discipline you choose, the basic skills of riding will be the same. Don't feel like whatever discipline you pick now will be what you'll be stuck with for life.

If you are unsure of which discipline to take, try them both and see which one you like best.

Another option is to find an instructor who teaches lessons on the trail. This instructor may have you ride either English or Western, and will conduct most of your riding lessons on the trail once you are competent enough to handle the horse outside an arena.

Before you start your lessons, it will be helpful to get a sense of what you will learn. Your instructor will probably start out with lessons on how to sit properly on the horse and how to hold the reins. Next, you'll learn how to make the horse go forward, how to stop the horse, and how to turn the horse.

As with most learning situations, you'll start out slow and work your way up to a faster speed. Your first several lessons will probably be only at the walk. This is the slowest gait for a horse, and will permit you the most security and control as you learn the basics.

Once you have developed a sense of balance in the saddle and are able to control the horse at the walk, your instructor will probably begin teaching you to ride at the trot. The trot is faster than a walk, and is a two-beat gait, similar to when you jog. Many beginners find the trot a bit difficult because it can be bouncy. Each horse has her own way of trotting, based on the way she's built and her personality. You may find yourself on a bouncy horse or a smooth horse. Either way, you'll probably find the trot a bit uncomfortable until you learn how to balance yourself and control the horse at this speed. (If you are learning one of the English disciplines, your instructor will teach you how to *post,* which will enable you to move up and down with the rhythm of the horse at the trot.)

Before you move up to the canter, which is a much slower version of the galloping you see at the racetrack, your instructor will probably work with you at the trot for an extended period of time to make certain you have a good sense of balance in the saddle. He or she will also want to be sure that you have mastered the ability to control your horse at the trot.

Each riding instructor has his or her own way of teaching, and methods will vary. Your instructor may have you ride without stirrups or on a lunge line to

Formal lessons with a qualified instructor are the best way to learn how to properly ride a horse.

help you learn balance in the saddle. He or she may have you do a number of other balancing exercises to help you learn to stay in the saddle. These types of exercises are more common among instructors in the English disciplines, although Western instructors also have their own ways of teaching balance and control to new riders.

Another important aspect of horsemanship that an instructor should teach you is how to handle the horse from the ground. You must learn to groom your horse, clean out her hooves, saddle her, bridle her, and lead her. You'll need to learn to "catch" a horse in her stall or paddock and put a halter on the horse. You should also learn to *lunge* a horse, which is a technique of exercising a horse without riding it. In lunging, you stand in the center of a circle with a long rope (around 25 feet) attached to the horse's halter or bridle. The horse goes around you in a circle at the three gaits of walk, trot, and canter, at your command. Lunging is useful in helping younger or excitable horses release extra energy before you get on their backs. It's also a valuable training tool.

If you have been working with your horse at a stable and riding in an arena all this time, you might be wondering when you can actually go on a trail ride! After all, that's what you really want to do.

It's important to realize that before you can safely take a horse out into the wilderness or on suburban trails, you need to learn how to control that horse in a controlled environment like an arena. If you have issues with balance or control, you'll want to get a handle on these problems while you are in the confines of an arena with an instructor who can help you, rather than out on the street with a cement truck careening in your direction.

FINDING A GOOD INSTRUCTOR

Probably the trickiest part about taking riding lessons is finding a good instructor. Unlike doctors, psychologists, or even hairdressers, riding instructors are not licensed in the United States. Essentially, anyone can hang up a shingle and call himself or herself a horse trainer or riding instructor. So how do you know if you are going to someone who knows what he or she is doing? After all, you are going to want an instructor who has good lesson horses so you can learn safely, is a good teacher so you'll understand what he or she is trying to tell you, and is someone who knows exactly what a beginner needs to learn.

Watching Horses

It's vital to get experience in the saddle before you embark on your trail riding career, but it's also important to spend time *watching* horses. You'll be amazed at how much you can learn about equine behavior and how to handle these beautiful creatures if you just sit back and take them in.

Seize the opportunity to study horses and their actions whenever you can. If you are taking riding lessons, come early or stay late just to hang out with the horses. Or go to a local riding stable and watch how the horses act when they are tied, waiting to be ridden. Study them in their stalls or paddocks, and watch how they act when they are under saddle. Get a picture of how they interact. The way horses behave toward one another is a good clue to what goes on inside the equine mind.

Just spending time sitting and watching horses will help you absorb the essence of these animals. You'll get a sense of their different personalities, their likes and dislikes, and how they express their emotions. Some of the greatest riders in the world acquired their deep understanding of horses just by being around them.

Observing horses will give you an innate sense of the animal you are trusting to carry you through the wilderness as you begin your endeavors in trail riding. Take a few moments to study them whenever you can. It will be time well spent.

Finding a good instructor is a three-step process. First, you need to get the names of one or more instructors. Next, you should visit these individuals, speak to them, and watch them give a lesson. Finally, take a lesson yourself with the instructor before you make your final decision.

The first place to look for a good riding instructor is with the Certified Horsemanship Association (CHA). The CHA is an organization based in Texas that certifies riding instructors in all the equine disciplines around the United States and Canada. CHA certification is voluntary on the part of the instructor, and requires that the instructor be evaluated by two CHA clinicians at a five- to seven-day certification clinic. Clinicians watch instructors teach at least four lessons, give a riding evaluation, take a written test, and participate in workshops on risk management, teaching techniques, and professionalism. This program ensures that the instructor knows how to teach horseback riding to beginners. (See appendix C, "Trail Riding Opportunities," for CHA contact information.)

CHA instructors are certified in Western, English, and/or Trail Clinic. The latter discipline involves learning to ride on the trail instead of in an arena. If you choose a certified trail instructor, you will most likely still learn the basics of riding in an arena before you hit the trail.

If you are unable to find a CHA-certified instructor near you, you can try contacting the American Quarter Horse Association (AQHA), which provides a list of horse trainers and riding instructors in both the Western and English disciplines. The professionals on this list subscribe to an oath of ethics that requires they conduct themselves with integrity in a professional manner. While all of the instructors listed with the AQHA work with Quarter Horses, they are not necessarily limited to this breed. (See appendix B, "Resources," for AQHA contact information.)

You can also find instructors on the Internet, in the telephone directory, and in local horse publications. You will find ads for riding instructors in your area in each of these resources. When searching these lists, seek out instructors who state that they teach the discipline you want to beginning riders. When you call to get more information, make certain these teachers have lesson horses available for instruction if you don't have your own horse.

Word of mouth is another way to get the name of an instructor in your area. If you have friends who ride, ask them if they can recommend an instructor for a beginning rider. If they give you a name, ask them what they know about this person. Have they ridden with the instructor themselves, or do they only know of this person through a third party? If you can, find out what your friend liked about the instructor—and what he or she didn't like.

Once you are armed with some names of instructors, it's time to meet the individual and observe some lessons. Call the person and find out if you can come and watch a beginner lesson. If the instructor says no for any reason, cross that person off your list immediately. You don't want to commit to riding with an instructor without first seeing him or her at work.

When you go to meet the instructor, spend some time talking to him or her and explain your goals as a rider. Gauge the response. If the instructor doesn't respect your goals to become a trail rider, this is not the person for you. If the instructor seems too busy to spend time talking to you, or you don't feel a chemistry with this person, cut your visit short.

If all goes well in the initial meeting, hang around and watch a lesson with a beginning rider. Look for the following:

- *Patience.* The instructor should be patient with the student and never lose his or her temper.

- *Clarity.* The instructor should explain what he or she is looking for in a clear way so the rider understands. If the rider is not catching on, the instructor should rephrase the instructions until the student is able to follow.

- *Attention to safety.* The instructor should require the student to wear a riding helmet and not push the student to trot or canter if the person doesn't seem secure with his or her riding. The horse should be quiet and relatively obedient, although keep in mind that some riders are so inexperienced, they can't properly cue the horse to act.

- *Respect.* The instructor should behave in a professional manner and treat the student with courtesy. The instructor should give 100 percent of his or her attention to the student and not be chatting with other people or training someone else's horse during the lesson.

If you like what you see when you watch the lesson, it's time to book a trial lesson of your own. Find out what the instructor charges for a trial lesson, and set one up to see how you two mesh.

During your trial lesson, look for the same points you watched for when observing a lesson from the ground. In addition, consider the following:

- Does the instructor make you feel secure on the horse and not push you beyond your limits of comfort?

- Does the instructor give you clear directions and explain something again when you don't understand?

- Do you feel comfortable with the instructor's teaching style and personality?

- When your lesson is over, do you feel as though you learned something?

- After your lesson has ended, are you looking forward to another one?

If you can answer "yes" to all these questions, then you have probably found the instructor who's best for you. If you are unsure whether the match is a good one, take one or two more lessons before you make up your mind. Once you think you have found the right person to teach you, consider booking a block of lessons since most instructors offer discount packages for a set of lessons purchased all at once, in advance.

The cost of lessons will vary depending on where you live and the experience level of the individual instructor. Some instructors charge as little as $15 a lesson; others charge as much as $150. Try not to choose your instructor based on how little he or she charges. Go with the best instructor you can afford.

GETTING THE MOST FROM YOUR LESSONS

It's important that you find a good instructor to teach you the nuances of riding, but in order for you to get the most out of your lessons, you must also be a good student.

A good student will do the following:

- Show up for lessons prepared and on time.

- Avoid canceling lessons and switching lesson times as much as possible.

- Listen carefully to the instructor and focus only on the lesson.

- Avoid arguing with the instructor. If you don't understand what the instructor is asking you to do, or can't feel a problem with your riding that your instructor is describing, verbalize this in a nonconfrontational way.

- Pay your bill on time.

If you have a good instructor, and you are a good student, you'll be riding well in no time!

Avoid situations where you don't receive instruction as part of your riding experience.

Other Ways to Get Riding Experience

In addition to formal riding lessons, beginning riders do have other ways to spend quality time in the saddle.

Vacation ranches that provide some instruction for trail riders are a good way to spend time in the saddle and get a feel for what trail riding is all about. Some vacation ranches that provide instruction to new riders in addition to trail rides are listed in appendix C.

Another way to spend time in the saddle is on a friend's horse. If you know someone who is an experienced rider and has a quiet, dependable horse, you may want to consider riding with him or her. If you go this route, it is vital that your friend be a good, patient teacher and that the horse be completely reliable. Also, if you don't have much or any experience riding, your time on this horse should be in an arena and not on the trail. Make certain your friend understands that you are a beginner and that you are just learning. Don't allow yourself to be pushed into doing anything that would be more suitable for an experienced rider, including going out on a trail ride and going faster than a walk, until you are ready. Learn to control the horse in the arena first before you embark on a trail ride.

Chapter 3

FINDING A HORSE TO RIDE

The single most important element in trail riding is the horse. Without a horse, you can't trail ride. And without a *good* horse, you can't enjoy trail riding. That's why it's crucial to have a good, safe mount for your trail riding activities.

While you are still learning to ride, the majority of your time on horseback should be spent on lesson horses whose job it is to help you learn the nuances of good riding. Once you have nailed down the basics, you will probably be itching for a horse of your own you can take on trail rides.

If you already have a horse and would like to start trail riding with him, but he has never been on the trail or has only done it a few times—in other words, if you have mostly been riding him in the arena—you need to evaluate whether your horse has what it takes to be a safe trail horse for you. Keep in mind that while your horse might be too much for you to handle on the trail, it doesn't mean he couldn't work as a trail horse for someone else. When it comes to pairing up riders and horses, it's all about making a good match.

Using Your Arena Horse

Most horses can become decent trail horses with the right training and exposure, so if your arena horse is a nervous Nelly on the trail, it's probably because he hasn't had much exposure to it. Your horse needs time and practice on the trail, and you may need a professional to help him get it if he's not safe on the trail or if you feel like you just don't know how to deal with him out in the open.

Each horse is an individual just as each human is an individual. Some horses take to trail riding faster than others. Some horses need just a few jaunts on the trail to get the hang of it, while others need six months or more of consistent exposure to be able to relax.

If you want to make your arena horse into a trail horse, and you are not a very experienced trail rider, it's a good idea to get help from an expert. A horse

Even a high-priced show horse can make a good trail mount.

trainer or a very experienced friend should take your horse out on the trail to evaluate whether he needs a lot of work before you get on and start trying to conquer your local trail system.

When evaluating your horse's trail worthiness, keep in mind that horses always feel more secure when they are with other horses. Take your horse out with another, more seasoned trail horse, one who is calm and relaxed and won't react if your horse starts to get nervous. Let your horse follow behind on rides until he relaxes, then try him out front next time around to see if he can handle being the leader. Some horses are fine when following, but get very uptight being the one in front. Eventually, your goal is to work up to riding your horse alone on the trail and having him be completely comfortable. Keep in mind that this may take a while, depending on your horse's personality. (For more, see chapter 8, "Preparing Your Horse for Trail.")

Finding a Horse for Trail

Many people believe that you must buy a horse in order to have one you can ride whenever you feel like it. Thanks to the little-known option of leasing, you don't need to commit to buying a horse just to have one you can ride. In fact, leasing is a much better idea for most beginning riders because it gives them a chance to find out if they will enjoy horse ownership. Owning a horse is a big responsibility, and leasing is sort of a dry run to see if you can handle it.

Leasing a horse is similar to leasing a car, although you may not have the option to buy at the end of the lease as you would with an automobile you leased from a dealer. Of course, this can be negotiated. Some people lease out their horses in the hopes that a lessor may ultimately buy the animal.

When exploring the option of leasing, you'll see two types of leases: a full lease and a half or partial lease. Each of these leases is very different. With a full lease, you take full responsibility for the horse. You pay the horse's board (which includes feed and stall cleaning), shoeing, and veterinary bills, along with a leasing fee. In return, you have complete access to the horse and can ride it every day. You can also show the horse, take it on trail rides, and do a variety of other activities with the horse, depending on what is permitted in your contract. Full leasing is a good choice if you can afford the maintenance on a horse but don't have the money to purchase one, or simply do not want to make the commitment to buy a horse outright.

A half or partial lease, on the other hand, limits your access to the horse to two to four days a week. You are not responsible for the board payment or the horse's vet bills (unless your negligence resulted in the horse's illness or injury). A half or partial lease is a good option if your time and finances are limited, but you want to ride the same horse on a regular basis. (See "The Leasing Process" later in this chapter for more details on leasing.)

CAN YOU HANDLE IT?

If you are certain you want to own your own horse, then you are in the market to buy. Of course, before you do so, make sure you can afford not only the purchase price of the horse but also the upkeep. Horse owners are responsible for the horse's food; board, if you don't have your own property; shoeing; veterinary bills, which includes regular vaccinations and dental maintenance; and other miscellaneous costs such as deworming products, fly repellent, brushes, saddles, bridles, halters, and other basic equipment.

As a horse owner, you are morally and legally responsible for the welfare of the horse or horses in your care. If your horse is kept in a small paddock, it's your job to make sure he gets daily exercise. You are in charge of keeping him healthy and happy, which is no small task. Horse ownership is a big responsibility. Make certain you are ready for it and have the time, money, and devotion to take it on.

If you aren't sure whether you can manage owning a horse, lease a horse first to see what it's like. Start with a partial or half lease, and if that works out, find a full lease or take the plunge and buy.

On the subject of renting, the hazards of renting a horse by the hour were covered in chapter 2, "Getting Experience in the Saddle." Essentially, renting a horse by the hour from a riding stable for a casual trail ride is rarely a good idea, especially if you are a novice rider. If you want to ride often but don't want to lease or buy a horse, find a trainer who will give you lessons on the trail so you can learn and enjoy the trail under supervised conditions.

Another option is to spend your vacations at a dude ranch or on a packing trip into the mountains. This will provide you with a concentrated amount of trail riding time without forcing you to commit to riding on a weekly basis throughout the year.

GETTING HELP

If you have decided you want to lease or buy a horse for trail riding, your first step is to find someone knowledgeable to help you with your selection. Even experienced riders can use the advice of a trainer or instructor when looking for a horse to buy or lease. Unfortunately, deceit is rampant in the horse-trading business, and it's very easy for a beginner in the horse world to get ripped off, especially during the buying process. Having a qualified professional walk you through the process will substantially decrease your chances of being duped by an unscrupulous seller.

If you have been taking riding lessons and you like your instructor, you are already a step ahead of the game. You are working with someone you trust who knows you and has a good feeling for the kind of horse that would be best suited to your needs.

Talk to your instructor about your desires to lease or buy a horse, and ask this person if he or she is available to help you find the right trail mount. Most instructors provide horse shopping as a service to clients. Those instructors who don't get involved in this end of the horse business should be able to refer you to someone who does.

If you aren't working with a riding instructor and don't have a connection to a professional in the horse business who can assist you, you need to find someone to help you before you start looking for a horse. See "Finding a Good Instructor" in chapter 2, and use those guidelines to locate a professional who can help you find a horse. You may even need to take a few lessons with this individual so the instructor can get a sense of your riding skills and personality. The better the instructor knows you, the more likely you'll end up with a horse who's good match.

Some people live in areas that are so rural, riding instructors are hard to come by. If that's the case, call a local equine veterinarian or horse-breeding facility—anyone who is a professional in the horse industry—and ask them if they can help you or refer you to someone who can. If you are looking to buy a horse, it's imperative you get assistance from someone who knows horses before you plunk down your hard-earned money.

What Makes a Good Trail Horse?

Whether you are planning to sign a full or partial lease or actually buy a horse, you'll need to look for certain qualities in your future equine companion if you hope to trail ride.

Begin by thinking about what breed you would like. As you come across the various breeds in your research and experiences with horses, you may have developed an interest in a particular breed. Perhaps you like the look of the American Quarter Horse, or are attracted to the spots on the colorful Appaloosa. Maybe the Paint's flashy appearance or the Tennessee Walking Horse's smooth gaits have tickled your fancy. If you think you'd like to explore a particular breed as a potential trail horse, concentrate your search among this breed, for starters. (Remember that each horse is an individual, and a horse of any breed can make a great trail mount.)

Next, look for a horse at least 9 years old. In fact, if you are a rank beginner, an older horse even into his 20s is your best option, as long as the horse is healthy. Older horses are more mature and tend to be quieter than younger horses, although many exceptions to this general rule do exist. With the right care, many horses stay sound and healthy well into their mid to late 20s.

Good ground manners are an important quality in a trail horse. Ground manners refer to the way the horse behaves when you are handling him from the ground, as opposed to being on his back. A horse with good ground manners stands quietly while he is being groomed, does not fuss or move around when you are saddling and bridling him, and walks quietly alongside as you are leading him. He picks up his feet willingly so that you can pick out his hooves, and tolerates fly spray application, baths, and just about anything else you might need to do to him on a daily basis.

Trail horses need to have good ground manners for a number of reasons. With a trail horse, you never know what kind of situation you might find yourself in. Trail riding by its very nature requires that you be away from your home base. The last thing you need is a horse you can't control if you are far from the stable. Emergencies happen on trail rides too. Horses can slip and fall into ravines, get stones embedded in their feet—just about anything can happen out there. If your horse has good ground manners, he is more likely to cooperate in an emergency situation if you have to dismount.

Good ground manners also come in handy on long rides or overnight excursions, when a horse must stand tied for long periods of time. Pawing, fussing, and pulling back in an attempt to break the halter and escape are unacceptable behaviors in a trail horse.

Under saddle, a good trail horse has many positive qualities. Trail horses are obedient and sensitive to their riders. They have a good work ethic, which means they know they have a job to do in this world, and they are willing to do it. The best trail horses are also virtually unflappable. Not much scares them, and if they do become frightened, they don't lose their minds but assess the situation instead of taking off in mad flight.

Good trail horses also get along well with other horses. They don't kick horses who are behind them on the trail, and they don't bite horses in

The best trail horses are quiet and sane, even in urban environments.

Basics of a Good Trail Horse

If you are a beginning rider, the horse you select for trail riding should possess the following attributes:

- *Calm in new situations.* The horse should be alert but relatively calm when exposed to new stimuli, such as a new trail or an object along a familiar trail.

- *Well rounded.* The horse should have some experience in different areas of riding, including arena and trail work.

- *Responsive to the rider.* The horse should respond quickly and easily to your cues under saddle.

- *Not prone to panic.* If your horse spooks, he should be able to compose himself quickly and resume a calm demeanor after determining that he is safe.

- *Good ground manners.* The horse must be good on the ground, leading quietly, standing for grooming, and lifting his feet when asked. He should not be prone to kicking or biting.

- *Sound.* The horse's limbs should be in good condition, and he should be sound at the walk and trot, at the very least.

- *Healthy.* Good health is imperative in a trail horse.

- *Loads willingly.* When it comes to getting into a trailer, the horse should not hesitate to load and unload.

front of them. They are equally willing to be in the lead or follow behind, depending on what the rider prefers.

Personality and behavior are very important in a trail horse, and so is soundness. If you are looking for a trail horse to do long, all-day rides, horse camping trips, or competitive events like competitive trail riding or endurance, you need a horse free from serious health problems. The health of a horse's legs and joints is crucial when it comes to trail riding because this activity requires a horse to spend a lot of time under saddle. Depending on where you live, the horse may be going up and down hills during trail rides, which can also put a lot of strain on the joints, tendons, and ligaments. Only sound horses can do this kind of work without developing problems.

On the other hand, if you only plan to do short rides of an hour or two on relatively flat ground, soundness is less of an issue. Many horses who are not sound enough to do other kinds of work can make excellent trail horses for light work.

Gender is another important issue when shopping for a trail horse. Geldings make good trail horses, and so do mares as long as they don't suffer from behavior extremes during their heat cycle—some mares do and some don't. Stallions are out of the question for beginning riders, and even for most intermediate riders. Stallions can be difficult to handle, and even the nice ones can pose a problem when it comes to boarding and going on group rides. Some boarding stables won't allow stallions on the property because of liability issues, and many group trail rides forbid stallions because many are unpredictable.

When it comes to what size horse you should buy, a good general rule is that a horse can comfortably carry 20 percent of its body weight. If you weigh 200 pounds and plan to do a lot of long rides on the trail, you need a horse who weighs 1,100 pounds.

When horse shopping, take a horse weight tape with you. These equine measuring tapes, available in tack and feed stores, can help you determine the weight of a horse, as well as the horse's height.

Costs of Horse Buying

Now that you know what to look for a trail horse, it's time to start shopping. Hopefully, you have an expert to help you with your search. If you don't, please go back and reread the section in this chapter on getting help finding a horse. Having help with this process is vital!

You'll want to start out knowing exactly how much you plan to spend on a horse. For some people, money is no object and they can pay whatever they need to find a good horse. Most horse shoppers do have limited budgets, however, and it's important to know your spending limits.

When determining how much you actually need to get the kind of horse you want, you must figure out exactly what you plan to look for. The breed of horse you seek will be a factor in how much you'll spend. If you have your heart set on a Friesian (a beautiful black horse who looks like he stepped out of a medieval tapestry), you can expect to spend anywhere from $15,000 to $30,000, depending on the age and training level of the horse. If you don't care if your trail horse is of a particular breed or is even a purebred, you can probably get away with spending anywhere from $1,500 to $5,000, depending on the age of the horse, the level of training, and the area of the country in which you live.

Another cost in horse shopping is the prepurchase exam. Prepurchase exams are conducted by equine veterinarians and include a check for basic health of the horse along with a lameness exam. If you are spending only a couple of thousand on a horse, you may not want to incur the expense of a full exam, including X-rays on all four legs, because this can run you nearly $500 or more in itself. While it's a good idea to ask for a full exam complete with X-rays, you can opt for only a lameness exam and see if the horse shows any signs of a problem on any of its legs. If so, you can opt to have those legs X-rayed, or else just walk away from the sale. Some people are so determined to buy a horse, they will do it anyway despite the vet's finding of lameness. This can be a bad move or a good move, depending on the horse's condition and the buyer's circumstances. If you just want a trail horse who can walk up and down your street carrying your 8-year-old grandson, then a mild lameness issue might not be a big deal. On the other hand, if you are looking for a horse with whom you can do serious trail riding for many years to come, it would be unwise to buy a horse with a lameness issue that is bound to get worse.

One more fee you'll need to pay when shopping for a horse is your instructor's time. The expert you hire to help you will charge you for time she or he spends going to see horses with you, riding the horse to do an evaluation, and accompanying you to the prepurchase exam, if necessary. This will most likely be a nominal fee and well worth every penny, since expert help will ensure you get the best horse for your situation.

The Buying Process

Purchasing a horse is similar to buying a used car—you really don't know what you bought until after you've had it for a while. You can take a used car for a test drive to get a sense of what the car is like, and likewise, you can ride a horse on the day you check it out to see what that horse is like. But until you have the horse in your possession for some time, you won't really get to know the horse.

The horse shopping experience can be broken down into two or three steps. First, you need to locate horses for sale so you can consider them. Thanks to the Internet, you can go online and see ads for horses all over the country. The search engines on these sites allow you to look for horses for sale in your area, and also allow you to search by breed, gender, price range, and even discipline. These ads often have pictures of the horse with the ad so you'll know what the animal looks like before you even see it in the flesh.

· Other sources for horses for sale are local equine publications, bulletin boards in tack and feed stores, and classified ads in your local paper. You can also ask your instructor to look for a horse for you. In return, the instructor will take a commission based on the sale price of the horse (usually 10 percent) if you ultimately buy the animal.

When you are looking at horse ads, pay attention to the age of the horse and whether the horse is listed as being good on trail. Since you are shopping for a trail horse, this latter piece of information is vital.

Once you have narrowed down your search to a few horses who sound promising, call the owners to find out more about the horses. Here is a list of questions you should ask, along with the answers you want to hear:

- *How old is the horse?* A good general rule is to look for a horse over the age of 8 and under the age of 25. If you want a horse for competitive events such as endurance, you'll want a horse no older than 12 or 13.

- *Does the horse have any health issues?* If the seller is honest, he or she will tell you if the horse has any lameness or other issues. If the seller says "no," take this with a grain of salt and let your vet decide if there is a problem during the prepurchase exam.

- *What kind of training has the horse had?* If you are a beginning rider, you want a horse who has had a lot of training, either formal or informal. You want a horse who is safe and obedient, and training is what gives a horse these qualities.

- *What is the horse like on the trail?* This is a crucial question since you are looking for a trail horse. If the buyer says the horse is excellent on the trail, ask if there is anything that frightens the horse. Find out how the horse reacts when he's frightened. If the horse is afraid of a lot of things and responds by rearing, spinning, and/or bolting, this is probably not the horse for you.

- *Is the horse suitable for a beginner?* If you are a beginning rider, this is an important question. Most sellers will tell you if the horse is difficult to handle and needs a more experienced rider.

- *Why are you selling the horse?* The purpose of this question is to determine if the seller is getting rid of the horse because it has problem behaviors, or if there are other circumstances unrelated to the horse. You'll need to gauge if the seller is being honest with you; if you go see the horse, you'll probably find out soon enough if the horse is a problem.

- *How are the horse's ground manners?* You want a horse with good ground manners, so the answer should be "good." No horse is perfect, and the seller might admit to something like "He doesn't like being clipped." This is your opportunity to ask more questions and find out exactly how difficult the horse is under certain circumstances. This is where your expert helper comes in; a knowledgeable horseperson can tell you whether the issue is a big enough problem to warrant walking away.

- *Does the horse load well into a trailer?* Nothing is worse than trying to stuff 1,000 pounds of unwilling horseflesh into a trailer. Some horses refuse to load without literally hours of battling. If you are buying a trail horse and intend to trailer the horse from place to place so you can ride— and don't want to spend time and money to have the horse retrained to load easily—stay away from a horse with trailer problems.

- *Does the horse have any stable vices?* Stable vices include habits such as weaving, cribbing, wind sucking, and pacing. These are all habits stemming from anxiety or boredom, and once a horse discovers one of these behaviors, it can be nearly impossible to break him of it. All of these problems are bad for the horse's health and can be destructive to the horse's stall or paddock.

- *Are you open to a trial period?* If you have determined that you won't buy a horse without at least a two-week trial period, then a "no" answer to this question means you are not interested in the horse. Many sellers won't agree to this arrangement if it involves taking the horse out of their possession for the trial period, for fear of something happening to the horse. Some of these sellers can be put at ease if you offer to give them a check for the full amount of the horse and sign an agreement saying you will return the horse to them in good health in exchange for your check should you decide not to buy the horse at the end of the trial period.

If you like the sound of the horse, make an appointment to go see the animal. Bring your instructor along with you so you have a pair of expert eyes to help you make a decision.

Evaluating the Horse

When you arrive at the horse's location, prepare the horse for riding, or watch carefully as the owner does this. Pay attention to see if the horse leads quietly without forging ahead or refusing to go forward, and stands still for grooming and saddling. Notice if the horse picks up its feet willingly and if he is easy to bridle.

Ask the owner to ride the horse in an arena first so you and your instructor can get a feel for what the horse is like. If the owner doesn't ride, then have your instructor get on the horse first. Pay close attention to whether the horse stands still during mounting, and after mounting until the rider asks the horse to move forward.

If your instructor thinks the horse seems safe, mount up and see how the horse feels to you. You want to make sure the horse responds willingly to each of your commands, and walks, trots, and canters in a controlled manner. Turn the horse in each direction, and back the horse up to see if he responds. The horse should obey you without resistance, and you should feel safe on the horse.

Because you are looking to buy a trail horse, it's important that you and/or your instructor take the horse on a trail ride. If the seller understands your main purpose in purchasing the horse will be to ride it on trail, he or she should be amenable to letting you take the horse on trail. The seller may want to ride with you. If that's the case, you'll need to let him or her know that you'd like your instructor to take the horse out alone too. You don't want to buy a trail horse who cannot go out on a ride without the company of another horse.

When trying out the horse, try to expose him to situations he might encounter should you buy him. If you must ride down a busy street to get to the trails, see if you can take the horse down a street. Ask the seller first if the horse is safe in traffic, and if so, have your instructor ride the horse on the street or do it with your instructor close by.

When the horse is being ridden on trail, look for a relaxed demeanor. The horse should be used to the area where he is being ridden since he lives in this locale, so if he seems uptight, he has not been ridden much on trail, or he is a flighty horse. Either way, if the horse refuses to walk away from the barn, will not walk but insists on jigging (an annoying cross between a walk and a jog), or repeatedly spooks at inanimate objects or refuses to pass them, this is not the horse for you. Politely thank the seller and leave.

If the horse is relaxed, and you have the opportunity while out on the trail, evaluate how the horse handles various trail obstacles. Ask the horse to cross a creek or other safe body of water. Trail horses frequently encounter water, and a good trail horse will walk willingly into a stream or calm river. If the horse does not want to cross the water, he will need training in this regard if he is going to be a good trail horse.

Ask the horse to walk over a log so you can see how he encounters obstacles on the trail. The horse should safely step over the log. If he jumps over it, he needs work on this aspect of trail riding.

Another point to note when trying the horse out on trail is whether the horse pays attention to the terrain and where he's going. A horse who is oblivious to where he's stepping will trip often and possibly put both himself and his rider in a dangerous situation.

Remember, the horse's disposition and behavior is the single most important element for you to consider if you are a beginning rider and want to participate in trail riding. A good horse will make you happy, build your confidence, and keep you safe. A badly behaved horse has the potential to damage your confidence, leave you with fear issues, and even cause you bodily harm. If you feel the least bit hesitant about the horse's behavior, walk away from the sale. Enough good horses exist out there that you don't have to feel like you need to settle.

Conformation

One of the most important factors to consider when purchasing a trail horse is the horse's conformation. You need to look at the horse with a critical eye to determine whether he will hold up to the rigors of the trail.

If you only plan to do occasional trail rides, or even daily rides that are only about an hour or so long on relatively flat ground, the way your horse is built is less of an issue. Just about any horse can do this kind of trail riding as long as he is sound.

If you have dreams of competing with your trail horse in competitive trail rides or endurance races, or want a horse you can spend many hours a day with on the trail, you will need to play close attention to the horse's conformation. A horse with poor conformation is more prone to lameness problems when ridden hard on the trail. Also, horses who are stocky and have a heavy build will have less stamina on the trail than a light, narrow horse.

To determine whether the horse you are considering has the right kind of build for trail riding, taking a close look at his legs. When the horse is standing square—that is, he is standing still with his legs directly under him, the front two lined up and the back two lined up—go to the side and look at his front legs. You should be able to draw an imaginary line through the point of his shoulder down through his knee through his fetlock and to the back of his heel. This line should be completely vertical. If the horse's front legs vary from this line, he is not properly aligned.

Check the back legs, too. Draw an imaginary line from the point of the horse's rump just below the dock of the tail through the back of the hock and down the back of the horse's leg to the ground. If the horse's leg varies from this horizontal line, he does not have correct conformation in his legs (see the following figure).

The problem with legs that are not properly lined up is that the constant concussion from trail riding will put too much stress on these ill-designed legs. The joints are not set up to take the stresses of hills and many hours of riding on

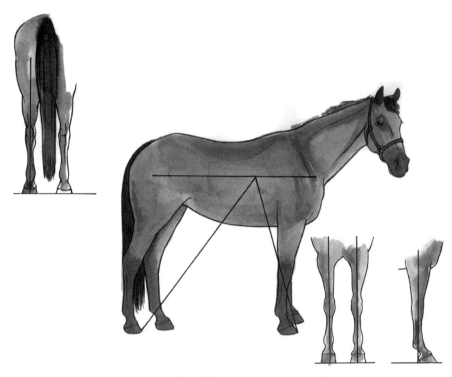

A horse with good conformation is well balanced and correctly angled.

hard ground, and the horse will develop lameness and arthritis way before his time.

Another important point of conformation is the angle of the horse's pasterns. Pasterns serve as the legs' shock absorbers, so if the angles of the pasterns aren't right, undue pressure is placed on the horse's joints and tendons.

Look for a horse who has a pastern angle that is 45 to 50 degrees in the front, and 50 to 55 degrees in the back. Keep in mind that the more upright the pastern, the more potential problems the horse will have with its legs, especially with hard work.

Trail horses should also have well-proportioned hooves. A horse with a very small foot is prone to unsoundness, especially when asked to do a lot of hill work.

Experts disagree on a number of other issues regarding conformation and whether these details can impair a horse's ability to remain a sound trail mount for years to come. One thing they all agree on, however, is that a heavily built, stocky horse will not have the endurance to do very long rides, especially those that include hill work. A horse who has a wide chest and a lot of muscling will get hot and tired much faster than a horse with a narrow chest and lanky build. Of course, plenty of horses fall in between these two body types and make very good trail horses. The only riders who should focus on buying a horse with a narrow build are those who intend to participate in endurance racing.

Keep in mind that no horse is perfect, and any horse you look at will have some physical flaws. The key is finding a horse with flaws you can live with. The level of riding you plan to do will be a key factor in determining whether a conformational problem is something you can ignore as you are considering purchasing the horse. The veterinarian who conducts the prepurchase exam should be able to give you plenty of guidance on making this decision.

Making the Purchase

If you like the horse you rode and your instructor agrees, your next step is to request a trial period. If the horse is located close to where you live, the owner should be agreeable to letting you come and ride the horse regularly over the next two weeks to make sure the two of you get along. If you don't live nearby, you will have to ask the seller if you can take the horse to your own property or a boarding stable near your home so you can spend time with the horse.

As mentioned earlier, this should be agreeable to the seller provided you sign a liability agreement stating full responsibility for the horse and give the seller a check for the amount of the sale. The seller should agree not to cash the check until you have officially agreed to buy the horse at the end of the trial period. If you decide to keep the horse, the seller is free to cash the check.

When asking for a trial period, two weeks is the minimum the seller should agree to. If you can get a 30-day trial period, that's even better. The more time you can spend with the horse, the better. Not only will the extended time permit you to get to know the horse so you can make a good decision, it will also reduce the likelihood of the horse's demeanor being affected by behavior-altering drugs. Unfortunately, the horse business has its share of unscrupulous sellers who will drug a horse to make it calmer. When the drugs wear off, the horse will be a completely different animal.

In the event the seller will not agree to a trial period, you must decide if you are willing to buy the horse regardless. You can ask to come back one or more times to ride the horse again before making a decision, but of course this will be difficult to do if you live far away. Also, you run the risk of another buyer purchasing the horse before you have made your decision. Despite these inconveniences, it is wise to ride the horse several times before deciding to go to the next level in the buying process.

The Vet Check

If you have found a horse you believe will make a good trail mount—and you have agreement from your expert helper—you should consider a prepurchase exam, or vet check, before you make your final decision.

Plenty of buyers opt to skip the prepurchase exam if the horse they are buying is relatively inexpensive. They reason that they are only spending a couple of thousand dollars on the horse, so why spend $500 or more on a prepurchase exam with X-rays?

On the surface, it may seem silly to spend money on an exam if the horse doesn't cost that much, but you may think otherwise when you consider the following: If you unknowingly purchase a horse with a medical condition, it can cost you a lot more than the price of the prepurchase exam to treat that animal. What's more, if the condition is serious, you may lose use of the horse and be out the money you spent on him. A wise buyer will put aside $500 or more of his or her horse-buying money to pay for a prepurchase exam, regardless of the price of the horse.

During a prepurchase exam, an equine veterinarian of your choosing takes a close look at the horse to determine if the animal is healthy. If the horse you are considering is in close proximity to where you live, ask your instructor for a recommendation for a veterinarian to do the prepurchase exam. Make sure the vet does not have the seller as a client, since this would be a conflict of interest for the veterinarian. Many vets will refuse to do the exam if the seller is a client, but some feel they can be unbiased regardless. The best approach for you the buyer is to find a vet who is completely neutral in the process, if you can.

If the horse is located out of your area, *do not* use the seller's veterinarian for the exam. The potential for conflict of interest is too great. Instead, shop around for another vet in the area who can do the exam. Call horse clubs in the area for recommendations for good equine vets who do not work for the seller.

On the day of the scheduled exam, the vet will look in the horse's eyes, listen to his heart and lungs, and check his gut sounds to make sure the digestive system is in good working order. Next, the vet will look for signs of lameness. This part of the exam is the most important if you are looking to buy a trail horse, especially if you plan to compete in trail-riding events (see chapters 14, "Judging on the Trail," and 15, "Racing on the Trail").

The lameness exam consists of the vet watching the horse trot on hard ground toward him or her, and away. The vet will then conduct a flexion exam, which involves bending each of the horse's legs and holding the hoof tight against the elbow or stifle for two minutes and then watching the horse's trot out immediately afterwards. This test helps determine if the horse has issues with one or more legs. The horse will limp on any of the legs that may have problems.

The vet will also conduct a hoof pincher test, which involves taking a tool called a hoof pincher and squeezing the top and bottom of the horse's foot. If the horse pulls away or twitches, this indicates pain, which in turn indicates a problem.

If the veterinarian finds some issues with any of the horse's legs during the lameness exam, your next step is to decide if you want X-rays to determine exactly what might be causing the problem. Some issues are minor and won't seriously affect the horse's long-term use as a trail mount. Other issues can be severe and indicate debilitating lameness down the road.

If you opt to skip the X-rays and the horse you are considering shows signs of lameness during the exam, you are taking a risk by buying the horse. Without knowing exactly what is wrong with the leg, you are potentially buying a horse who could become unsound. Be aware that you are taking a big risk.

If the horse seems completely sound on the lameness exam, and you have the money to spend, consider having the horse's joints X-rayed nonetheless. If you plan to keep the horse for a long time and/or want to use the horse in competitive trail events, it's a good idea to get a full set of X-rays so you can find out if any hidden problems are lurking.

After the lameness testing, the exam is over unless you want the veterinarian to do blood work. Blood work can consist of a basic blood panel, where the vet checks the horse's red and white blood count, thyroid levels, and other areas of the blood that will indicate overall health. This type of test is particularly important if you are purchasing an older horse in its 20s. You may also request a drug test to determine if the horse you are considering has been given any behavior-altering medications, including pain relievers, to mask a problem in the legs.

Finalizing the Sale

Once you have completed the prepurchase exam and have discussed the results with the veterinarian and your instructor, it's time to make your decision about the horse. If you opt to buy the animal, think about how much you are willing to pay for the horse. Something may have come up on the prepurchase exam that leaves you feeling that the horse is worth less than the asking price. Or you may simply want to offer the seller less money if you think he or she will be amenable to a lower price. Make your offer to the seller and let him or her decide if the price is negotiable.

Once you and the seller agree on a price, make sure you sign a contract with the seller indicating the name and description of the horse, the purchase price, and any other stipulations of the sale, such as the inclusion of a saddle and bridle. Keep a copy of this document for yourself and hold onto it. It is your legal rights to the horse you have just purchased. (Remember: Horses are not like toasters. Once you buy the horse, it's yours. The only exception would be if you have something in writing from the seller stating that he or she will buy the horse back if you change your mind.)

If the horse you bought is a registered purebred, the owner should provide you with the horse's registration certificate and a signed transfer of ownership form obtained from the pertinent breed registry at the time money changes hands. You will then need to countersign the transfer form and send it to the breed registry with the transfer of ownership fee in order to have the horse's registration switched to your name.

Once your new horse is in your possession, give him a day or two to get settled before you start riding him. Remember, he's in completely new surroundings with new people and so needs a bit time to adjust. Give him lots of love and start enjoying him on the trail once he's settled in. And congratulate yourself— you are now the owner of a trail horse!

The Leasing Process

If you have wisely decided to try out horse ownership by leasing before making the commitment to buy, start looking at ads at local stables and in the papers for trail horses for lease. Ask your instructor if he or she has a trail horse for lease or knows of any. Instructors are often willing to work out half or partial leases of their lesson horses, which would enable you to ride the horse on your own for two or three days a week.

A full lease will give you a better sense of what it's like to own a horse, since you will be the person who is fully responsible for the care of the horse. Choosing a trail horse to lease is a lot like buying one, although you won't need to go through the expense of having a full veterinary exam with X-rays to determine if the horse is healthy. Most lessors will want you to sign an agreement saying the horse was in good health when you leased it, so if you want a vet to examine the horse beforehand to make sure the horse doesn't have any problems, this is a good idea. However, unless any health problems that arise in the horse are the result of your negligence or because of an injury sustained while you are leasing the horse, the lessor, if honest, is unlikely to hold you accountable.

When it comes to leases, each situation is different, depending on what the lessee and lessor agree to. Some lessors may want you to simply pay for the horse's regular maintenance, including vet bills and shoeing costs, along with a nominal fee for use of the horse. Others may require that you purchase insurance for the horse in case something happens to the animal while he is in your care. Other leases have restrictions on what you can do with a horse during your lease. If you are leasing a horse for trail riding, make certain you are allowed to take the horse out on trail, and are allowed to trailer the horse off the property for trail rides, if you plan to do this.

Once you and the lessor have agreed to the terms of your lease, get everything in writing. Pay close attention to the details of the contract, since this is a legal document that will be presented in court should a dispute arise. In other words, read the fine print and be sure to hold up your end of the contract.

Chapter 4

TACKING UP

Aside from the actual horse, equipment is your next priority if you want to get into trail riding. Not only will you need a saddle and a bridle, but basic necessities such as a halter, lead rope, and grooming tools are a must for all horse owners.

Trail riding is the act of riding a horse outside the arena, on a trail. If you are a casual trail rider and just plan to take your horse out for an hour at a time to take a break from arena work or merely for enjoyment, it doesn't really matter what kind of tack you use. You can trail ride—or *hack,* as English riders call it—in a hunt seat saddle, dressage saddle, or saddle seat saddle. People who spend most of their time riding out on the trail usually use Western saddles. Those riders who compete in endurance riding or simply spend a lot of time riding in rugged terrain often opt for endurance saddles, which are a cross between an English and a Western saddle.

If you are already riding in a particular discipline and feel most comfortable in that saddle, then you should probably stick to this type of riding when you go out on the trail. If you are thinking of switching saddles for trail riding, or if you are just learning to ride and are trying to decide which discipline to pursue, you'll want to take an in-depth look at each one of these different saddles and its use on the trail. Keep in mind that a trail saddle should be comfortable for both you and the horse, and should make you feel secure when riding out in the open.

English Saddles

The three types of English saddles—hunt seat, dressage, and saddle seat—are all suitable for trail riding. In fact, riders all over the world hack on the trails in these saddles. Hunt seat saddles and saddle seat saddles were originally designed for riding out in the open. Dressage saddles were designed for schooling horses in more of an arena setting, but plenty of people trail ride in dressage saddles. English saddles are most popular for trail riding in the eastern U.S. and Canada, and in Europe.

Let's take a closer look at each one and its suitability for trail riding.

HUNT SEAT

Hunt seat saddles—and their closely related cousins, the all-purpose English saddle—feature a relatively shallow seat that holds the rider in a forward position. Originally designed for jumping, and still widely used for this purpose, the hunt seat saddle is usually ridden with short stirrups during arena work. Hunt seat saddles allow you to post at the trot—that is, rise up and down with the rhythm of the horse—making them a saddle of choice for riders with horses who have fast, bouncy trots. Hunt seat saddles also give you good contact with the horse. There is very little leather between you and the horse, which enables you to give the horse clear signals with your seat and legs and lets you feel the horse's back beneath you. This can be handy when approaching a scary object on the trail. In a hunt seat saddle, you will feel your horse tighten up more quickly and will have ample warning if she is about to react.

The negatives of riding on the trail in a hunt seat saddle include the fact that you don't have much to keep you in the saddle if your horse spins, rears, bolts, or does something dangerous as a response to fear. You have to be a very good rider to stay on board a horse who is behaving like this if you have nothing between you and your mount except a hunt seat saddle.

Because hunt seat saddles hold the rider's body in a more forward position, some riders find them uncomfortable during long trail rides. Lengthening the stirrups can be helpful in making the ride more comfortable, although the hard seat found on most hunt seat saddles starts to wear on most riders' backsides after a while. You can purchase a soft sheepskin or gel seat cover to help soften the ride.

DRESSAGE

Dressage saddles are similar to hunt seat saddles in appearance, but once you ride in one, you'll see a big difference between the two. Dressage saddles have a deeper seat than their hunt seat counterparts, and position the rider's body in a more upright position. Dressage riders wear their stirrups longer than do hunt seat riders, which is more conducive to long hours on the trail.

The positives to dressage saddles are similar to those of hunt seat saddles. Riders have more contact with the horse in a dressage saddle than they do in a Western saddle. English saddles are relatively light, and dressage saddles are no exception, giving the horse less weight to carry.

The downside to trail riding in a dressage saddle is the lack of something to grab on to should you lose your balance. Although a dressage saddle has a deeper seat than a hunt seat saddle, it won't hold you in the way a Western saddle will.

SADDLE SEAT

Saddle seat saddles, also called show saddles, are usually seen only in the show ring, with certain gaited breeds (horses who possess a four-beat gait in lieu of the trot) and certain types of classes for "trotting breeds," such as the Morgan and Arabian. Most popular in the South where these saddles were developed, show saddles are not often seen on the trail. The exception to this would be riders who ride their horses in saddle seat in show competition and want to go for a trail ride to keep their horses' minds fresh.

Saddle seat saddles have very flat seats compared to other English saddles, making them less likely to keep a rider in the saddle during an unpleasant episode on the trail. On the other hand, saddle seat saddles are comfortable to sit in, and are ridden with longer stirrups. If you are most comfortable in a saddle seat saddle, there is no reason not to use this same saddle to ride on the trail.

Western Saddles

The most popular saddle for trail riding is the Western saddle. Designed to carry cowhands for many hours at a time, and keep them secure in the saddle while roping, cutting, and herding cattle, Western saddles do a good job of keeping the rider on the horse. The seat is deeper than most English saddles, and the presence of a horn provides something to grab on to should you lose your balance.

Western saddles feature large fenders that protect the rider's leg from direct contact with the horse. This can be useful when riding over many miles of terrain on a sweaty horse. The stirrups are worn long on a Western saddle, which many riders find most comfortable on the trail.

Another benefit to riding in a Western saddle is that Western riders hold the reins with only one hand, usually the left. This leaves the other hand free, which many riders find to be very convenient. With your right hand free, you can easily reach into your saddlebag and pull out a snack, grab your water bottle for a swig, or even take pictures while on horseback.

The biggest drawback to trail riding in a Western saddle is its weight. Western saddles are substantially heavier than English saddles and can weigh as much as 25 pounds.

Western saddles come in a variety of different styles designed for various types of Western riding. Whether a Western saddle is designed for barrel racing, roping, or pleasure riding, any of these styles is fine for a jaunt down the trail.

Endurance Saddles

Serious trail riders—those who participate in competitive trail rides and/or endurance racing—use endurance saddles. Inspired by Australian saddles designed for cattle work in the Outback, endurance saddles look like a cross between an English saddle and a Western saddle.

Endurance saddles come in a number of different designs. Some have high pommels (the front area of the saddle), while others have virtually no pommel. Some have very deep seats, while others have seats that are shallower. Some have stirrups designed like those of a Western saddle, while others have traditional stirrup leathers like those found on English saddles.

The great thing about endurance saddles is that they are designed for riders who spend many hours on the trail. A good endurance saddle is so comfortable, you can easily see yourself sitting in it all day.

Endurance saddles are also lightweight, and are much easier to lift than Western saddles. This makes the rider easier for the horse, and makes tacking and untacking easy for the rider.

The benefits of endurance saddles are many, and also include more flexibility in the stirrup for better comfort when going up and down steep hills. When you are negotiating this kind of terrain, you need to be able to get your leg far out in front of you on the downhill, and behind you on the uphill. An endurance saddle will allow you to easily swing your leg in either direction.

Endurance saddles are designed to give riders the proper position for trail riding, and therefore, a comfortable ride. They also feature a number of D-rings in various places to give you plenty of spots where you can clip on sports bottle holders, saddle packs, and anything else you want to take along with you on the ride.

Well-made endurance saddles also do a lot to protect the horse by evenly distributing the rider's weight through wide panels and special design. Taking care of the horse's back is a priority in trail riding since many riders spend many hours in the saddle at a time.

Serious trail riders have come up with all kinds of girth riggings, breast collars, and other accessories to help endurance saddles fit better and be more comfortable for the horse. If you explore the websites and catalogs listed in appendix B, "Resources," you'll discover a wide variety of endurance saddles and accessories.

Buying a Saddle

Once you've decided which type of saddle you'd like for trail riding, think about whether you want a new or used saddle. A new saddle will cost you more, of course (anywhere from $400 to $2,000), and will be in excellent condition. On the other hand, you'll need to break in a new saddle and spend time oiling it to soften the leather. The exception to this would be if you purchase a synthetic saddle. Saddles made from synthetic materials are becoming more popular because they are lightweight, durable, easy to clean, and less expensive than leather. Some are even adjustable so they will fit any horse. Whether you buy a leather saddle or a synthetic saddle is a matter of personal preference. Many trail riders prefer the tradition of leather and opt for a leather saddle rather than a less expensive synthetic model.

If you prefer to get a used saddle, you'll find plenty of deals out there. Look in the classified section of your local paper, or in your local equestrian publication for people selling used tack. Visit a tack consignment shop, and keep an eye out on the bulletin boards of your local stable and feed store. Many riders are also finding good deals on Internet auction sites, too.

When buying a used saddle, it's important to make certain the saddle does not have a broken tree. This can be tricky, so take the saddle to a saddle repair shop or to your instructor or other professional horseperson to see if they can

Western saddle   All-purpose English saddle

Endurance saddle

Examples of a Western saddle, an all-purpose English saddle, and an endurance saddle.

help you make this determination. A broken tree renders a saddle useless because it will not provide the kind of support the horse needs between herself and the rider.

Whether you are considering a new saddle or a used one, it's vital that you make sure the seller gives you a trial period so you can try the saddle on your horse to see if it fits. A poor-fitting saddle can be a disaster for your horse, causing back problems, leg problems, and ultimately attitude problems. Poorly fitting saddles are one of the leading causes of muscle pain and soreness among horses, and in extreme situations, can even result in permanent damage to the horse.

Not every saddle fits every horse, and properly fitting a saddle to a horse can be a complicated endeavor. You'll need the help of an expert horseperson to help you determine if the saddle fits the horse. Make certain you position the saddle properly on the horse first; the front of the saddle should be placed just behind the horse's shoulder blades. When you attach the girth, the strap should fall about four inches behind the horse's elbow when the horse's foreleg is stretched out. (You can do this by standing in front of the horse, and lifting and pulling the horse's leg forward.)

Basic rules of thumb for saddle fitting include sliding your hand under the front of the saddle where it meets the horse's shoulder. Have someone do this for you while you are sitting in the saddle. Your helper should be able to fit his or her hand between the saddle and the horse's back. If the fit is so tight that your helper can't get a hand underneath, the saddle doesn't fit.

Regardless of the type of saddle you are considering, you should also look for three fingers' worth of room between the underside of the pommel and the horse's withers. The top of the pommel should not be touching the horse's withers. If it does, the pommel will rub on the horse and cause pain and eventually an open sore.

A variety of other methods can be applied to determine if a saddle fits right, and the best person to evaluate this is an expert in your discipline. Have a professional take a look at the saddle you are considering to help you judge if it's a good fit for your horse.

Keep in mind that a saddle that fits properly is a must no matter what your riding discipline, but it's particularly important in trail riding. Trail horses spend hours wearing their saddles, and if the saddle doesn't fit, the horse is in for all kinds of pain and physical problems. Poor saddle fit can impede a horse's ability to move properly, cause her to move with a hollow back, and create open, oozing sores.

Horses can't talk, and the only way they have of letting us know they are in pain is to misbehave. If your trail horse is acting up, take a good look at your saddle and how it fits.

Bridles

A saddle is not the only piece of equipment you need for trail riding. The bridle you use on your trail horse is also important. If you ride your horse in the arena and she goes well in a particular bridle and bit, then this equipment should be fine for trail riding. However, if you are serious about trail riding and want to spend many hours on the trail, you might want to consider an alternative bridle for riding out in the open.

Trail riders use all kinds of bridles and bits out on the trail, but two of the most commonly seen among long-distance riders are hackamores and trail bridles. Some very serious trail riders even have custom bridles designed for their horses.

Hackamores are bitless bridles that work by exerting pressure on the horse's nose. Many trail riders like hackamores because the absence of a bit in the mouth means the horse can easily graze and drink out on long trail rides without interference. A horse can still eat and drink while wearing a bit, but these tasks are more comfortable for the horse in a hackamore.

Unlike hackamores, trail bridles utilize bits, but also include a built-in halter. Trail bridles allow riders to easily tie a horse to a tree or other safe object from a halter that is part of the bridle. Since it is unsafe to tie a horse by the reins because the horse's mouth could be damaged if he pulls back, trail riders who will need to tie their horses on a long ride must carry a halter. A trail bridle with a built-in halter eliminates the need to carry an extra halter on the saddle or have the horse wear a halter under the bridle. Trail bridles usually have reins that are connected in the middle, a setup that lends itself to riding with two hands, although Western-style reins can replace the English style.

The type of bridle you ultimately choose for your trail riding activities is a matter of personal preference. If you ride English in an arena and don't want to buy another set of tack just to trail ride a few times a week, then your English bridle will do fine. On the other hand, if you plan to do very long trail rides and even overnight camping rides, you'll want a bridle that is most conducive to your future activities. This may include a simple Western bit and bridle, an English bridle with a bit, or a hackamore or trail bridle. The choice is yours.

The bit you use for your bridle (assuming you are not using a hackamore) will depend on your horse and her training level. Some horses use very mild bits, while others require a stronger bit for more control. Your instructor or another equine expert can help you decide which bit is best for your horse on the trail. Some horses need stronger bits on the trail than they do in the arena, and some need lighter bits. It's all about your individual horse's needs.

Other Trail Tack

Tack manufacturers have designed a number of other items that can come in handy for trail riders. These tack accessories can be useful if you spend a lot of time riding on the trail.

These types of accessories are available in different materials, from leather to Biothane. You may have to experiment a little to find the material that does not chafe your horse. Endurance riders report that Neoprene and Biothane products seem to be most comfortable.

GIRTH

The girth (or cinch, as it's referred to in Western circles) is the piece of equipment that holds the saddle onto the horse. Casual trail riders use any girth that is meant for their type of saddle, usually made from leather, while hardcore trail riders experiment with synthetic materials that are easier to clean than leather or sheepskin girths. Some riders also believe certain synthetic materials can be more comfortable for the horse.

Girths made specifically for endurance saddles often feature different types of rigging (the way the girth is attached to the saddle), some very unique. Many serious trail riders also change the rigging on their saddles to create their own custom designs.

BREAST COLLAR

Horses who travel up and down hills in their trail work can benefit from a breast collar. The breast collar attaches to the front sides of the saddle and the girth underneath the horse, and works to hold the saddle in place when going up hills. Without a breast collar, some saddles slide back on the horse and end up in the wrong position after the horse finishes the climb.

The cinch is the piece of equipment that secures the saddle to the horse. Have an experienced horse person teach you how to properly tie it around your horse.

Breast collars are made for English saddles, Western saddles, and endurance saddles, and come in a variety of materials from nylon to polyurethane. They also come in a variety of colors and designs. The breast collar you use is a matter of your own personal taste and what works best for your horse's comfort.

SADDLE PAD

You must have a saddle pad between your saddle and your horse to protect your horse's back from chafing from the saddle, to protect the saddle from dirt and sweat from the horse's back, and to provide extra support for the horse. If you are a casual trail rider using an English or Western saddle, you can use any pad designed for your saddle type. Western pads tend to be thick and rectangular, while hunt seat pads usually take on the shape of the saddle. Dressage pads are often quilted, and saddle seat pads can be square quilted pads or thicker pads that mirror the shape of the saddle.

Serious trail riders using endurance saddles experiment with saddle pads, and often ride with pads that are designed especially for the sport of trail riding. These pads provide extra support for saddles being used on horses who spend many hours on the trail, and come in everything from sheep's wool to gel. If you want to get into long-distance riding, talk to other people in the sport and see what they prefer. You may even be able to borrow a pad from another rider to see how you like it before you make the investment. (If you do this, be sure to wash the pad before and after you use it to avoid spreading possible skin conditions from one horse to another.)

CRUPPER

The crupper is a device that attaches around the base of the horse's trail and connects to the back of the saddle. The purpose of the crupper is to keep the saddle from sliding too far forward when a rider is going down very steep hills. Most cruppers are designed to be used with endurance saddles, which feature D-rings on the back of the saddle for attachment. You probably don't need a crupper unless you plan to do a lot of riding on steep hills.

Choose a style and material that will not chafe your horse and that only tightens when you are going downhill. When your horse is on level ground, the crupper should be slack.

ACCESSORIES

When it comes to accessories, few equine sports can keep up with the plethora of items available for trail riders. Here's a look at a few of the more popular accessories.

Saddle Packs

If you plan to be out on the trail for many hours, you'll want to have a saddle pack attached to your saddle. Most saddle packs fit on the back of the saddle, although some packs are designed to sit on the front. Saddle packs come in a wide variety of shapes and sizes. Almost all feature holders for sports bottles, and all have at least one large pouch where you can put your lunch, sunscreen, cell phone, horse treats, or anything else you want to carry along.

Water Bottle Holders

For shorter rides where a saddle pack isn't necessary, trail riders can opt for a water bottle holder designed to clip onto one of the D-rings located on the front or back of most saddles.

Seat Covers

Long hours on the trail can be tough on your hind end. Trail riders often equip their saddles with seat covers, made from sheepskin (or fake sheepskin) or gel. Seat covers are designed for Western, English, and endurance saddles, and come in a wide array of prices.

GPS Devices

Trail riders were using Global Positioning System (GPS) technology long before auto manufacturers were making them standard fare in higher-end cars.

GPS devices designed for use by sailors and other navigators can be attached to the saddle to help serious trail riders determine how many miles they have ridden at a time, as well as where they are located on difficult trails, by using satellites that orbit around the earth.

Heart Monitors

Many serious endurance riders use equestrian heart rate monitors to help them gauge their horse's heart rate during training on the trail. Knowing the horse's heart rate helps riders determine how the horse is doing in his training, and also gives them an idea of how the horse will fare in upcoming endurance rides.

Hoof Boots

A hoof boot can be a trail rider's best friend. If you are out riding on a rocky trail and your horse suddenly loses a shoe, a hoof boot can come to the rescue. Designed to slip over the horse's hoof and protect the bottom of the foot from rocks and hard terrain, a hoof boot can get your horse back home safe and sound.

Many serious trail riders keep a hoof boot in their saddle pack just in case of emergency. Some even use hoof boots when riding on concrete or rough terrain just to protect the horse's feet.

Before purchasing a hoof boot, measure your horse's hoof to determine which size will fit best. Follow the manufacturer's instructions on measuring. See appendix B for contact information on hoof boot manufacturers.

Rump Rugs

For trail riders who work in inclement weather, something called a rump rug can be helpful. This attaches to the back of the saddle and lies over the horse's rear end to help keep the muscles warm in cold and/or wet weather. Rump rugs are made from water-resistant materials that help keep your horse's hindquarters dry. They also allow your horse to cool down more slowly after a workout in cold weather.

Miscellaneous Goodies

All kinds of items are available to make the trail rider's life easier. Foldaway water buckets for horses, portable corrals, straps to hang and attach to saddle packs, combination sponges and bags, folding hoof picks, portable water tanks . . . you name it, it's out there!

The best place to buy unique trail tack is through catalogs specializing in trail items. You'll find a list of these catalog and online retailers in appendix B.

Halter and Lead Rope

While all this stuff is fun and great for trail riding, you'll also need the most basic of all horse owner tools: the halter and lead rope. The halter is your most fundamental tool for controlling your horse, and will be your most often used piece of tack. The lead rope is a close second since a halter isn't much good without a lead rope.

Go into any tack store or visit any catalog or online tack retailer, and you'll see many different kinds of halters. While there are numerous colors and patterns on halters these days, you'll see three basic types of materials: leather, nylon, and cotton rope.

Most horses only wear their halters when they are being groomed, but trail horses often wear theirs when they are working. Unless you plan to buy a combination bridle and halter, you'll want to keep your horse's halter on his head when you go on long rides, with his lead rope attached. The reason for this, as I've mentioned, is that it's unsafe to tie a horse by the reins of the bridle, and if you need to stop and tie your horse to a tree, you must do it with your lead rope. In fact, some trail-riding competitions require that the horse be wearing a halter and lead rope (the rope is tied to the saddle) during the judging.

So how do you know what kind of halter and lead rope to get? Leather halters are the fanciest and most expensive, and look the nicest. Nylon halters come in a vast array of colors and designs, and are very durable. Cotton rope halters are the least expensive and are light as a feather but also durable.

Ultimately, the choice is a matter of personal preference. Any one of these halters will do. Keep in mind that if you plan to keep the halter on under your horse's bridle while riding on the trail (and that's how your horse needs to wear it), a nylon or cotton rope halter will be the least bulky.

As for lead ropes, twisted cotton ropes are the easiest on your hands should the horse pull back when you are holding the rope. Nylon lead ropes are inclined to burn your hands as they slide through. For this reason, some riders don't use them. On the other hand, if you are a big fan of color coordination, you'll find that many nylon halters also have nylon lead ropes in matching colors and patterns.

Leather lead ropes are not really practical for trail riding, although they look nice if you are showing your horse or if you plan to take pictures.

Caring for Your Tack

If you're the type of rider who is comfortable using synthetic materials, caring for your tack will be easy: Simply hose your stuff off when it gets dirty! Of course, if you have leather tack—or even if it's just a leather saddle, with synthetic girth, breastplate, crupper, and bridle—you need to take special care of the leather so it stays strong and in good condition.

True fanatics about leather care clean their saddles after every ride to keep dust, dirt, and mildew from slowly destroying the leather. Since this amount of

If you take good care of your tack, your bridles and saddles will last for many years.

work is not practical for most riders because of time constraints, you can help keep your leather saddle in good condition by at least dusting it off after every ride and keeping it covered when you're not using it. (You can buy saddle covers designed to fit English and Western saddles, some of which also fit endurance saddles.) Whenever you have time after a ride, apply leather conditioner to the saddle to keep it plush and moisturized. Be sure to clean off any sweat that may have accumulated on the saddle using water and saddle soap, or a leather cleaner, before you apply the conditioner.

At least once a month, give your leather saddle a good, thorough cleaning. Using saddle soap and a tack sponge (available at tack stores), scrub down the entire saddle, including the stirrup leathers. Be sure to get into the nooks and crannies of the saddle, where dust and mildew gather. If you have a Western saddle with tooling, a toothbrush can help you get into the detail to clean it out.

After you have finished scrubbing down the saddle, go back over it with clean, damp tack sponge to remove the saddle soap, and let it dry. Once the leather is dry, you can apply leather conditioner to make the saddle supple.

If you have other leather tack, like a bridle and breast collar, now is the time to clean that, too. You may need to take your leather bridle apart to really get at all the dirt that accumulates. Just take a good close look at how it looks before you dismantle it so you can easily put it back together.

Part II

CARING FOR
THE TRAIL HORSE

Chapter 5

BASIC CARE

T he care you give your trail horse will help determine how long your equine friend will be able to carry you over hill and dale. Horses have been known to continue trail riding into their 30s if they received good care when they were young.

An important part of horse care is stabling and feeding. Your horse's environment and what you feed him will help determine his overall health and mental well-being, and is something you should make a high priority. Grooming is another aspect of basic care, and should be attended to on a regular basis.

Options for Housing

Once upon a time, all horses were kept on the family farm or in the household stable. In today's world, not all horse owners have that option.

Those of us who are fortunate enough to have what real estate agents call "horse property" can keep our equine charges right in our backyards. Your horse property might be a quarter-acre lot in a suburban neighborhood that is zoned for horse keeping, or it might be a 250-acre pasture in God's country. Either way, if you keep your horse on your own land, you have ultimate control of that horse's housing and feeding—and ultimate responsibility.

Horse owners in urban environments must usually keep their horses at boarding stables, where they pay a monthly fee in exchange for the horse's stall or paddock, feed, and stall maintenance.

Advantages exist with both of these methods. Having your horse at home means you have complete control over everything in his surroundings. You control the amount your horse eats, how often and what time his stall gets cleaned, and who is stabled next to him. You don't have to drive to get to your horse, and you can always keep an eye on him to make sure he's doing okay.

If you board your horse, someone else does most of the work for you. A stable hand or the owner of the property where you board feeds your horse and cleans his stall. The boarding stable management or the property owner pays for repairs to the facility and hauls away the manure (or pays a service to haul it away). If you can't make it down to the stable one day, it's not a crisis. Your horse will still be fed and cleaned up after, and there is always someone around to give him a bucket of grain or other special feed if he needs it.

You can find plenty of disadvantages to each of these situations, too. Keeping your horse at home means a lot of work. You have to be around at certain times of the day to feed him, and you have to clean his stall every day. If something breaks in your horse's stall, you have to fix it. And if you live on a small property, the flies that come with every horse will drive you nuts.

On the other hand, if you board your horse, you can't just go out in the backyard and hop on. You'll need to drive to get to your horse. You also won't be able to check on him through the day and evening to make sure he's okay, and you won't be able to control exactly how much food he is getting—which can be a real problem if you are trying to manage your horse's weight. And then there's the money. In addition to the rent or mortgage on your own living quarters, you must spend money for a boarding fee as well as for gasoline that you use to go back and forth to wherever you keep him.

If you have horse property, you may think it's a simple decision as to whether or not to board your horse. But if you are a serious trail rider, think again. Do you have access to trails where you live? Or must you put your horse in a trailer every time you want to go on a trail ride? The answer to these questions may determine whether you want to keep your horse on your own land or at a boarding stable with close proximity to good riding trails.

HOUSING DETAILS

Whether you opt to board your horse or keep him at home, you need to consider what type of housing your horse will have.

In the horse world, the box stall is considered the equine equivalent to the luxury apartment. Usually measuring anywhere from 12 by 12 feet to 18 by 16 feet, box stalls are just what they sound like: a stall in the shape of a box. Many horse owners opt to put their horses in box stalls, provided they can afford it, reasoning that the horse will be happier. Good box stalls are filled with clean wood shavings, so the horse always has a soft place to lie down, and horses who live in box stalls stay cleaner longer. They are also protected from wind, rain, snow, and harsh sunlight, and bites and kicks from other horses.

While box stalls might be most appropriate for certain show horses and racehorses because of the value of these animals and their owners' wishes that these horses never have a scratch on them, most trail horses don't need a box stall, regardless of the climate. Trail horses are rugged, hardy creatures who do well outdoors. In fact, the ventilation in barns that contain box stalls is often less favorable than outdoor enclosures, and often contributes to respiratory problems in the horses who live there. Horses who live in box stalls are also more prone to leg problems because they don't move around as much as horses in outdoor enclosures. Stall-bound horses sometimes develop stable vices such as cribbing and weaving in response to the boredom of being kept in a box stall as opposed to outdoors.

Which brings us to the first of two outdoor options: the paddock. Paddocks are areas usually anywhere from 12 by 24 feet to five times that size. Most paddocks have a shelter or covering of some sort to protect the horse from the elements. They consist of a dirt floor, hopefully with good drainage so the dirt doesn't turn to mud when it rains. Paddocks are often linked together, so horses stabled in these kinds of enclosures often have a horse next door whom they can touch and interact with.

Most trail horses do very well in paddocks. Paddocks allow them to move around more than most box stalls do and provide them with closer proximity to nature and to other horses. The good news is that paddocks are almost always cheaper than box stalls when it comes to boarding or building one on your own property.

The next and most ideal housing for trail horses is the pasture. Pastures can be any size, from a quarter-acre to 500 acres. Pastures typically have grass that the horse can eat whenever the mood strikes him (which is often, since horses typically graze for 18 hours a day).

Pastures are the best option in housing for trail horses. A pasture environment allows the horse to graze at leisure, which is the most natural way of living for a horse. It's healthy for the horse's digestive system as well as for the horse's joints since the horse is always moving, leaving joints well lubricated.

If you can't ride more than a couple of times a week, a pasture is the best place for your trail horse because he'll have plenty of room and won't feel cooped up. A horse kept in a box stall or small paddock who is not exercised nearly every day is bound to start storing energy, which will be unleashed the next time you ride. Since trail horses should be calm and obedient, the last thing you want is a pent-up trail horse.

The good news is that in most areas, pastures are the least expensive place to keep a horse. The disadvantages are that your horse will inevitably get dirty and you'll spend time cleaning him up every time you take him out to ride. (See "Grooming," later in this chapter, for details.) If he is living with other horses in the pasture, he is at risk for being kicked or bitten. Your horse may also be difficult to catch out in a pasture, although this is a bad behavior that can and should be remedied with training.

IF YOU ARE BOARDING . . .

If circumstances dictate that you board your horse, shop carefully for a boarding situation. You'll want a place you can afford, of course, but don't skimp on quality just to get a good price. Your horse's well-being depends on the care he receives at a boarding facility. If you opt for cheap at the cost of quality, your horse will suffer for it.

You'll find two options in boarding facilities: the commercial stable that houses a number of horses owned by different people, and the private home that is open to a boarder or two or three. Advantages exist to both.

Commercial boarding stables often have amenities that you can't find at most private homes with horse property. These include riding arenas (including lights so you can ride at night), round pen enclosures for training and lunging, and wash racks. You'll also find help in the form of one or more trainers who will probably be affiliated with the stable. This can be a great resource if you run into trouble.

A commercial stable should also be a bit more professional than a private person renting out a stall, and will have hired help to make sure important jobs like feeding and stall cleaning get done at the same time every day.

At a commercial stable, you'll meet other riders and will make friends, many of whom will be happy to trail ride with you. This can be important if you have a nervous horse you are trying to "break" to trail.

Private properties have their advantages too. A personal touch accompanies most private boarding facilities. You and the owner will get to know each other and may even end up riding together, if the owner has his or her own horses. If the owner lives on the property, you'll know someone is always around to keep an eye on your horse. Private boarding situations tend to be less expensive than commercial boarding stables, in large part because these small facilities lack the amenities of a riding arena, round pen, and other features commonly found at large stables.

Whichever type of situation you choose, make sure you keep the following points in mind when you are making your decision:

- *Proximity to trails.* If you are reading this book, trail riding is important to you. Unless you have no problem trailering your horse every time you want to go on a trail ride, make certain the boarding facility has access to trails. Before you sign a boarding agreement, hike some of the trails to make sure they are safe and well maintained. Be certain the trails are long enough to give you a decent ride. Remember, your horse will travel about four miles an hour at a walk, so the more trails you have, the longer you can ride and the more variety you will have in your trail riding.

- *Access to a riding arena.* Even though you are going to be trail riding, it's important to have access to an arena where you can train. If you are considering a private home that doesn't have arena access, find out if the community has a common arena where you can ride. If not, look around for boarding and training stables in the area and see if they have an arena they might lease you for a monthly fee. Even the most well-mannered trail horse might need to be lunged once in a while, get a turnout, or require some schooling under saddle in an enclosed environment. Don't discount the need for an area just because your number one preference is trail riding.

- *Good maintenance.* Make certain the facility is well maintained before you sign a contract. Walk around the grounds and look at the stalls, paddocks, and pastures. Check to see that the buildings are in good shape and the horse areas are free from debris that could be harmful to a horse. (Horses are great at hurting themselves on seemingly innocuous objects.) Look to see if the stalls are clean and well kept. If your horse will be out in a pasture, check the fencing to make sure it's secure. (Avoid facilities that use barbed wire for pasture fencing because this type of fencing is dangerous to horses.) If the facility provides automatic waterers, check a number of stalls to see if they are working. If water is provided in a trough, make certain it is full and clean. Also, find out if the stalls are cleaned every day, and how often. Don't keep your horse at a place where the stalls aren't cleaned at least once a day. And be sure to check the amenities such as riding arenas and round pens to be certain they are in good working order.

- *Feeding.* If your horse will be getting fed at the facility, find out what kinds of feed are available. Next to pasture grass that the horse can graze on, hay is the best staple for most horses, including trail mounts. Some facilities only feed pelleted food and swear by it, but most veterinarians prefer a diet of grass or hay for their equine clients. Find out what kind of hay is available to your horse, and discuss these options with your veterinarian. Frequency of feeding is important too. Since horses were designed to eat most of the day, the more feedings a horse receives each day, the better. The minimum number of feeding times should be two, but three is even better. Take a peek at the hay supply at the stable and see if the quality is good. (See "Feeding Your Trail Horse," later in this chapter, for advice on judging hay quality.)

- *Health requirements.* Large boarding stables should require that your horse be vaccinated against the most common contagious diseases, such as influenza/rhinopneumonitus and equine encephalomyelitis. This is to protect not only your own horse, but the other boarders as well. Certain contagious diseases are more common in different parts of the country, so it's a good idea to ask your vet what he or she would like to see at a local boarding stable in terms of vaccines.

- *A place for tack.* Many boarding facilities allow boarders to keep a tack locker by their horse's stall, or even have individual or group tack sheds available for rent. This is a nice touch if you can find it. Otherwise, you'll have to lug your saddle, bridle, grooming tools, and everything else you need for your horse in your car every time you come to ride.

- *Professional behavior.* Last but not least, expect professionalism from the people who run the facility. They should give you a contract to sign, and if the facility is a commercial stable, a list of stable rules. They should be friendly and polite, and act as if they care about your business—and your horse. Remember, if you have a problem that needs addressing, such as a waterer that doesn't work or a special need for your horse should he become sick or injured, these are the people you will have to deal with, and probably under stressful conditions.

Boarding facilities offer a variety of housing options, from basic outdoor corrals to indoor box stalls.

KEEPING YOUR HORSE AT HOME

If you have property where you can keep your horse at home, you are one of the lucky ones. Most horse owners dream of being able to have their horses close by, although some prefer not to do the work.

And work there is. If your horse is at your home, you'll need to supply facilities for him. You'll have to buy his food, feed it to him at least twice a day, and clean his stall daily. The tradeoff is that your horse is just out your back door, ready for a trail ride any time the mood strikes you.

If you have property without horse facilities, you'll need to provide either a barn with box stalls, a paddock, or a pasture for your horse. The details of building these enclosures is beyond the scope of this book, but you'll find plenty of good sources for information on horsekeeping on the Internet and in your tack store's book section. Regardless of which type of enclosure you choose, be sure to hire a qualified professional to build or install the enclosure if you don't plan to do it yourself. Get referrals from other horse owners in the area to find out who is the best contractor in town for this type of work.

If space allows, consider adding a riding arena to your property so you can school your horse under saddle or in the lunge line in an enclosed space. If your horse is living in a stall or paddock, he might appreciate some turnout time in an arena, too.

You should also plan for tack storage. A small 6-by-8-foot tack shed is more than enough room to store tack for two horses. You'll be able to organize your bridles, saddles, and all the other accessories you'll need for your horse.

Hay storage is something else you will need to have on your property. The amount of space you need for this depends on how many horses you are feeding. A 4-by-6-foot area is big enough to store about 12 bales of stacked hay, which can last you over a month if you have only one horse on the property. You won't need to build a cover for your hay storage area if you don't mind protecting the hay from wet weather with a tarp. If you don't like the idea of having to cover the hay stack, then add a permanent cover to protect your hay from getting wet and moldy.

A wash rack is also a handy addition to any property where horses reside. A wash rack can be a simple concrete slab, around 12 by 12 feet with a hitching post or crossties cemented in and plumbing nearby for

Keeping your horse at home means doing the dirty work yourself.

a garden hose. On hot days when you come back from a long trail ride, your horse will appreciate a bath to get the sweat out of his coat.

Living in an equine community, you should have manure pickup as part of your sanitation options. If your local trash company does not provide manure hauling, you'll need to find a way to dispose of your horse's waste. Some people compost the manure, although this can be a smelly way to get rid of it, especially if your property is small. The number of flies on your property is bound to increase as well if you keep a pile of composting manure around.

Although it costs money to get your horse facility up and running, you'll find that keeping your horse at home is cheaper in the long run. Boarding facilities typically charge more than double what it costs to keep a horse at home.

Feeding Your Trail Horse

When it comes to determining what your trail horse should eat and how much, your first reference should be your equine veterinarian. Your horse's vet is an expert at equine nutrition, and knows the types of feed that are most accessible in your area. Your vet will also be able to access your individual horse's needs and give you the best advice on how to feed your trail mount.

That said, your vet is likely to recommend that your horse's diet consist primarily of hay. Hay comes in two basic types: grass and legumes. The most often seen grass hays in North America include Bermuda, bluegrass, fescue, orchard, rye, timothy, barley hay, oat hay, and prairie grass. Common legumes are alfalfa,

Quality hay should make up the bulk of your trail horse's daily feed ration.

clover, soybeans, and bird's-foot trefoil. By the far the most popular of these legumes is alfalfa.

The basic differences between grass hays and legumes are that grass hays have more fiber and provide less energy. They can be good for horses who tend to put on weight easily since they are less likely to cause weight gain. Depending on the particular grass hay, they can be safe to feed in large quantities, allowing horse owners to provide a more natural state for horses, who are designed to have food moving through their systems on an almost constant basis.

If you have a horse who needs more energy or has trouble keeping weight on, a legume hay such as alfalfa can be a good choice. Legumes have more protein and more calcium than grass hays. This can be good or bad, depending on your horse's age and health issues. Your vet can tell you if legume hay or grass hay is most appropriate for your particular horse.

If your horse is in a pasture and grazes on a quality pasture grass all day, he may not need supplementing with hay. However, it's important to discuss your horse's needs with his veterinarian before you assume he doesn't need hay in addition to pasture grass.

Because trail horses put in a lot of hours at work—especially if they compete—concentrated feeds can sometimes help them keep weight on and give them more energy in the form of concentrated fats and carbohydrates. These feeds come in sweet feed form and pelleted form. Sweet feeds are just that— sweet because of the addition of, most commonly, molasses. Pelleted feeds are usually more digestible than sweet feeds because of the way they are processed,

Treats Galore!

Horses absolutely adore treats, and trail horses are no exception. Nothing says "thanks for the great ride" better than a good treat once you are back at the barn.

Here is a list of some of the most popular treats among horses. While no official polls have ever been taken on this subject, it's not hard to figure out that these are the top equine favorites:

- *Carrots.* It's hard to find a horse who doesn't love carrots. Something about the sweet taste really appeals to them. Carrots are healthy for horses in moderation. If your horse likes to gobble his treats, cut up the carrots in small pieces so he doesn't eat too much at once.

- *Apples.* Red apples are high up on the list of equine favorites, but many horses like green ones, too. Cut apples up in pieces to help the horse out. Many horses will happily try to eat a whole apple—but that's not only difficult for them, it could pose a choking hazard.

- *Peppermints.* Horses love peppermints, especially the red-and-white ones you see around Christmas. These should be fed in moderation because they are high in sugar.

- *Sugar cubes.* Speaking of sugar, everyone knows that horses love sugar cubes. It's not the best treat in terms of equine health, but an occasional sugar cube never hurt anybody.

- *Commercial treats.* Your local tack store is loaded with all kinds of commercial horse treats, made from oats, corn, and other assorted grains, usually mixed with molasses. Horses usually love these, and aren't very discerning. If you offer it, chances are they will eat it.

and contain similar ingredients to sweet feeds. Pelleted feeds usually contain two or more of the following ingredients: corn, oats, and wheat.

If your horse is older, has trouble keeping his weight up, or gets lots of exercise, he might benefit from a concentrated feed in his diet. These feeds are also useful for mixing in dietary supplements, such as joint powders, vitamins, and other compounds. However, before you start giving a concentrated feed to your horse, talk to your veterinarian. If your horse doesn't need the excess energy to do his job, you may find yourself with a problem animal on your hands if you start giving him concentrated feeds. (Sort of like giving sugar to an already hyperactive child.) The expression "feeling his oats" is more than just a saying—horses who eat oats and other concentrated feeds can get pretty feisty. The last thing you want is a crazy horse out on the trail, caused by unnecessary feeding of concentrated feeds.

DIETARY SUPPLEMENTS

A visit to your local tack and feed store will reveal a plethora of dietary supplements designed for horses. These supplements are most often made from natural ingredients and are meant to keep horses healthy and enhance their performance.

Because they are not drugs in the technical sense, dietary supplements are not approved by the Food and Drug Administration (FDA), and some do not have significant studies to support their worth. However, anecdotal evidence is strong indicating that many dietary supplements do work to help horses stay sound and healthy.

Only your veterinarian can advise you on which, if any, supplements your horse needs. That said, here's a rundown of some of the dietary supplements most commonly given to trail horses:

- *MSM.* Short for Methyl-sulfonyl-methane, MSM is a sulfur compound that occurs naturally in the body. It is reportedly helpful in preventing and treating inflammation, arthritis, and muscle pain. MSM is believed to be most effective when taken in conjunction with glucosamine and chondroitin.

- *Glucosamine.* Glucosamine sulfate, an amino sugar produced from the shells of chitin, a shellfish, is reported to help reduce inflammation and arthritis by stimulating joint function and repair. Glucosamine is often combined with chondroitin for maximum benefit.

- *Chondroitin.* Chondroitin sulfate is a natural substance found in the body. Its job is to help build and support cartilage. As a supplement, it is given for arthritis and joint health.

- *Yucca.* Obtained from the yucca plant, which grows naturally in southwestern U.S. deserts, yucca supplements are reportedly useful in decreasing inflammation.

- *Electrolytes.* Salts that are found naturally in the body, electrolytes can be supplemented to help replace minerals lost while sweating. Electrolytes also encourage horses to drink, which reduces the likelihood of colic. Azoturia, or tying up, can also be prevented with electrolyte supplements.

- *Probiotics.* Compounds that encourage the growth of "good" bacteria in the gut, probiotic supplements contain certain bacterias meant to replace whatever necessary organisms might be missing in the horse's intestines as a result of antibiotic use or stress. Probiotics are thought to help prevent colic and diarrhea.

Keep in mind that if you plan to compete in endurance racing with your horse (see chapter 15, "Racing on the Trail"), a dietary supplement may give you a positive result on your horse's drug test. Discuss any supplement you are considering for your horse with an official of the sponsoring endurance event to make sure you don't get disqualified.

Grooming

Even though your trail horse may not be a show contender, you should still keep him clean and well groomed. You want your horse to look good even if all he's doing is carrying you through the woods. Also, a clean coat underneath the saddle is better for your horse. Dirt and debris between the horse's back and the saddle pad can cause sores and irritation.

You'll need a set of basic equine grooming tools to get the job done. These include a stiff body brush, a soft face brush, a mane and tail brush, a currycomb, a sweat scraper, and a hoof pick. While you are shopping for these items, pick up some horse shampoo and conditioner for days when you are going to give your horse a bath.

Groom your horse before and after every ride. Before the ride, give him a vigorous rubdown with the currycomb to dislodge loose hair and dirt, leaving his face and legs alone. Then go over him with the stiff body brush to sweep the hair and dirt off his coat, and be sure to brush his legs, too. Give him the once over with the soft brush, including his face.

Clean out your horse's feet with the hoof pick every day before you ride. This will not only keep your horse's hooves healthier, but it will give you a chance to examine his feet for any nails or stones that may be lodged there.

After your ride, clean out your horse's feet again, taking special care to look for stones and any other objects he may have picked up on the trail. If your horse is sweaty all over, or even just under the saddle pad, hose him off to get the sweat out of his coat. If the weather is cold, don't use water on him. Instead, wait for the sweat to dry and then scrub it out of his coat with a currycomb.

During warm months, bathe your horse every so often using horse shampoo to make his coat extra clean. Wash his mane and tail with horse shampoo, and then follow with conditioner to make it soft and silky. Avoid putting conditioner on your horse's back since this may make his coat slick and cause your saddle to slide.

When you are finished with the bath—or even if you just hosed off his dirty spots—use a sweat scraper to press the excess water out of his coat. This will help him dry faster and will flatten his hair so he looks good once the water has evaporated.

If your horse lives in a dirt paddock, make certain he is completely dry from his bath before you put him back in his stall. Otherwise, he's bound to roll and make mud out of your hard work. Throwing him a flake of hay can help distract him while he's drying out in his paddock, but some horses make rolling a priority before eating.

Clipping

Show horses get clipped extensively, losing nearly every hair from their ears, muzzles, and fetlocks. Trail horses have the luxury of remaining au naturel, depending on the whims of their owners. No rules exist in any trail riding competition stating that trail horses must be clipped.

Grooming Tools

Every trail rider needs basic grooming tools to keep the horse clean and in good shape. Make sure your grooming tote contains the following items:

- Plastic or rubber currycomb (for getting out embedded dirt)
- Shedding comb (for removing loose hair during shedding season)
- Hard bristle brush (for body brushing)
- Soft bristle brush (for body finishing and face brushing)
- Mane and tail brush
- Sweat scraper (to remove excess water after bathing)
- Hoof pick (to keep hooves free of stones and debris)
- Electric clippers (to keep your horse neat and trim)

In the interest of beauty, many trail riders do clip the whiskers on their horses' muzzles, as well as their fetlock hair. Clipped muzzles do make a neater appearance, as do clipped fetlocks. However, this is purely a matter of choice.

When making your decision about whether to clip or not to clip, it may help to know that some trail riders feel trail horses need both their whiskers and their fetlock hair to do their jobs. Horses use their whiskers to help them sense their immediate environment, and this can be useful on the trail, especially in dense brush or woods. The shape of fetlock hair helps direct water away from the hoof as it runs down the leg, something valued by some trail riders. On the other hand, some experts believe that it's good for the hoof to get wet as it aids in keeping the hoof moisturized. So this one is a toss-up.

One thing trail horses *don't* need is their eye whiskers clipped. An eye injury in a horse is a very unpleasant thing to deal with, and if eye whiskers can help keep a horse from coming into contact with an object that will potentially injure his eye, then the whiskers should stay.

Trail horses don't need the hair on the insides of their ears clipped either, something show horses have done to them on a regular basis. Gnats and other assorted flying insects prey on horses who are out on the trail, and the hair inside the ear is the only barrier between these biting insects and the horse's delicate skin.

Full body clipping, on the other hand, is a practice that some trail riders perform on their horses, especially in warmer climates. In states like California and Florida, where winters can be warm and even occasionally hot, horse owners will clip down all the hair on their horses' bodies. The reason for this is that many horses grow very thick coats in the winter, and when they are worked hard, those coats become drenched with sweat and do not easily dry off. By giving a horse a full body clip and then blanketing him at night to help him stay warm after the sun goes down, riders avoid dealing with a horse who becomes drenched with sweat during workouts and is difficult to cool down.

The very nature of trail riding lends itself to what is most natural for the horse, and most trail riders do not perform a full body clip on their mounts. Trace clips, where a section of the hair is removed to facilitate cooling down, are more popular among trail horses. If the trace clip is truly minimal, as it should be, the horse may not need blanketing in the winter unless the animal is dealing with a very harsh northern climate.

To do a trace clip on a horse, the animal must be clean and completely dry. Using chalk you can buy at a tack and feed store, draw the outline of where you will be clipping. Start at the bottom of the horse's jaw, where his head attaches to his neck, and continue down his neck, about four inches above where his foreleg attaches to his chest and across his side all the way to the end of thigh. Draw another chalk line about four inches below both chalk lines on his front and hind legs, and then do the same on the other side. Essentially, you'll be clipping the underside of the horse's neck, the entire front of his chest, and a four-inch strip just above his foreleg and just above his hock. His entire belly will be clipped too.

Once you trace-clip your horse, you'll see how much easier it is to cool him down after a long trail ride. If you are in a warm climate, you'll find that he doesn't sweat as much when you are riding and seems generally more comfortable.

Many trail riders don't clip their horses at all, and simply deal with the long winter coats. You certainly have that option if you prefer to keep your horse au naturel.

For more on basic horse care, see the books listed in appendix B, "Resources."

Chapter 6

PREVENTATIVE CARE

---

s with most things in life, preventing trouble before it starts is much better than trying to fix it later. This is especially true when it comes to
equine health. Good care can go a long way toward keeping your horse
healthy, and keeping vet bills at bay.

If you love your horse and want the best for her, it shouldn't be hard to do
what's right in the realm of good care. Trail horses in particular need adequate
care because of the difficult job they do. Carrying riders over rough terrain for
hours on end can take a toll on a horse who isn't getting the kind of preventative care she needs.

Finding the Right Vet

The person you choose to provide your horse's veterinary care is important. The
right vet can make the difference between a healthy horse and a tragedy.

While some people simply pick a vet out of the phone book, you'd be wiser
to do some homework and find someone who is good. Just as with human doctors, some veterinarians are more skilled than others. You want an animal doctor who really knows his or her stuff.

The most obvious thing to look for in a veterinarian is a specialty in treating horses. Most veterinarians specialize in one type of vet medicine. Most treat
cats and dogs, while others add rodents, rabbits, and other small animals to their
list. In most cases, horse vets treat only horses (and mules and donkeys). The
exception to this are some vets in remote rural communities, who treat just
about everything, including cats, dogs, goats, sheep, cattle, and horses.

Most small-animal vets won't even consider treating a horse, but even if you
could find one who would, you are better off looking for someone who works
exclusively with horses. Horses have a unique physiology and problems all their
own, something a small-animal vet may not be familiar with. Experience is
everything when it comes to choosing a good veterinarian, and a seasoned horse
vet is your best bet.

Of course, within the world of horse vets, talent varies. If you have a choice among vets, ask other horse people in your area whom they prefer. One of the best ways to choose a vet is to get referrals from other horse owners. Make sure you talk to as many people as possible before you make a decision, since you'll always find someone who doesn't like a particular vet. You are looking for a consensus to help you make your decision.

Since trail riding is the most popular equine activity in North America, you shouldn't have trouble finding a vet who knows how to treat trail horses. Still, if you can find someone who works with competitive trail riders and endurance racers, you'll most likely get state-of-the-art care when it comes to lameness and other problems that typically affect trail horses.

Once you've selected a vet you would like to use, call his or her office and ask a few questions. Find out what kind of services the vet provides, and get a sense of whether the office staff is professional. Keep in mind that many horse vets run very small practices, and may only have one individual on staff, or perhaps just an answering service. Your goal is to find out how easy it is to reach the vet in the event of an emergency, and to make sure you are treated with courtesy.

It's a good idea to meet the veterinarian before you make a commitment in your mind to use him or her on a regular basis. If your horse is due for vaccinations or to have her teeth checked, make an appointment for the vet to come see your horse so you can gauge the vet's bedside manner and reliability. If your

A good equine veterinarian can be your trail horse's best friend.

Equine Maintenance

Your horse needs regular preventative care in these areas to stay healthy:

- *Inoculations.* Talk to your vet about which shots your horse should receive and how often. Most vets recommend equine influenza, encephalitis, West Nile virus, and strangles vaccines be given regularly. Your vet may suggest other vaccines as well, depending on where you live.

- *Tooth care.* Have your vet check your horse's teeth at least every six months (more if your horse is younger or older). Don't skimp on tooth care, since tooth problems can result in pain for your horse and difficulties under saddle.

- *Deworming.* Deworm your horse every three months or as often as your veterinarian recommends it. You can buy quality dewormers in your local tack store or through Internet equine supply sites.

- *Hoof care.* Have a qualified farrier trim your horse's feet every six to eight weeks (the exact frequency will depend on your horse). If your horse is shod, have the shoes replaced with every trim.

horse doesn't need shots or anything right now, it couldn't hurt to ask the vet to do a basic exam just to check your horse's general health. Not only will this give you an opportunity to see if you like the vet, but the vet will consider you a regular client if you suddenly have to call for an emergency appointment. Horse vets have very busy schedules, and often give priority to their regular clients when called for emergencies.

Vaccines

The pharmaceutical industry has developed a vast number of vaccines for use in preventing infectious disease in horses. The vaccines your horse needs will vary depending on the environment in which she lives, the type of work she does, and your area of the country.

Your veterinarian will recommend the vaccines your horse should get on a regular basis. Most likely, your horse will need one or more of the following vaccines:

- *West Nile disease.* A relatively new illness in the world of horses in North America, West Nile disease is caused by the West Nile virus, an organism that is spread to horses through the bite of an infected mosquito. Although most horses bitten by infected mosquitoes don't show symptoms of the disease, one-third who are bitten suffer from severe neurological symptoms that can result in death. Most veterinarians are recommending inoculations for this disease annually or biannually. West Nile disease has been seen in all of the forty-eight continental states and Canada.

- *Equine encephalomyelitis.* Also called sleeping sickness, encephalomyelitis is caused by a virus spread by infected mosquitoes. This potentially fatal disease has different names in different regions, since different parts of the continent have unique strains. Western equine encephalomyelitis (WEE), Eastern equine encephalomyelitis (EEE), and Venezuelan equine encephalomyelitis (VEE) all have unique annual vaccines to combat this illness.

- *Tetanus.* The same disease that affects humans and causes extreme muscle stiffness and fever, tetanus in horses can result when a horse receives an injury that becomes infected with the tetanus bacteria. Tetanus bacteria is found in soil, dust, and manure, so horses are particularly prone to this illness because of their environment. Since trail horses are susceptible to injury while riding on the trail, this is a particularly important inoculation for horses doing this kind of work. Tetanus shots are usually recommended for all horses on an annual basis.

- *Influenza/rhinopneumonitis.* This contagious respiratory illness is most common among horses who live in close quarters with a lot of other horses, or who attend competitive events such as horse shows and endurance rides. The airborne virus attacks the mucous membranes of the respiratory tract and causes runny nose, difficulty in breathing, and fever. Similar to the human flu, equine influenza and rhinopneumonitis is cyclical and comes around to make horses sick nearly every winter. Vets usually recommend inoculating for flu/rhino every few months if the horse lives at a boarding stable or regularly attends competitive events with other horses. Horses at a lower risk of contracting the viruses that cause this illness will need the vaccination less often.

Eliminating Parasites and Other Pests

If you have a dog, you are probably familiar with the problem of intestinal parasites. Most puppies are born with roundworm, and likewise, most horses are plagued with the horse version of the same parasite. Horses are also affected by a host of other internal parasites, more commonly called worms.

While many experts believe that nearly all horses carry around a normal load of parasites in their guts, having too many of these organisms can take a heavy toll on a horse's body. Worms can drain the horse of nutrients and cause weight loss, lethargy, and in extreme cases, death. Worms can be particularly harmful to trail horses since horses who do this kind of work need all the energy they can get to perform their jobs.

It used to be that horse owners had to call out the veterinarian to have their horse dewormed every few months to keep these parasites at bay. These days, pharmaceutical companies and other manufacturers in the equine industry are offering excellent deworming products available over the counter to horse owners.

You'll find a large variety of deworming products out there on the market. Before you plunk down your money on the one with the most convincing packaging, talk to your veterinarian to see what he or she recommends for an over-the-counter deworming product. Your vet may recommend a rotation schedule, where you use one dewormer one month and a different one three months later. Or your vet may prefer to keep your horse on the same dewormer for an extended period of time. Even though your vet won't be administering the medication, don't hesitate to talk to him or her for advice on how best to handle deworming your horse.

The other incredibly nasty parasite that plagues the domestic horse is the fly. The flies that annoy horses come in several different species, most notably the stable fly, face fly, housefly, and horsefly. Each of these flies has its own particular way of bothering horses, which can include feeding on the horse's eye and mouth secretions or biting the horse and drinking her blood. (Some horses suffer from fly allergies, which I'll discuss in the next chapter.) Tiny gnats called no-see-ums also drive horses crazy by getting into their ears and biting the insides.

As a trail rider, you not only have the task of keeping flies at a minimum in your horse's living quarters, but also out on the trail. You'll never get rid of flies completely in the stable, but you can do a lot to keep their numbers down by cleaning up manure frequently and storing it in a covered container. You may also want to use biological fly control. This involves releasing a tiny fly predator into your horse's environment. The predator will eat the larvae of developing flies and reduce the number of adult flies that attack your horse.

The equine marketplace is filled with a variety of products designed to combat the fly problem, including sprays, wipes, shampoos, insecticidal collars, and sticky traps. You'll need to experiment with some of these products to see how they work on your particular horse and in your particular facility.

Another way to combat flies is to cover up your horse. Fly masks do a good job at preventing flies from getting to your horse's eyes, where they will feed on the moisture and potentially spread disease. You can also cover your horse with a fly sheet, which is a mesh blanket designed to provide good ventilation to your horse's skin while keeping flies from being able to bite.

You may also want to consider fly leg wraps, which will keep flies from biting your horse's legs. (Be aware that some horses won't keep these wraps on and will pull them off with their teeth.)

When trail riding with your horse, it's a good idea to bring along some fly repellent if you will be riding in an area with a lot of biting insects, such as in the woods. If you can't carry it with you, at least apply some of the product to your horse before you embark on your ride. Deerflies can attack a horse out on the trail and drive the horse crazy, and large horseflies have no qualms about biting a horse while you are riding along on the trail. See chapter 7, "Health Concerns," for more information on fly control.

Another flying pest you need to worry about is the mosquito. If you live in an area where mosquitoes are rampant, or if you do a lot of trail riding during the summer, do whatever you can to protect your horse from being bitten. As I mentioned earlier, mosquitoes carry West Nile virus and equine encephalomyelitis, two potentially fatal diseases. When riding on the trail, make sure your horse has been protected with a repellent that works for mosquitoes. This is especially important if you are riding at dawn or dusk, when the majority of mosquito species do most of their feeding. To keep mosquitoes from biting your horse at home, get rid of standing water where mosquitoes breed. If your horse lives in a box stall, put up a fan to circulate air in the stall; mosquitoes won't land when there is a breeze. (It's a good idea to wear mosquito repellent yourself, since humans are also susceptible to West Nile virus.)

Shoeing

In the wild, horses do not wear shoes and many of them get by just fine. Horses living in the human world usually do wear shoes, however, for better or worse. Most horses, as a result of breeding, diet, and/or environment, don't have hooves tough enough to withstand rigorous trail riding. The rocks, concrete, and hard ground horses encounter on the trail can chip and break their hooves if shoes are not worn for protection.

Chances are, your trail horse will need shoes. If you are fortunate enough to own a horse with really tough feet, you may be able to get by without them. Some breeds, like the Appaloosa and the mustang, are known for having hard feet and can sometimes go barefoot for trail riding. Most other breeds need the help of shoes to protect their feet from injury on tough trails.

The person responsible for the trimming and shoeing of your horse's feet is the farrier. Farriers usually provide a mobile service, traveling from facility to facility to take care of horses' feet. Many farriers study at special trade schools for horseshoeing, while others learn through apprenticing.

Just as with any profession, some individual farriers are better than others.

Quality farrier care is crucial to keep your trail horse sound.

It's imperative you find a farrier for your horse who is good, because a poor farrier can ruin your horse's feet.

Finding a good farrier can be tricky, and a case of trial and error. To avoid having to go this route, talk to knowledgeable horse owners in your area about who they use for shoeing. Try to get referrals from people who trail ride a lot, since that is your activity of choice. Talk to trainers in the area, too, to see whom they prefer. Trainers hire shoers to care for the feet of many different types of horses, and they quickly get a feeling for which ones are the best.

Once you've found a good farrier, let that person know you are a trail rider and have him or her take a look at your horse's feet. If your horse needs some fixing as a result of a poor shoeing job in the past, the farrier may recommend corrective shoeing on a temporary basis. The goal is to get your horse's feet where they should be and then go back to normal shoeing.

If your horse has problems with her feet or legs, your farrier should offer suggestions on how to trim and shoe the horse to help with these problems. Keep in mind that although corrective shoeing can help a horse with leg problems to some degree, the shoer cannot and should not try to change the horse's basic physiology.

Depending on how fast your horse's hooves grow, you will probably need to put your horse on a shoeing schedule of every six to eight weeks. If your horse is going barefoot, you'll still need regular trims on this same schedule. Ask your shoer to put you down for a regular appointment every six to eight weeks so you don't need to remember to call and make a date for the work to be done.

Most horses who do a job wear steel or aluminum shoes, although some trail riders have begun experimenting with different types of shoeing material, such as plastic and nylon. Be aware that these materials are experimental right now when it comes to horseshoes, meaning that not enough horses have used them to determine whether they can really help a horse stay sound. If you are interested in using an alternative to steel or aluminum, discuss the possibility with your farrier.

Another alternative movement in the area of horseshoeing is the barefoot movement. This controversial philosophy of hoof care dictates that the horse be kept without shoes and trimmed a certain way to allow for maximum balance, and therefore maximum soundness. Barefoot horses need special living conditions in order for their hooves to strengthen to the point of not needing shoes, including water soaks for ten minutes a day, paddocks or pastures with similar footing to where they are ridden, the ability to graze for long periods of time, and more. For many horse owners, providing this type of environment is difficult to impossible, which eliminates the option of going barefoot for a lot of horses.

The barefoot philosophy calls for a particular trim that can only be given by a shoer who subscribes to this method of hoof care. Most shoers who give barefoot trims do not work with horseshoes, and only do barefoot work.

Taking Care of Teeth

Unlike humans, who need their teeth cleaned regularly and must get a filling now and then, horses have a different problem with their teeth: they grow continuously, to the point where they can actually become uncomfortable. Horses also develop dental problems similar to what humans experience.

Both young and older horses alike suffer from a variety of dental maladies. The results of teeth gone wild are problems like sharp edges on the molars that rub the horse's tongue or cheeks, creating ulcers; abscesses caused by trapped food; misaligned teeth that make it hard for the horse to chew; cracked, infected teeth; gum inflammation; and molars that interfere with the placement of the bit.

Horses with neglected teeth suffer a host of problems, including weight loss, drooling, head shaking during eating, and tongue or gum sores. Horses with bad teeth can have chronic problems with colic, and can develop behavior problems under saddle as a result of pain in the mouth caused by the bit.

To ensure that your horse does not suffer from teeth problems, have your vet check her every six months for trouble. If the vet notices issues such as abscesses or sharp points, he or she will treat your horse by filing down the teeth, a procedure called *floating*. Regular floating of the teeth will remove sharp points on the horse's molars, thereby eliminating a number of potential problems from developing, like impaction colic and mouth ulcers.

The Importance of Exercise

The term "weekend warrior" applies to folks who sit behind a desk all week and are gung-ho athletes on the weekends. Many trail riders fall into the category of weekend warriors, which would be fine except for one thing: Horses need exercise every day.

Unless you are keeping your horse in a pasture with other horses, where she is walking around as she grazes and interacting with her pasturemates, you have an obligation to get your horse moving on a daily basis. This is particularly true if your horse lives in a box stall. Not only is it inhumane to leave a horse standing in a small stall for days on end, but it's bad for the horse's health.

In nature, horses graze for many hours a day, slowly moving as they work their way through the grass. This constant movement keeps their joints lubricated, their muscles loose, and their minds active.

In a stable situation, horses are restricted in their movement. This is not only detrimental to their legs, but also to their minds.

Unless you are lucky enough to have your horse in a pasture, you will need to provide some exercise on a daily basis. This is especially true if you are a trail rider. It's incredibly unfair to ask a horse to stand in a stall all week and then go on a four-hour trail ride on a Saturday. The horse will end up stiff and sore, and you run the risk of the horse developing lameness and azoturia (one of several

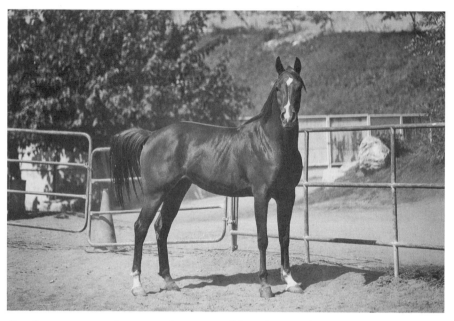

Regular turnouts are important for your trail horse's mental and physical well-being.

illnesses that can strike when a horse is worked beyond her limits). Your horse will also develop a bad attitude about being ridden if every trail ride results in her being exhausted and sore because she's not up to it.

If you don't have time to ride during the week, even a twenty-minute hand walk can help your horse stretch her legs, get her blood flowing, and stimulate her mind. If you board your horse and absolutely can't get down to the stable to do even this much, consider hiring someone to take the horse out for you. You can employ a trainer to ride the horse anywhere from three to five times a week. Not only will this assist in your horse's exercise and conditioning, it will result in a more highly trained horse.

If you can't afford to pay a trainer, hire a high school kid just to take the horse out and walk her every day. If your horse is easygoing and safe, you might even want to half-lease her to someone you trust who will trail ride her or even cruise around in the arena several days a week. That way, when you show up on the weekend to ride your horse, she won't feel like she's being let out of prison only to be tortured on a ride that she's not physically capable of handling.

When you do ride your trail horse, be sure to warm her up first at the walk for at least ten minutes before you start trotting or cantering. Before you put her back in her stall or pasture, cool her down by walking for at least ten minutes or longer, depending on how hot and sweaty she feels to the touch.

Whatever you do, don't take your horse on long strenuous rides if she has not been conditioned for this kind of work. If you have not done the work necessary to get your horse ready for long trail rides, see chapter 8, "Preparing Your Horse for Trail," for details.

Chapter 7

HEALTH CONCERNS

Horses are strong animals, but they are surprisingly fragile too. Their legs carry the vast weights of their bodies, and when you add a rider to that, you put a huge burden on the joints and tendons. The horse's digestive system is delicate as well, most likely because of the unnatural conditions in which they are kept in domesticity. Unlike wild horses who graze for most of the day and night on low-quality feed, our horses eat just a couple or a few meals a day of high-quality food and concentrated feeds.

The result of these realities is that horses frequently suffer problems in their legs or in their digestive tracts. The mere fact that they are horses also makes them susceptible to a variety of other health problems. While good preventative care can go a long way in keeping problems at bay, as discussed in chapter 6, "Preventative Care," some conditions are simply unavoidable.

Trail horses can get the same illnesses and diseases as all other horses, but are particularly prone to certain issues because of the nature of their work. Long hours on the trail over rugged terrain can take their toll on a horse's legs, stressing joints, ligaments, and tendons. Other issues related to the extreme physical rigors of competition on the trail are also of concern in trail horses.

This chapter covers a number of conditions that affect trail horses in particular as a result of their work, as well as problems that can affect a horse's ability to do his job on the trail.

Lameness

The biggest worry for trail riders are leg problems that result in lameness. Trail horses are expected to carry their riders for long periods of time, often up and down hills and across rugged terrain. Soundness is imperative in the trail horse. Without healthy legs and feet, a horse cannot perform his duties as a serious trail horse.

A variety of lameness can plague trail horses. Prognosis for a horse suffering from one of these conditions depends on the individual horse and the particular condition.

NAVICULAR DISEASE

A small bone in the foot called the navicular bone is the focus of this crippling condition. The navicular bone is a sort of hinge that connects the deep flexor tendon and the coffin bone. Veterinarians commonly believe that decreased blood flow to the navicular bone and subsequent degeneration causes cysts and channels to form within the bone. Vets aren't sure what causes this condition, which usually presents itself as lameness in both front legs, specifically the heel. Some experts believe navicular disease has a genetic component, which means the condition can be passed from sire and dam to the resulting foal.

Researchers have yet to discover a cure for navicular disease, but vets are able to manage the disease through a variety of treatments. Therapeutic shoeing that provides more support to the heel is often recommended, as well as medication that can increase blood flow to the navicular bone. Anti-inflammatory drugs and painkillers may also be prescribed. Nerving is another option for horses with severe navicular disease that no longer responds to drugs. See the "Ringbone" section on the next page for more on this option.

Trail horses with navicular disease can still lead productive work lives for as long as the disease is well managed. Your vet may recommend reduced activity for your horse to help cut down on the amount of concussion to the affected heels. That would mean shorter trail rides on more gentle terrain.

LAMINITIS

Laminitis, also known as founder, is a dreaded disease in horses. The condition affects the sensitive lamina within the hoof, which serves as the connective layer between the hoof and the coffin bone. When laminitis strikes, the coffin bone separates from the hoof wall as a result of inflammation of the lamina.

A number of situations can cause laminitis, but the good news is that most of them are avoidable. Poor shoeing where the feet are trimmed too short is one cause of the disease. Excessive galloping on hard ground can also bring on laminitis, as can using bedding made from black walnut shavings, which is toxic to horses. Other causes include colic brought on by eating too much grain (horses who have escaped from their stalls and raided the grain bin are usually affected), obesity, feeding too much pasture grass without properly acclimating the horse, overfeeding alfalfa, and the use of steroid medications.

Horses suffering from mild laminitis walk gingerly on their feet, as if stepping down too hard will cause pain. More severe cases cause the horse to rock back on his haunches to take weight off his front feet. Horses suffering severe pain from laminitis are reluctant to walk, and may even spend a lot of time lying down to get the weight off their feet.

The way veterinarians treat laminitis depends on the severity of the condition. Stall rest on soft footing is one method, along with therapeutic shoeing and a low-carbohydrate diet. Vets also prescribe nonsteroidal anti-inflammatory drugs for the condition as well as medications that help increase blood flow to the hoof.

Once a horse has suffered from laminitis, he is prone to relapses. Very severe bouts of the disease can even cause death, and most horses with laminitis are lame for life. Trail horses diagnosed with this disease are usually retired from work. Horses with mild cases may still be able to do some very light trail riding on soft, even ground, but more than that puts them at risk for pain.

RINGBONE

A form of equine arthritis, ringbone is the growth of extra bone on or within the coffin or pastern joint. Caused by poor conformation, specifically upright pastern angles, and/or poor shoeing, ringbone is progressive and results in permanent lameness. Upper ringbone, which affects the pastern joint, and lower ringbone, which affects the coffin bone, can be treated with corrective shoeing. A skilled farrier can rebalance the horse's foot so less stress is placed on the affected area. This can slow down the progression of the disease, but does not eliminate the problem.

Another treatment for ringbone is the injection of sodium hyaluronate to the affected area, which can help lubricate the joint and reduce inflammation. This method can help reduce pain and lameness for a period of time.

Horses with severe ringbone can also be helped by a procedure called posterior digital neurectomy, commonly known among horse owners as *nerving*. This procedure permanently blocks the nerves in the affected area, eliminating the pain the horse experiences. This eliminates the lameness on a temporary basis, but doesn't erase the problem. Eventually, the pain returns as the disease progresses.

Trail horses diagnosed with ringbone have limited careers ahead of them. The disease can take many years to progress to complete lameness, or it can happen more quickly, depending on the horse.

DEGENERATIVE JOINT DISEASE

Sometimes called nonspecific arthritis, degenerative joint disease refers to any form of arthritis that develops in the horse's joints that does not have a distinct or identifiable cause.

This is the most common type of arthritis, and starts out mild, gradually progressing as the horse gets older. The mild version of the condition begins with an inflamed joint capsule and often worsens with erosion of the cartilage in the joint and ultimately fusion of the joint. This happens as a result of a cycle of inflammation, where the normally thick, slippery joint fluid becomes thin. Once this happens, the joint surfaces are not as protected, and they get irritated, causing more inflammation, more destruction of joint fluid, and further irritation of the joint surface. This irritation causes lameness, and as it progresses, the joint surfaces, which are made of cartilage, begin to erode. The body tries to heal this erosion by laying down more bone.

In the early stages, when the joint capsule is mildly inflamed, it is often referred to as serous arthritis. The horse will be only mildly lame, and no joint surface damage occurs. This is usually the case when the arthritis was originally caused by a trauma such as a fall, a kick, or a heavy concussion during work.

Often the joint responds by producing more joint fluid, which can stretch the joint capsule, making the joint appear like it has developed lumps around it. This is known *as bog spavins* in the hocks or *windpuffs* in the fetlocks. This form rarely causes lameness, or if it does, it is mild and can be treated with rest and anti-inflammatory drugs (such as phenylbutazone) in order to stop the cycle of inflammation and let the joint return to a healthy state.

If the cycle of inflammation continues, however, the arthritis progresses, causing more joint damage and bone development. Once the joint starts to develop bone, the arthritic condition is called osteoarthritis. This is a more serious type of arthritis that calls for more treatment and results in more lameness. It can also be a career ender for some performance horses. In the beginning, the bone development is mild and appears as small spurs off the edges of the bones. These spurs are called *bone spavins*. As the disease progresses, the joint space begins to decrease and bone begins to fill in the joint until the whole joint fuses into one big chunk of bone. Once the joint fuses, the pain and lameness usually goes away.

Horses of any age can be diagnosed with degenerative joint disease, with varied causes including the toll of many years of hard work, poor conformation, trauma to the joint, and old age. Most of the time, the hocks are affected, with the knees a close second. The fetlocks and stifles can also be affected by the disease, although this is usually less serious.

Veterinarians treat degenerative joint disease according to its severity. Drugs are used to control inflammation and encourage healthy production of joint fluid and joint surface cartilage. Injections of hylauronic acid often help repair the joint in severe cases.

Many vets also recommend supplementing an affected horse's diet with chondroitin sulfates and glucosamine, two amino building blocks of cartilage.

While it may be impossible to prevent your trail horse from eventually developing arthritis (nearly every older horse has it in some form), you can do a few things to keep the condition at bay. Make sure your farrier is visiting regularly and doing a good job with your horse's feet, and keep your horse from becoming overweight. Some horse owners give their horses daily supplementation with chondroitin sulfates and glucosamine in the hopes of preventing arthritis in the future.

The severity of the arthritic condition determines how much work a trail horse can do. Horses with mild arthritis benefit from trail riding on footing that is not too hard, and do well when given exercise on a daily basis. Leaving an arthritic horse standing in his stall day after day is a sure way to aggravate the problem, as the joints become stiff and inflexible without regular movement.

BOWED TENDONS

A leg problem that sometimes plagues trail horses is a bowed tendon, or tendonitis. This problem is considered an injury, and happens when the back of the horse's leg overstretches, causing it to become strained or torn. The result is a swollen leg that is hot and painful. Horses with bowed tendons are usually lame on the affected leg.

Bowed tendons are caused by hard riding and usually occur when a horse is jumping or galloping, especially in deep footing. Trail horses who gallop through deep sand are particularly susceptible to bowed tendons.

Veterinarians treat bowed tendons with ice, poultices, and nonsteroidal anti-inflammatory drugs, as well as stall rest. Bowed tendons can take a long time to heal, and affected horses need to be laid up for six months to a year, with restricted exercise. Pushing a horse with a bowed tendon before the injury has healed completely puts the horse at risk for a recurrence of the condition.

To keep your trail horse from getting a bowed tendon, make sure he is getting good farrier work, and that you are riding him in good conditions. Avoid galloping through deep sand and slippery mud out on the trail.

BRUISED SOLES

Trail horses often work in rocky terrain, and are susceptible to bruised soles, also called stone bruises. This problem occurs when a horse steps on a hard object, which bruises the underside of the hoof. Some horses don't need to step on a particular object to suffer from bruised soles; their thin soles or flat feet make them prone to bruising on any kind of hard ground.

A horse with a bruised sole will show lameness on the affected foot. A veterinarian should examine the horse to diagnose this problem since a bruised sole can also be confused with a hoof abscess, a more serious condition discussed in the next section.

Horses with bruised soles tend to be prone to a recurrence of the problem, so your veterinarian may recommend special shoes to protect the bottoms of your horse's feet. This might include full pads or rim pads on your horse's shoes to cover the sole of the foot. Shoeing that provides extra support for the foot might also be prescribed.

To ensure your horse stays sound, conditiontion him with arena work before you start taking him on long trail rides.

If your horse has a tendency to develop bruised soles, avoid riding him on hard, rocky trails.

Hoof Abscess

A hoof abscess is an infection of the hoof that begins in the sole and works its way up to the lamina and then eventually to the coronary band. Puncture wounds to the hoof often result in hoof abscesses since they allow bacteria to enter the foot.

If your horse is sound one day and lame the next, he could be suffering from a hoof abscess. After an exam to verify the abscess, your vet will open up the underside of the hoof with a hoof knife to expose the abscess. This will allow the abscess to drain. You'll need to soak the hoof in Epsom salts daily to help the infection clear from the foot, and also give your horse nonsteroid anti-inflammatory drugs and painkillers prescribed by your vet.

The infection will most likely clear up in three to five days, and your horse will be able to get back to trail riding soon after.

Other Issues

Trail horses are susceptible to a host of other conditions because of their line of work. The good news is that most of these conditions can be prevented or managed with the help of a veterinarian.

Azoturia

Also called tying up, azoturia is of particular concern to trail riders. This condition affects the muscles of the horse, and is the result of high amounts of lactic acid in the horse's body. Muscle breakdown results, and kidney damage can also occur.

Experts used to believe azoturia resulted when a horse who had not been exercised for several days but was fed grain during the period of no exercise was suddenly asked to exert himself. The stored energy from the grain, when used by the horse, instantaneously created high levels of lactic acid as a by-product. Today, newer theories on hormonal, genetic, and nutritional causes are being explored.

Horses suffering an attack of azoturia experience anxiety, profuse sweating, and a fast pulse rate about fifteen minutes to an hour into their workout. Shortly after, the horse becomes stiff and uncoordinated and may collapse.

Horses with azoturia should not be asked to move, but should be treated by a veterinarian immediately. The vet will administer a tranquilizer to relax the horse, and then give him an intravenous anti-inflammatory drug to loosen his muscles. This treatment will continue for several days after the attack to help the horse recover. If the horse does not respond to the initial treatment, he may require hospitalization.

It's imperative to get veterinary treatment right away for azoturia, since severe kidney damage and possible death can result if the horse doesn't get immediate help.

The good news about azoturia is that it can be prevented. To avoid ever having to deal with this frightening situation out on the trail, give your horse daily exercise to help eliminate lactic acid from building up in his body. During times when he won't be getting out much, such as during periods of bad weather, cut back on his protein and carbohydrate intake. Take time to warm him up before long rigorous trail rides (ten minutes of walking and trotting should do to trick), and cool him down by walking toward the end of your ride. (See chapter 8, "Preparing Your Horse for Trail," for more information.) Your vet may also suggest feed supplements to ward off future attacks, such as rice bran, Vitamin E, and/or selenium.

Remember that once a horse has suffered an attack of azoturia, he is very prone to future attacks. Keep a cell phone with you when you ride so you can call a vet if your horse is stricken out on the trail, and be sure to take preventative measures.

IMPACTION COLIC

All horses are prone to colic, which is a generic term for a number of digestive problems. Trail horses are particularly at risk for impaction colic, which occurs when dry, hard manure becomes trapped in the horse's large intestine.

Impaction colic is often the result of dehydration, which is what makes it a risk for trail horses. Long hours of working on the trail, particularly in hot weather, can result in a dehydrated horse. Some horses are poor drinkers on the trail and won't take in enough water during the ride. In some situations, water is not available on the trail, and a horse may go hours without a drink, even if he's thirsty.

Impaction colic has the same symptoms of other types of colic, including biting at the flanks, pawing, kicking at the belly, pacing, repeated rolling, standing with legs stretched out, straining to defecate, profuse sweating, and anxiety. These are all signs of abdominal pain, and should be taken seriously.

If your vet suspects impaction colic, he or she will administer a painkiller to your horse, give him a rectal exam, and give him large amounts of mineral oil through a nasogastric tube. Once the hard manure passes, the horse should be okay. In severe cases, the horse may have to have the impaction surgically removed.

The best ways to prevent impaction colic is always to encourage your horse to drink on the trail. If your horse is reluctant, help him out by taking him to a water source where he doesn't have to share with other horses and so won't be intimidated. If you are riding in a group, ask the other riders to wait patiently nearby as you ask your horse to drink. Your trail buddies should not let their horses push into the trough or creek alongside your horse, nor should they ride off and leave you while your horse is contemplating a drink as this will cause your horse to abandon the water to keep up with his trail companions.

You can also encourage your horse to drink on a trail ride by giving him electrolytes before or during the ride. Available in tack and feed stores, these powdered products can be mixed with your horse's feed or given in paste form. The salts in the electrolyte mixture will make your horse thirsty and encourage him to drink more water.

Other ways to avoid impaction colic include providing regular exercise to your horse (this keeps his digestive track moving), feeding frequent smaller meals (this is a more natural way for a horse to eat), feeding high-quality hay as opposed to a diet high in carbohydrates (the fibrous particles in hay stimulate the horse's intestines), and providing good tooth care, as described in chapter 6 (horses with bad teeth do not chew their food properly and are more prone to impaction colic).

HEAVES

The equine equivalent to human asthma is chronic obstructive pulmonary disease, or heaves. Horses with heaves have difficulty breathing, especially when they exert themselves. The condition is the result of inflammation and spasm of the lungs. Horses with heaves become short of breath when exercising, and will cough and wheeze.

Heaves seems to be caused by allergies, just as with most cases of human asthma. Poor ventilation in the barn or repeated exposure to allergens such as dust and certain types of hay can aggravate the condition, reducing the horse's ability to perform under saddle. Heaves is a chronic condition, and certain horses are born with a predisposition for it.

Horses diagnosed with heaves are treated with a bronchodilating drug to help open the airways. If this treatment works, the horse may be put on a regular treatment program of bronchodilators. If a secondary bacterial infection is suspected, the vet will also give you antibiotics to treat the horse.

In serious cases, your veterinarian may prescribe steroids, since these drugs are known for reducing the cycle of inflammation in the horse's lungs. While steroids have been traditionally given through the mouth, a new way of administering steroids is now being applied: A nebulizer attached to a specially made inhaler that fits like a mask over the horse's muzzle releases an inhaled steroid. The inhaler can also be used to administer bronchodilating drugs. Although there is some debate over how well these nebulizers work, many horses appear to have been helped by this treatment.

Sometimes drug therapy doesn't work for heaves, but something as simple as moving the horse's residence to a different location will do the trick. Feeding the horse from a ground feeder helps drain mucus from the airways, and providing an open-air, low-dust stall can help. Soaking the hay in water before feeding it can also help a horse with heaves by removing most of the dust that settles in the hay when it's baled.

Heaves is rarely fatal, but it can affect your horse's ability to be ridden on the trail. Horses with heaves often have trouble negotiating steep hills and going faster than a walk.

Fly Allergies

As mentioned in chapter 6, flies are an unfortunate way of life for horses. No matter how clean your stable, you are bound to have flies pestering your horses. To make matters worse, some horses have allergies to these annoying pests. During fly season, they experience itchy, flaky, scabby skin. In severe cases, the horse can start to lose his hair and appear bald in places.

Trail horses with fly allergies find their nemesis not only at home in their stalls or pastures, but out on the trail. In some parts of the continent, large and vicious biting flies lurk in the woods and near streams and rivers, and are more than happy to prey upon horses passing by.

If you have a trail horse with a fly allergy, you can do a lot to protect your mount from being bitten:

- *Use fly repellent.* Pay a visit to your local tack and feed store and you'll find a plethora of fly repellents to choose from. Most are in spray form, while others come as wipes, roll-ons, and "spot-on" products that are applied to the horse once every two weeks. These products can do wonders to minimize the number of flies that land on your horse's body. Follow the directions on the label when applying them to make sure you don't overdose your horse.

  Some horses with fly allergies are also allergic to fly repellents, so keep a close eye on your horse after applying the product. If your horse is allergic to the product, he will develop hives or scabs on his skin. Should this happen, try another product, one that is water-based and labeled as having all-natural ingredients.

- *Use cover-ups.* Fly sheets, leg wraps, and fly masks can serve as barriers between your horse and biting flies. Cover your horse up while he's in his stall, using all of these barriers. You can also use a fly mask while riding if flies attack your horse's eyes, ears, and muzzle out on the trail. Specially made masks for riding are available in tack stores, and through catalogs and the Internet.

- *Practice good stall hygiene.* The more manure and urine in your horse's stall, the more you'll have a problem with flies. Clean your horse's stall at least once a day, twice if you can manage it. If you use shavings, replace soiled bedding with fresh bedding at least once a day. Avoid using straw as bedding since this material attracts flies. (A host of bedding materials is available on the market these days, including wood shavings and recycled paper products, eliminating the need for straw.) Keep manure in a covered container until you can remove it from the property.

- *Consider biological fly control.* An environmentally friendly way to control flies is through the use of fly predators. These tiny wasps feed on the larvae of the fly before it can turn into a winged pest. Fly predators are tiny and unnoticeable to people and horses, yet do wonders to keep fly populations under control. New fly predators must be released in the horse's environment once a month during fly season to keep up with the fly population. Since these tiny predators are susceptible to fly repellents, horses should be sprayed away from the area where the predators are released. Fly predators can be purchased from the companies that produce them, through your local feed store, or online.

- *Use fly traps.* A variety of sticky and baited traps are available for placement in or near horses' stalls. These products lure flies to them and trap them with a sticky surface or inside a container. They are a good tool for keeping fly populations down.

- *Get help from your vet.* Horses suffering from severe fly allergies need help from a veterinarian. Your vet may opt to give your horse allergy shots to help desensitize him to flies. The vet may also prescribe antihistamines, and in extreme cases may recommend cortisone shots to reduce itching and inflammation.

HIVES

Horses get hives just like people do, usually in response to an allergic reaction. Hives are small lumps that cover the entire body or a section of the body. They can be anywhere from half an inch to a few inches in diameter and are usually uniform in shape. Hives give to pressure when you touch them, and may or may not be itchy. A horse's face and eyelids sometimes swell up when hives are present.

Trail horses with skin allergies are particularly prone to hives because they often come into contact with different types of plants out on the trail. If a horse is allergic to a plant that rubs up against his body while you are riding, he is likely to break out in hives. Horses can also get hives from eating something that causes an allergic reaction.

If your horse develops hives, call your vet. He or she will determine the cause of the allergic reaction, and may recommend an intradermal skin test, which will positively identify the allergens in your horse's environment. If the offending allergen is an airborne pollen, you won't be able to do much to keep your horse from inhaling it except to avoid trail riding in areas where this plant is prevalent.

If the allergen is airborne, your vet might recommend allergy shots to help desensitize the horse's immune system. If the allergen turns out to be something like cigarette smoke or the dust from a particular type of bedding, or something the horse is eating, you will need to remove the substance from the horse's daily life or be sure to keep your horse from ingesting the plant when you are riding.

In either case, your vet might want to inject your horse with cortisone to reduce or eliminate the hives until the cause of the problem can be addressed.

THRUSH

If you take good care of your trail horse's feet, you shouldn't have to deal with the problem of thrush, a bacterial infection of the foot. Horses whose hooves are chronically packed with manure or mud can develop this condition, which can be crippling if not treated. The infection can spread deeper into the foot and can damage the horse's tendons.

You can tell if your horse has thrush by the foul smell and black discharge emanating from the bottoms of his feet. When you scrape the bottoms of your horse's feet, a clay-like material will slough off and leave grooves in the horse's feet.

Most diligent horse owners catch thrush in its early stages where odor and some discharge indicate the first signs of the condition. Tack and feed stores sell over-the-counter thrush medication that can kill the bacteria with a few applications. Infections that don't respond to this treatment require the attention of a veterinarian. The vet will treat the thrush by pulling the horse's shoe and removing the affected area of the hoof. He or she will then apply an antiseptic to the foot such as iodine, formalin, or some type of antibiotic. The horse's foot will then be bandaged. You will need to repeat this treatment yourself every day for the next few days and then a couple of times a week after that. Your horse may even have to temporarily wear a special bar shoe on the affected hoof. While your horse is receiving treatment for thrush, it's important to keep the animal in a dry stall or paddock.

The most effective way to prevent thrush is to keep your horse's feet clean and dry. Pick your horse's feet at least once a day, and before and after every trail ride. Don't make your horse stand in mud, manure, or soiled bedding for hours on end—this is the kind of environment that encourages thrush.

THUMPS

Thumps is the common name for a condition called asynchronous diaphragmatic flutter. Thumps is essentially a contraction of the diaphragm that synchronizes with the horse's heartbeat. Thumps is a result of an electrolyte imbalance, and can be seen in horses who have undergone strenuous exercise. Thumps presents itself as a twitch or spasm in the flank. The twitch sometimes produces a thumping sound, hence the name of the condition. Other signs of the problem include a stiff gait, a tense facial expression, a drooping third eyelid, and twitching or quivering muscles.

Thumps can be a precursor to a very serious situation. A horse with thumps is experiencing a metabolic imbalance, and may become seriously ill as a result of not enough water, chlorine, sodium, potassium, calcium, phosphorus, and magnesium in the body. Horses with thumps who are forced to continue work and do not receive treatment are at risk of death.

If you suspect your horse is experiencing thumps, stop exercise immediately and offer the horse small amounts of water at five-minute intervals. Administer an electrolyte paste, and contact a veterinarian right away. Do not continue on your ride; doing so puts your horse at great risk.

To prevent thumps, encourage your horse to drink water on long trail rides, and avoid exhausting him. Give him electrolytes before, during, and after the ride if you are riding under hot, strenuous conditions that are causing your horse to sweat profusely.

EXHAUSTED HORSE SYNDROME

Horses who are asked to do more than their conditioning permits are at risk for exhausted horse syndrome. Caused by a severe metabolic breakdown resulting from overexertion, horses with this syndrome will show signs of tying up, thumps, erratic heart rate, lethargy, shortened stride, a dull eye, dehydration, elevated temperature, loss of appetite, and loss of thirst. Horses with this syndrome may also show signs of colic and can collapse. Without immediate veterinary intervention, which includes the intravenous administration of fluids, horses at this stage of the condition will die.

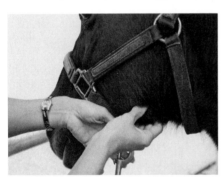

Learn to take your horse's pulse so you can determine whether he's at risk of becoming exhausted on a long ride.

To avoid putting your horse through the horror of exhausted horse syndrome, make sure your mount is properly conditioned before you take him on a long trail ride. Give him electrolytes before the ride and encourage him to drink along the way. If you sense your horse is having difficulty, stop and give him a long rest, as well as water and electrolytes. If this doesn't seem to perk him up, discontinue the ride and make arrangements for a trailer to come and retrieve him. It's not worth risking your horse's life just to finish the ride.

SHIPPING FEVER

If you haul your horse long distances to trail rides, he's prone to a condition called pleuropneumonia, or shipping fever. An infection of the respiratory tract, shipping fever results from poor ventilation in the trailer, keeping the horse's head tied for long periods of time so he can't lower it, and the stress of travel.

> ## Call the Vet!
>
> Whenever you suspect any medical problem in your horse, contact your veterinarian immediately. No matter how knowledgeable you are, it's never a good idea to perform your own diagnosis and administer your own treatment since only a veterinarian can tell for certain exactly what is going on with your horse.
>
> Prompt treatment by a vet is the best way to handle any equine illness. Don't wait until your horse is really sick before you call your vet. The longer you wait, the harder it will be for your vet to make your horse well.

Horses who spend many hours in a trailer under these conditions can develop shipping fever, which results in nasal discharge, coughing, fever, loss of appetite, and lethargy. If not treated, the condition can turn into fatal pneumonia.

A horse with shipping fever usually shows signs of the condition immediately upon arrival at its destination. If you trailer your horse a long way for a ride and discover that he's not feeling well when you arrive, don't ask him to work. Instead, contact a local veterinarian right away. The vet will likely prescribe antibiotics to combat the bacteria and want the horse to rest. If you are horse camping and must tie your horse while he's recovering, make sure he's able to lower his head. This will help the mucus drain from his respiratory tract.

To avoid having to deal with shipping fever on a long haul, make sure your horse travels in a well-ventilated trailer. Keep the windows open, even if the weather is cold. If you are worried about your horse in the cold, blanket him before shipping. If you can, secure him so he can lower his head. If this isn't possible, make frequent stops and untie him so he can put his head down to clear his airways.

Encourage your horse to drink plenty of water when he's traveling. Dehydration can make a horse more susceptible to shipping fever.

First Aid for Trail Horses

One of the most exciting aspects to trail riding is exploring new places with your equine companion. The downside of this is that you never know what you might encounter.

Should you run into trouble on a trail ride and need to give first aid to your horse, keep the following points in mind:

- Keep your horse calm if he's injured. Injured horses are sometimes very frightened. Try to get your horse to relax so you can take a look at the injury. Talk to him and pet him, and use "whoa" to get him to stop moving. Keep your own safety in mind. If your horse won't settle down, don't put yourself in harm's way.

- If your horse is seriously hurt, call for help. Use your cell phone to call 911, or if you can't get service, ask another rider to go for help. Stay with your horse and keep him calm until help arrives.

- Make sure your horse is up to date on his tetanus vaccine (see chapter 6). The vaccine will protect him in the event of an injury that breaks the skin. If your horse has not had a tetanus vaccination in six months prior to being wounded, he needs a tetanus vaccination immediately.

- Carry a first-aid kit, which is a must on long trail rides, for both horses and humans. See chapter 10, "Safety on the Trail," for details on putting together a first-aid kit.

COPING WITH WOUNDS

Of all the creatures in the animal kingdom, horses seem to be the most accident-prone. This is especially true for trail horses, who are out in the open dealing with all kinds of hazards on the trail.

The first thing you need to do when your horse hurts himself is determine what kind of wound your horse has suffered, and then act accordingly. Here are some types of wounds horses typically incur and the action you should take with each:

- *Puncture wounds.* These are usually the most serious wounds because they penetrate deeply into the horse's flesh. Horses sometimes get puncture wounds in their hooves after stepping on protruding objects like nails. If the wound is in the back third of the hoof, around the frog, bacteria may get into an area called the navicular bursa. If this occurs, infection can travel up the entire leg and the horse could lose his life.

  What to do: because of the seriousness of puncture wounds, it's important to call a veterinarian right away. This is especially true if the wound is in the hoof. The vet will probably opt to give the horse a series of antibiotic injections.

- *Lacerations.* A laceration is a simply a cut anywhere on the horse's body. It can be large or small, superficial or serious, depending on the size and amount of bleeding.

  What to do: for minor lacerations, use water to flush out any foreign objects that may be inside. Use water and Betadine scrub on a sponge to gently remove any particles that persist. (Have someone hold your horse as you do this, since it will be uncomfortable for the animal.) If the wound isn't serious, apply antibiotic ointment to it and let the wound heal on its own. If the laceration is deep or very large, do not attempt to treat it yourself. Instead, call a vet. Sutures and antibiotics may be required.

  Sometimes even small lacerations get infected and need veterinary attention one or two days after the wound occurs. If the area becomes swollen, hot, and painful to the touch, it's time to call the veterinarian.

- *Abrasions*. Abrasions are superficial wounds that happen when a horse scrapes itself on a rough surface. Most abrasions are not serious, although they can be very painful.

  What to do: once the bleeding has stopped, cleanse the area with Betadine scrub and apply an antibiotic ointment. Sometimes a veterinarian-prescribed anti-inflammatory ointment may be needed. Do not bandage the area. If the abrasion was caused by the horse falling, call your veterinarian since the horse may have internal injuries as well.

TREATING BITES

Horses sometimes bite each other on the trail, and sometimes these bites can be severe. Horses can also be bitten by other animals out on the trail, such as dogs and wildlife.

If the bite came from another horse and it's severe, call the vet. A bite from any other animal requires a call to the vet, too. Bites can become easily infected, and your horse might need an antibiotic. Don't worry about superficial horse bites since these will heal on their own.

If your horse is bitten by a snake that you know is poisonous (poisonous snakes in North America include rattlesnakes, copperheads, cottonmouth water moccasins, and coral snakes), don't panic. Most snakebites in horses are not fatal. They should be taken seriously, though, since they can result in severe swelling of the face, pain, and lameness.

Keep your horse calm and call for help immediately. A trailer that will take your horse home will be a godsend since you don't want your horse to move too much. Keep him calm while you are waiting, and lead the horse very slowly to the trailer once it arrives.

If you can't get help, you'll have to walk your horse slowly back home. Before you do, you can do some things to help your horse. If he was bitten in the face, and you carry two six-inch pieces of garden hose in your first-aid kit (see chapter 10 for details on putting together a kit), insert these into the horse's nostrils after lubricating them. The hose will keep the horse's nostrils open so he can breathe.

Veterinarians have differing opinions about whether it's wise to apply a tourniquet to a horse with a snakebite. Talk to your vet beforehand to get advice on this.

When you get your horse home, call the vet immediately. Your horse may need treatment for shock, as well as antivenom.

Prevent snake bites on the trail by checking grassy areas under trees before tying your horse. If you see a snake on the trail, give it a wide birth. If you are approaching a snake on the trail and it is coiled and threatening to strike, turn around and go the other way.

Part III

ON THE TRAIL

Chapter 8

Preparing Your Horse for Trail

I n the wild, horses spend plenty of time on the trail. In fact, wild horses often make their own trails as they forge through the brush on their way to watering holes and in search of better grazing. Foals born to wild horse herds grow up in the great wide open, and for them, traveling dirt trails becomes second nature.

Domesticated horses are a different matter. Because most saddle horses grow up in stalls, paddocks, and enclosed pastures, they feel most secure when surrounded by fencing and familiar surroundings. Horses who have spent most of their lives in these kinds of conditions need to learn to be confident out on the trail.

If you want to start riding your horse on trail, you'll have to begin by conditioning her mind first. Once she is mentally prepared for the trail, you can start to work on her body.

Basic Training

Before you begin acclimating your horse to the trail, you need to be confident that she is responsive and obedient to you in the arena. A horse whose first instinct is to obey her rider is going to be a lot more manageable on the trail than one who doesn't pay much attention to the signals coming from the person on her back.

Spend some time riding your horse in the arena with a critical eye. Ask her to stop, stand quietly, go forward, turn, and back up. She should do all of these things without hesitation. If you can, try to test her on these basic training issues when other horses are in the area or there are distractions outside the ring. If she listens to you well under these circumstances, she is ready to begin serious trail training.

If your horse does not respond to these important commands the first time around, even in the presence of distractions, she needs more basic training before you set foot on trail. This is for both your safety and hers. You want her to be focused on you when you are riding in the open, and you need her to be a reliable mount so you can control her.

WORKING ON THE ESSENTIALS

If you have a horse who won't listen to you in the arena, it's imperative that you work on getting her to pay attention to you before you go out on trail. If you are an experienced rider, you can work on these issues yourself. If you are a beginner, get the help of a riding instructor, horse trainer, or experienced friend.

Work on the following commands to get your horse trail-ready. You will have to use these commands on the trail when you are riding, so it's imperative your horse knows to obey them.

·If your horse obeys the commands without an argument, give her plenty of praise. If not, work with her until she performs the commands the first time around.

- *Stop.* Your horse must respond immediately to the word "whoa," accompanied by a gentle pull back on the reins. The horse should stop in her tracks the moment the verbal and rein cues are given. If your horse ignores your stopping cues, she needs serious retraining by a professional.

- *Stand quietly.* After stopping, your horse should stand still until given the signal to go forward. The longer you ask your horse to stand still, the more likely she is to start to move off on her own. Start out asking her to stand for a few minutes. If she does this without a problem, give her plenty of praise and gradually increase the time you ask her to stand until she has learned to remain still until you ask her to move. If your horse refuses to stand still at all, you will need the help of a professional or a very experienced horse person to teach her that she must stand until told otherwise.

- *Go forward.* Your horse must be willing to go forward when you squeeze her with your legs while holding her on a loose rein. If you have a particularly slow horse, you might need to cluck to her to wake her up and get her to move forward. If she refuses to move, she needs a lot of retraining to respond to your cues.

- *Turn.* From a stop, ask your horse to make a 180-degree turn to the left. Then ask her to make the same turn to the right. Ask her to do the same while walking, then trotting, and finally cantering. The turn doesn't have to be sharp or fancy, just a decent response to your cue. If your horse doesn't turn when you ask her to, have a professional or experienced horse person watch you as you ask for this maneuver. The problem may be your horse's training, or it may be the way you are asking. If you are asking properly and your horse doesn't respond, she needs work by a professional. If your cues are the problem, you should take some lessons on your horse to learn how to deliver the turn cues properly so your horse can understand them.

Obedience under saddle isn't the only criteria you need to look for in your horse before you take her out on trail. Good ground manners are also important when trail riding. You never know when you might have to get off your horse, lead her, tie her, and get back on again. You may have to do this under difficult circumstances, such as on a steep and narrow trail, or in a rocky ravine, or in running water. Dealing with an uncooperative horse in these situations will make you wish you'd never left the barn.

A good trail horse knows the following basic ground manners:

- *Standing for mounting.* Your horse should stand completely still while you are mounting, and not move until you give the cue to go forward. If your horse starts walking away while you are getting on, or moves out as soon as you get into the saddle, work with her so she learns to stand. You may need a helper for this to hold her bridle and make her stand. Do not let her go forward until you have cued her to do so. You may need professional assistance if you can't make progress on your own.

- *Standing for dismounting.* Most horses will stand still for their rider to get off, but some won't. You'll need the help of a trainer if you have horse who starts moving off while you are trying to dismount. This is a particularly dangerous behavior that needs to be fixed before you can safely take your horse out on trail.

- *Leading quietly.* Horses who drag their handlers when being led need reschooling. This is particularly important if you plan to take your horse on trail rides. If you need to get off her and lead on a narrow trail or through a difficult situation, you need a horse who will follow quietly and not drag you down the trail. A variety of methods can be used to train a horse to lead properly. Again, seek the help of a trainer or experienced horse person for this task.

- *Tying.* If you plan to take your horse on long trail rides, you will probably need to tie her at some point, either to a horse trailer or to a tree or hitching post. Horses who pull back when tied are particularly dangerous on the trail. A loose horse on the trail or in a campground can put herself, as well as other horses and humans, in jeopardy. If your horse repeatedly pulls back and breaks halters or lead ropes, she has developed a bad habit that needs to be trained out of her. Seek the help of a trainer for this task. Teaching a horse to stop pulling back is a difficult task to tackle on your own.

Venturing Out

Once you've determined your horse is safe and well mannered in the arena and on the ground, your next step is to get her used to the idea of trail riding. If you have only ridden your horse in an arena, you'll need to acclimate her to the concept of trail riding.

The first time you attempt to trail ride on your arena-bound horse, you'll probably find yourself on a nervous, spooky creature who is acting as if a horse-eating monster is about to leap out at her from behind every bush. If you are encountering a new trail for the first time on a horse you have ridden on other trails before, you might get this same reaction. This is typical horse behavior; many horses react with fear and nervousness when in a new situation. Instinct tells them predators might be lurking anywhere in this new place, and they need to stay on guard.

Start Slow

The key to getting your horse to relax is to gradually get her used to the idea of trail riding. It's amazing to see experienced trail horses react with calm and even enthusiasm when they are asked to negotiate a trail they've never seen before. Extensive experience with new trails has taught these horses that monsters aren't lurking everywhere outside the arena, and that exploring new trails is fun and stimulating. To get your horse to that point, you'll need patience and plenty of time spent out on the trail.

Work on your horse's obedience on the ground before you take the horse out on the trail.

The first step to acclimating your horse to the idea of trail riding is to get her out of the arena. Start easy, with just a brief ride outside the ring *after* a good workout so your horse has burned off her excess energy. You can ride your horse around the outside of the arena, following the rail. If she seems relaxed while doing this, extend your ride to a little bit beyond the fence line. Once you sense your horse tense up (her head goes up, her ears go forward, and her muscles stiffen), understand that you are pushing her outside her comfort zone. Ask her to work just a few minutes while she's uptight, and if she refrains from blowing up and still listens to you, reward her with praise and take her back to where she's comfortable.

You'll need to repeat this exercise until your horse is no longer tense when you take her to a new area outside the arena. When you sense she's relaxed, take her a little further until she tenses up again. Ask her to work a short time with this tension and then reward her by taking her back to where she's comfortable. If you take your time and do this slowly, your horse should gradually get used to the idea of working outside the arena. Hopefully, you'll avoid any incidents like spooking and bolting.

If your horse is very high-strung and gets extremely worked up at even the slightest venture outside her comfort zone, you'll need plenty of patience to continue to work with her. Don't risk your safety, however. If your horse is behaving dangerously (rearing, spinning, bolting) and you don't have the skills to deal with these issues, get help from a professional trainer.

Eventually, if you take gradual steps, your horse will learn that it's okay to be outside the arena. Your next move is to go on a short trail ride with a buddy.

Hitting the Trail

Finding the right trail buddy is key at this stage of the game. You need someone with a seasoned, quiet trail horse who will give confidence to your neophyte trail mount. You don't want to go out with a buddy horse who will react to your horse's nervousness and start misbehaving too. Horses have a tendency to feed off each other's nerves. If your horse is uptight, and this makes your friend's horse nervous, you will soon both be dealing with nervous horses who are getting themselves more and more worked up over time. The object here is to teach your horse that going on out trail is a safe, relaxed way to work. A buddy horse who feeds on your horse's nervousness will communicate just the opposite.

It's also important that you choose a riding partner who understands that you are trying to train your horse to trail, and is willing to ride at a slow pace. Until your horse is completely comfortable with trail riding, you should walk for the entire ride. You can eventually work up to trotting and then cantering, but in the beginning, a walk is all your horse can handle. If this sounds boring, just remember that the faster a horse goes, the spookier she becomes.

Once you find someone helpful to ride with who has a calm, unaffected trail horse, plan a short ride of anywhere from thirty minutes to an hour. Pick a trail that does not have any water crossings or other challenging obstacles. Be prepared to turn around and come back if your horse gets nervous to the point of being out of control. Hopefully, if you've done your homework and your horse is a good trail prospect, you will only have to deal with a tense animal who's a bit on the spooky side.

Before you go on your first trail ride, give your horse a good workout. This can either be a ride in the arena, a good workout on the lunge line, or a turnout. You want to get your horse's excess energy out so she is feeling mellow when you go out on trail. Eventually, when your horse is comfortable with trail riding, you won't need to work her out before your rides.

Ask your trail buddy to be in the lead as you ride, since horses new to trail riding feel more secure when they are following along rather than walking in front. Your horse should be allowed just to walk along in the back as the other horse assumes the role of leader.

Your horse will probably be a bit nervous the first time out, but will learn that all is well when she returns home to the barn in one piece. Her disposition, along with the way you handle her spookiness, will help determine how soon she relaxes on the trail. Some horses are more naturally alert and nervous than others, and take longer to get used to trail riding. Others are easygoing and virtually fearless, and take to this type of riding very quickly.

If you find yourself on a spooky horse who is jumping sideways at rocks and bolting when a bird flies up out of the brush nearby, you'll need to handle her reactions appropriately. Your job is to reassure her that everything is okay while at the same time letting her know that she needs to listen to you.

Handling Spooks

Different riders have different ways of handling spookiness in horses. The most common and effective way is to help the horse understand that whatever she's afraid of will not hurt her.

Horses react differently when they are afraid of something. Some will back up in an effort to avoid going toward whatever scares them. Others will spin away from the object. Yet others will dance around whatever it is in an effort to avoid approaching it, while some will simply plant their feet and refuse to move. (This latter maneuver is often followed by a spin if the rider keeps insisting that the horse go forward.) Some will agree to pass the object, but will prance by it, their heads pointing slightly toward it, with the ear closest to the object cocked. The idea here is to keep a close watch on the object should it decide to come to life and try to eat them.

The type of behavior your horse exhibits when she's afraid will depend largely on her personality. Each horse has her own way of reacting whenever she's scared.

It's important to realize that your horse is allowed to be afraid of something out on trail. Horses are built to be vigilant, and you can't change that aspect of your horse's personality. As long as your horse is alive and breathing, you can't reasonably expect her to be forever fearless. The goal when dealing with spookiness is to keep your horse controllable, even though she's afraid of something. In other words, she's allowed to be scared, but she's *not* allowed to become uncontrollable at the same time.

The work you do in the arena to enhance your horse's basic training will do a lot to help you keep your horse controllable out on the trail. Listening to you should become second nature to your horse. Responding to your cues should be a natural reflex to your horse. Once you have achieved this, repeated exposure to trail riding and positive experiences on the trail should help your horse be reasonably calm when you ride her outside the arena.

You can do a lot to help your horse stay calm and confident on the trail, especially when she's approaching something that seems scary to her. Here are some tips:

- *Don't focus.* First off, keep yourself from focusing on the scary object. Horses are incredibly perceptive, and if you start looking at whatever it is that's up ahead in anticipation of a spook, you will give subtle cues to your horse that she's got something to be afraid of. Instead, look past the obstacle to whatever lies beyond, and think to yourself, "We are going to walk past that thing and get beyond it without a problem."

- *Exude confidence.* Although it can be hard, stay confident. Hopefully, you have spent time taking lessons and riding your horse enough so that you feel you know what you are doing. If you are generally fearful and worried that you can't control your horse, your horse won't have confidence in you. Horses need to feel like they have a leader, and that leader should be you. Act like you are the one in control.

- *Relax.* It can be very difficult to stay relaxed on a nervous horse, especially when you sense your horse tensing up and getting ready to spook. If your horse feels you tense up, she will become even more nervous. After all, her rider is scared, so why shouldn't she be, too? To help relax yourself when you are approaching something that you believe might spook your horse, concentrate on taking long deep breathes. Count backward from fifty between each breath to relax your muscles. You can also try singing out loud. This will distract you and may also give your horse something else to think about.

- *Calm your horse.* When your horse is afraid of something, do whatever you can to help her relax. Talk to her in a soft voice and tell her it's okay. Unless you have a very strong bond with your horse developed after many years in the saddle, your voice won't be enough to completely relax her, but it will definitely help.

- *Distract your horse.* If you are about to pass an object on the side of the trail and your horse is starting to look at it as if she might spook, change her focus by pulling her head around to the opposite side of the object. In other words, if the scary item is on your right, pull your horse's head around to the left. Your horse will become distracted by this and won't be able to see the object. This works best with completely inanimate objects that won't potentially make any sounds.

- *Let your horse investigate.* Many horses feel better about approaching an object if they can touch and smell it first. If your horse is looking at something as if she doesn't want to pass it, ask her to stand in front of it and look at it. She may reach out her nose to touch it and smell it. Chances are, she'll realize it's not going to eat her and she will be willing to walk past it afterward. She might still keep a close eye on it as she passes, but that's okay—the point here is to get her past it in a controlled manner.

- *Ignore it.* Another approach preferred by some trail riders is to ignore the obstacle. If your horse seems willing to pass the object but seems afraid of it at the same time, dancing and prancing by it, just ignore the behavior. Acting as if the object is no big deal will help your horse realize she has nothing to be afraid of. Odds are the next time she passes it, she will be less worried, and eventually will come to ignore the object, just like her rider did the first time around.

- *Face it.* If something spooks your horse from behind, turn her around to face it. If your horse can see whatever it is, she is less likely to react to it—and is less likely to bolt and run.

- *Ride through the spook.* If all else fails and your horse spooks despite your best efforts, ride her through. Sit deep in the saddle and back on your pockets to maintain your balance. Keep a firm hold on the reins and keep your cool. If your horse bolts and runs, remember that she will eventually stop. Horses are sprinters, and will usually only run as far as they need to in order to put a safe distance between themselves and the scary object. If your horse is running out of control for an extended distance, pull her head around to one side to slow her down to the point where you can control her. Do this gradually and with a pulsing movement on the reins so you don't throw her off balance.

- *Reward.* Remember always to praise your horse when she successfully overcomes her fear enough to go past an obstacle. Pet her and tell her she's a good girl for doing as you ask, despite her fears. Most horses want to please their riders, so a bit of praise goes a long way in persuading the horse to trust you.

- *Understand the horse's mindset.* It's important to keep in mind throughout your ride that horses usually spook because they are afraid for their lives. Occasionally, they will act spooky if they are bored or are trying to get out of work, but a savvy rider who knows his or her horse can usually tell the difference between a genuine spook and a "fake" one. Remembering that the horse is operating out of fear rather than obstinacy will help you remain patient and understanding as you teach your horse to trust you out on trail.

- *Take note of the weather.* Horses react strongly to their environment, and are particularly sensitive to changes in the weather. Many horses become frisky when the air first becomes cool and brisk in the fall, and become particularly spooky when the wind is blowing. Keep these realities in mind when you are trail riding with your horse. Warm days are usually the best times for trail training, since inexperienced horses are less likely to act up if it's hot out.

Sensory Training

If you ride out in the countryside and rarely have to negotiate anything other than an occasional deer or an errant piece of trash, you probably won't have too much trouble keeping your horse calm on trail once she gets used to the idea of riding in the open. But trail riders living in urban areas have a lot more to contend with than wild life and the occasional plastic bag. Urban riders and their mounts are frequently confronted with an assortment of "horse-eating monsters," including roaring motorcycles, waving flags, intimidating garbage trucks, kids on skateboards, giant Halloween decorations, and a host of other things.

In order to help urban riders desensitize their horses to the sights and sounds of city life, sensory training clinics are cropping up around the country. Organized by former mounted police officers or professional trainers, these clinics introduce your horse to frightening stimuli in a controlled learning environment.

Most sensory training clinics are based on training programs designed for police horses, who have to deal with an incredible amount of stimuli all at one time when doing their jobs. While most urban trail horses won't have to engage in crowd control, they often have to deal with issues that are similar to what a police horse encounters on the job. A car backfiring sounds a lot like a gunshot, for example, and the urban trail horse who has been desensitized to this noise is a safer mount. Horses in sensory clinics are asked to stand quietly while firecrackers are set off, simulating the sound of a car backfiring. After hearing this noise at the clinic and learning that the sound is harmless, a horse hearing this same noise out on the street is less likely to react.

Conducted in the safety of an arena, sensory clinics give riders the opportunity to find out how their horses will react to scary stimuli on the trail. With the help of instructors, the riders learn how to deal with their horses' reactions. Riders also discover their horses' weak areas and are often encouraged to practice dealing with these same issues at home. Repeated exposure to stimuli is the key to desensitizing your trail horse.

- *Consider your horse's diet.* If you find yourself with a horse who is incredibly spooky and high-strung, talk to your veterinarian about the horse's diet. Items such as grain or alfalfa can make some horses act pretty crazy. (See chapter 5, "Basic Care," for more on feeding your trail horse.)

- *Get help.* Some horses can become downright dangerous when they are afraid of something. If your horse runs away with you, rears up, bucks you off, or does anything you can't handle, don't hesitate to get professional help from a qualified horse trainer.

Dealing With Common Obstacles

Horses are cautious creatures by nature, and some of the typical obstacles horses encounter on trail can send them into a tizzy. Even the most courageous and willing trail horse will probably balk the first time she's asked to cross running water or pass a strange object she can't identify.

As a rider, your job is to gain your horse's confidence so she can muster up the courage to negotiate the obstacle and to teach her how to safely and efficiently cross or pass or whatever lies before her.

Winning your horse's trust is something you'll develop along the way as you deal with her fear. Specifics on how to handle individual obstacles must be learned by you and transferred along to your horse.

Let's take a look at the most common obstacles horses must confront on trail, and how they should be handled over each.

WATER

Most horses are nervous the first time or two they are asked to walk through water. Whether it's a small puddle or a raging river, the typical horse will resist the rider's attempts to get her to cross. This is a matter of survival for the horse, who has no concept of how deep the water might be and where her legs will go once she steps into it.

By working on common trail obstacles from the ground first, you can safely acclimate your horse to these objects.

Horses learn with repetition to trust their riders on water crossings. After a horse has repeatedly walked through a creek, puddle, or river and come out the other side unscathed, she learns that water is safe and that it's okay to cross it. This is true of almost all horses. If a horse has a scare while in the water (she sinks into wet sand and can't get out, or loses her balance and falls), you will have a problem the next time you try to cross.

When teaching your horse to cross water, it's important she have a good experience the first time around. Make sure the first body of water you attempt with your horse is a safe one that you have ridden through before, or at least walked through. This includes both creek and riverbanks. Watch out for quicksand, and keep in mind that although you might not sink when you walk through it, your horse weighs a lot more than you do and might not be able to get out.

Keep in mind that if you are not an experienced and confident rider, you might want to ask a professional to handle teaching water crossings for you. Some horses can be extremely frightened when asked to cross water the first time, and if they have ever had a bad experience, your horse's reactions might be too much for you to handle. Also, you want to make sure that once you ask your horse to cross, you make certain she actually does it. This might mean forty-five minutes or more of repeated requests to move forward into the water before your horse even puts one foot in. If you give up and let your horse turn around and go back to the barn, your horse has learned that resisting means she doesn't have to do as you ask.

It's also important to choose that first body of water carefully. Pick an area that has a wide, clear bank and isn't overgrown with brush or trees on either side. If your horse has never walked through a small stream, don't ask her to tackle a wide, fast-moving river as her first attempt at water. Start small. You may even want to create some puddles in your horse's pasture or in the barn arena with a garden hose or bucket and ask her to walk through these puddles, first with you leading and then with you in the saddle.

When you are ready to attempt crossing your first real body of water with your horse out on trail, you'll find the tricky part is getting her to take the first step into it. If your horse tries to spin and bolt, dances sideways, backs up, or refuses to move, be firm and insist she go back to her original position and try it again. Continue to ask with your legs and voice for forward motion. Most likely, your horse will deny your requests several times and repeat her evasive maneuvers. You need to keep insisting until your horse realizes that she's not going home and you're not going to stop bugging her until she does what you ask.

Be aware that if the body of water is small enough, your horse may decide to jump over it. If you feel your horse bunch up beneath you, she's probably getting ready to launch herself. This is not behavior you want to encourage. You may need to get off and lead her through the water so she learns that she has to step through it. If you get the sense she is going to jump it while you are leading her, you need to reassess the situation and get help from a more experienced horse person.

Water is an obstacle that most trail horses have to encounter sooner or later. Teaching your horse to calmly walk through water will make life easier for both of you.

One way to avoid a fight with your horse is to ask the other person or people you are riding with to cross the water ahead of you. Many horses will follow if they see another horse walking through the water without a problem. The fear of being left behind is a concern to many horses and is often enough to convince a reluctant newbie to take the plunge. Of course, it's important that you are riding with people whose horses step easily into the water. The last thing you need is for the other horses to begin resisting their riders too. This will fuel your horse's notion that water cannot be trusted and encourage her to resist even more.

When your horse finally steps into the water, talk to her and praise her generously. If she wants to stop and drink, let her. If she starts to paw at the water, pull her head up and firmly ask her to move forward toward the other bank. Some horses like to roll in water, and pawing is a sure sign that rolling is on her mind.

Once your horse makes it across the water, praise her even more. Ride for at least a while on solid ground before you ask her to cross the water again on her way home. The second time around should be a lot easier because she's done it once already, and also because home is on the other side of the water. If she's still reluctant to step in, go back to your previous methods of getting her to walk through.

If all else fails when it comes to getting your horse to cross water, consider getting off and walking her through it the first few times. This won't be pleasant since you are bound to get wet, but your horse will be more likely to step into the water if you are in the lead. By following your lead, she will learn that water is safe.

If the water you plan to cross is so deep that your horse will be forced to swim, reconsider crossing it—particularly if the water is moving. This can be dangerous to both you and your horse, especially if you are inexperienced at this kind of water crossing.

In my years as a trail rider, I have seen fellow riders spend considerable amounts of time trying to get a horse to step into a body of water. One friend had a horse who was so fearful of water she had to have two other people ride alongside her, each holding the end of a rope that ran across her horse's rump to literally push him forward. This was the only way they could get the horse to cross the river. Others have persisted with their horses for well over an hour to get the horse to cross.

Horses are born knowing how to swim, yet they are instinctively afraid of entering bodies of water. For this reason, it can take plenty of courage and patience to go head to head with a resistant horse when it comes to water crossings. Keep in mind that some horses never learn to like water, and will always be reluctant to step into it. Your horse has the right to dislike water, but she is still obligated to listen to you when you ask her to cross it. If you think your horse might give you trouble and you aren't sure you have what it takes to win the battle, ask a professional or an experienced rider to handle the situation for you.

BLOCKED TRAILS

Trails that are not regularly maintained may be blocked by fallen trees or large limbs, sometimes for long periods of time. Or a large tree branch may happen to fall the day before your ride. If you have a horse who won't go over fallen timber, you won't be able to travel past the point where the tree is blocking the trail.

The best way to teach your horse to step over logs and other obstacles on the trail is to work in the arena first. Using poles that are made for jumps, you can teach your horse how to step over objects.

Start by putting a pole down and lead your horse up to it. Let her sniff the pole so she gets a good look at it, and then ask her to step forward with you as you step over it first. Most horses will step over the pole, possibly brushing it with their hooves as they do. Some may try to trot over the pole, while others may want to jump it. Your goal is to get your horse to step quietly over the pole without hitting it. If she does this, praise her heartily. If she doesn't quite get it, ask her to do it again until she gets it right. After she has negotiated her first pole without a problem, set up several poles in a row, about six feet apart, and ask her to step over each of these in succession. Once she is able to step over these poles effortlessly, you can try the same exercise under saddle.

When riding your horse over poles, ask her to step over them at the walk. You want her to learn to pick her feet up, so if she steps over the poles without knocking any of them, give her plenty of praise.

Once you have worked on this in the arena, you are ready to tackle fallen logs on the trail. When you see such an obstacle on the trail, ask your horse to approach it. If she wants to stop and sniff it, let her. Then ask her to go forward. If the log is small, she should step over it. If the log is too big to reasonably step over it but not so big that you can't see what's on the other side of it, expect your horse to jump it. If you are unsure of how to sit on a jumping horse, just grab a hold of your saddle horn (assuming you are riding Western) and let your horse make the leap. If you are riding English, go into the two-point position before your horse jumps. (Two-point is a seat position you should have learned in your lessons.) Be careful not to jerk back on the reins when your horse lands, regardless of which discipline you are riding.

Another option when encountering such obstacles on the trail is to go around them. If you have room to leave the trail and go around a fallen tree, do so as long as you know it's safe to walk off the trail. The brush might be thick, and your horse might be uncomfortable pushing her way through it. But if you gently nudge her forward and encourage her, she should be able to figure it out.

WARDROBE CHANGES

When riding on trial, be aware that the weather can change. It's a good idea to wear layers of clothing so you can remove items when you get warm and put them on when you get cold. Of course, in order to do this without having to get off your horse each time, you need to have a horse who is safe when you are putting on a sweatshirt, jacket, or rain slicker.

If you aren't sure if your horse is okay with a rider who is taking clothing on and off while sitting on the horse's back, start on the ground to see how she reacts to the item of clothing. Approach her quietly with a jacket or rain slicker, and let her sniff the item. When she seems relaxed, talk to her and gently rub the item of clothing on her body. Be prepared for her to react with fear if she initially seems uncomfortable with the item. If she pulls away and seems very afraid, stop what you are doing, talk to her until she's calm, and try again. If she refuses to calm down, try arming yourself with some carrots and see if you can feed her at the same time you are rubbing the clothing on her body. She should make the association between the food and the clothing and eventually realize she has nothing to fear.

The next step is to be able to put the clothing on and take it off while you are sitting on your horse's back. Do this part in an arena in case your horse spooks. You don't need a runaway horse on the trail. It's important to have someone help you with this exercise too.

Mount up on your horse and ask the helper to approach the horse while holding the jacket or slicker. Talk to your horse all the while and help her feel relaxed. If she begins to tense up at the sight of the clothing, ask your helper to approach very slowly and let the horse sniff the jacket or slicker. The horse should realize that this is the same article of clothing she was exposed to when you were working with her on the ground, and should stand still.

Next, ask your helper to hand the jacket to you. If your horse shies away when you try to reach out to take the slicker, it's time to get off and start over with the groundwork. The horse needs to feel completely comfortable with the jacket before you can even think about putting it on while in the saddle.

If your horse doesn't react when your helper hands you the jacket, take the item and rub it on your horse's withers and shoulders. Ask your helper to stand at your horse's head and hold the reins as you gently reach around and let the jacket brush against your horse's hindquarters. If your horse tries to scoot out from under the jacket, your helper will be at her head to keep her from bolting.

Continue this until your horse seems completely relaxed. Again, if she is very wound up about the whole thing, you need to take a step back and start working with her from the ground to get her used to the jacket.

The next step is to put the jacket on. Have your helper stand at the horse's head while you do this to prevent the horse from bolting forward. You will need two hands to put the jacket on, so it will be hard for you to control the horse if she starts to move forward.

If your horse stands quietly while you put the jacket on, praise her and let her stand for a few minutes. Then take the jacket off, with your helper standing at the horse's head. If your horse doesn't react to the jacket coming on or off, you have a horse who is reliable when you need to do a wardrobe change mid-ride.

Conditioning for Trail

If you plan on only taking your horse for short rides of an hour or less on trail, then you don't have to worry about conditioning her for the work. Any healthy, sound horse can handle that much trail work without physical preparation. But if you plan longer rides, and particularly competitive distance rides, you need to make sure your horse is in proper physical condition.

Conditioning a horse for trail involves building up her body to withstand the rigors of hours under saddle in wilderness terrain. In order for a horse to remain sound and healthy when ridden for long periods of time, she must be in good shape. You wouldn't run a marathon without training first, and the same goes for trail horses.

If you plan to go on a long ride with friends, or just want to start trail riding for several hours at a time, the best approach is to give your horse frequent exercise, on a regular basis, starting at least two months in advance of the event. Don't leave your horse without exercise for two weeks at a time, since this will impair the conditioning you've given her up to that point.

If your horse is sound and healthy and has been receiving regular exercise, you can start increasing her time under saddle in fifteen-minute increments each week. For example, if you have been riding her three times a week for forty-five minutes each time, increase that to three times a week for sixty minutes each time. You can also add another day of exercise to her routine. The more exercise

Good Behavior

Teaching your horse to be relaxed on trail and negotiate obstacles along the way is an important part of trail training. But so is good behavior. The following basic rules should apply to your horse when you are trail riding. As the rider, it's your job to enforce these rules with quiet insistence:

- *No eating.* Don't allow your horse to snack along the way as you are riding. While it might seem mean to stop her from just taking a nibble along the way on a trail ride, allowing her to do so will result in a horse who spends more time eating on rides that she does walking. She may also inadvertently take a bite out of a plant that is poisonous to horses. If you are on a long ride and want to give your horse some grazing time, dismount and let her eat so she understands the difference between taking a break and snacking whenever she feels like it.

- *No jigging.* Jigging is an annoying behavior that lies somewhere between a walk and a jog. A jigging horse refuses to walk, and instead does a walk/jog combination that can be extremely frustrating to a rider who wants a horse who calmly walks along. Jigging is a difficult habit to break, and is best handled by a professional trainer. If your horse is already a jigger, chances are you will need help breaking her of this habit. Don't let your horse become a jigger if she isn't one already. Make sure she *walks* the last fifteen or twenty minutes of every trail ride. Allowing her to trot or gallop home will get her in the mindset of speeding her way back to the barn. Then when you ask her to walk one day, she'll be loathe to do it.

- *No horse-determined detours.* Sometimes horses have their own notions about which way the trail should lead. This might be a shortcut

you give her, the more fit she will become. Just remember to add the exercise gradually so you don't overwhelm her and make her sore or lame.

If you are planning to attend an all-day ride and are prepping your horse for this event, remember that the general rule is to train up to about half the time you intend to ride on the big day. So, if you plan to ride with your friends for eight hours one day in a couple of months, you should build your horse up to the point where you are taking her on four-hour rides. Do this by gradually building up the time you spend out on trail, slowly adding more time to the rides.

Becky Siler of Clermont, Florida, a long-time competitive trail and endurance rider and president of the Florida Horseman's Association, has specific recommendations for conditioning a horse for long-distance trail riding. She suggests that if you have been riding your horse for at least half an hour to an hour two days a week, you need to add at least one more ride during the week. The extra day of riding will help condition your horse slowly instead of home, or perhaps around a puddle of water in the middle of the trail. Remember that you are in charge when you are riding, and all decisions should be yours. If you let your horse take control of the situation, you might find yourself banged up against a tree as your horse swerves to avoid a puddle or else fighting with her at times when she wants to go one way and you want to go the other.

- *No aggression toward other horses.* Horses have different personalities, just like humans, and some horses just simply don't get along. Often one horse is more of a troublemaker than the others and will repeatedly pick fights. If your horse is one to make trouble, she will likely try to bite or kick other horses you are riding with. This is a tough problem to deal with since it's hard to get a horse to change aggressive behavior toward other horses. Your can do a lot to prevent injuries to other horses from your horse by warning other riders about your horse's dislike for other horses, and by getting after your horse every time she acts aggressively toward another horse. Most acts of aggression are preceded by flattened ears, so pay attention to the signs. If she puts her ears back at another horse, give her a verbal correction or perhaps even a tap on the shoulder with a riding crop to warn her that aggression won't be tolerated.

- *No charging up hills.* It's easier for a horse to negotiate a hill by charging up it than it is to walk it. However, it's safer for the horse to walk. Teach your horse that she has to walk up hills and not charge them. This not only makes things easier on your horse's legs, but is also a courtesy to those riders behind you. If your horse races up a hill, you can be sure their horses will too, whether they want them to or not.

putting her through a difficult workout only on the weekends. According to Becky, a horse can build stamina quickly just being ridden three days a week.

The best way to condition your horse is on the trail, according to Becky. She recommends mapping out a couple of trails in your area that are five or six miles long. Use a vehicle or a Global Positioning System (GPS) to get an accurate reading. (See chapter 4, "Tacking Up," for details on GPS.) Keep in mind that the average horse walks one mile in about twenty minutes and trots one mile in nine to twelve minutes. Find out the distance of the ride you'll be taking so you know how much your horse will be doing that day.

When prepping for your all-day ride, Becky suggests giving your horse approximately four to six weeks at three rides per week to build up her conditioning. During the first two weeks, go the distance and pace you've been doing, but add a third day. You can spend time doing arena work or trail riding on the third day, anything that will be fun for your horse and keep her from getting bored.

When you get into week three, add five minutes of trotting five or six times during the ride. During weeks four and five, continue to add longer distances on one day of riding at the same pace until you are eventually riding fifteen miles in about four hours. The month before your ride, do these longer rides only a couple of times before the ride you are training for. It's helpful to know that during training, your horse only needs to be able to cover about 75 percent of the distance she'll be doing on the one-day ride.

By week six, your horse should be getting fairly fit if you've kept to your schedule. If you miss a day here and there in the training, don't worry about it. According to Becky, horses are usually athletic and adaptable enough to not have this affect their overall conditioning.

GOOD CANDIDATES FOR DISTANCE RIDING

A horse needs to have the following characteristics to hold up to long-distance riding:

- *Youth.* Not that an older horse can't do long distances, but horses 20 years and older who have never done this type of work may not hold up to it. Talk to your vet before conditioning a horse of this age for distance riding.

- *Soundness.* Horses with chronic leg problems or old injuries may have problems going long distances on trail. If your horse suffers from navicular disease, arthritis, or any other chronic joint problem, she's not a good candidate for distance riding. (See chapter 7, "Health Concerns," for more information.) If your horse suffered a bowed tendon or ligament injury in the past, talk to your vet before beginning a conditioning program.

- *Overall health.* A horse who is struggling with hypothyroidism, Cushings disease, or any other chronic health disorder may have a hard time when asked to do distance work. If your horse is just getting over a bout with any kind of illness, the stress of distance riding may cause her to relapse. If you aren't sure if your horse's health condition can be made worse by riding long distances, talk to your veterinarian.

PULSE AND RESPIRATION

An important aspect of conditioning your horse for trail riding is measuring her pulse and respiration rates. Before you begin conditioning your horse for trail, learn how to read your horse's pulse and respiration so you can measure her conditioning along the way.

Your horse's pulse is your key to understanding how efficiently her heart is working with exercise. Just as your pulse quickens when you jog, your horse's pulse will quicken as she works. The key to a well-conditioned horse is one whose pulse rate rises to a certain level during exercise and then recovers quickly after the work stops.

Most horses reach a pulse rate of 100 when they are exercising and slow down to the normal post-exercise rate of about 60 after five minutes or so of rest. When a pulse rate of 60 is reached, the horse has recovered from the exercise. A well-conditioned endurance horse can recover to 60 in a matter of seconds.

A resting pulse rate is anywhere from 32 to 44 for mares and geldings. If you plan to do trail rides of a few hours or less with your horse but don't plan on competing in distance rides, don't worry about getting a 60 recovery rate within a matter of seconds. Only competitive equine athletes need to have that kind of conditioning because they are being asked to go fifty to a hundred miles in a day.

To take your horse's pulse, you can use a stethoscope or just do it by hand. You'll also need a watch with a second hand.

Trot your horse for a few minutes and then look for her pulse. You should be able to feel it behind the horse's girth on the left side, the inside of the fore-leg, or under the jawbone, below the jowls. It can take some time to locate the beat, so don't give up easily or get frustrated. It takes practice to locate it on many horses. (Be careful not to use your thumb for this because you may confuse your own pulse with that of your horse's.)

When you find the pulse, start counting the beats for fifteen seconds. Multiply the number you get by four and that is your horse's heart rate per minute. As you work to condition your horse, check her pulse rate weekly to see if she recovers faster as you put more time into her training. The quicker she reaches the 60 rate, the more fit she is becoming.

Respiration is another way to judge if your horse is recovering quickly from a workout. For fifteen seconds, measure your horse's breaths by counting the number of times her flanks expand outward. Multiply this number by four and you have her breaths per minute. Before you start your exercise program, measure your horse's respiration at rest, and then after a good workout. Check it weekly as you condition your horse to make sure her fitness is improving. The more fit your horse, the faster her respiration rate will return to normal after exercise stops.

Warming Up and Cooling Down

When riding any kind of horse, it's important to have a slow warm-up and an adequate cool-down. Don't jump on your horse and take off at a gallop down the trail without warming up first, and don't leap off your horse and put her away hot and sweaty. This might be how they do it in the movies, but what you don't see is that someone is warming up and cooling down these horses off-camera.

The need to warm up and cool down is easy to understand when you think about your own body. Imagine going to the gym for a workout or outside for a jog. If you began a rigorous workout cold, without stretching or walking first to warm up your muscles, you would not only have a harder time during your workout but you would also likely hurt yourself or at least be sore the next day.

Your Horse's Diet

As your condition your horse for longer trail rides, you'll need to keep a close eye on her weight. The extra exercise will cause her to burn more calories and she may start to drop pounds. If she was overweight when you started, this is a good thing as long as it doesn't happen too rapidly and the weight loss doesn't continue past the point of her appropriate weight.

If your horse is at a good weight and starts to lose more as a result of her conditioning, she will need more calories to keep her from becoming underweight. Some trail riders supplement their horse's diet with carbohydrates such as grains for more energy and weight, while others switch to a richer hay. Still others will go with a supplemental feed designed to put weight on a horse. Ultimately, the decision of what to give your horse to keep her weight up for long distances and more work should be discussed with your veterinarian. Your vet can assess your individual horse's needs and make the most educated suggestion as to how to increase her calorie intake.

The same goes for horses. If you have a horse who is standing in a stall or paddock all day long, warm her up with at least five minutes of walking and five minutes of slow trotting before you ask her to really start working hard. This includes going up hills on trail, since hill work is the most rigorous aspect of trail riding. Basically, the longer you can warm up your horse, the better. On cold, damp days, your horse will appreciate a longer warm-up even more.

Cooling down is also important. A horse who has been asked to work hard and is hot and sweating needs time to cool down slowly. Tying a heated horse up for a long period of time or putting her back in her stall when she's overheated and breathing hard will take its toll on your horse. Instead, walk her for ten minutes or longer, depending on how hot the weather is and how thick her coat is. If the weather is warm, it will take longer for your horse's body to expel the heat. Keeping her walking while she does this enables her muscles to cool gradually and will prevent your horse from getting stiff and sore. It will also do wonders for your horse's attitude. Horses who are repeatedly "put away wet" grow to dislike their work.

Trailer Loading

One of the most important aspects of preparing your horse for trail riding is teaching her to ride in a horse trailer. If you only plan to ride your horse locally from whatever trail heads you can reach by horseback, then you won't need to worry about trailering to rides (although you may find that you want to start venturing farther once you have ridden all your local trails). However, all horses should know how to load into and ride in a trailer for their own safety. Illness or emergency may necessitate that a horse get into a trailer in a hurry, and time spent training for this is inevitability well spent.

If your horse already loads well and rides quietly, you don't have to worry about training her for this aspect of her job. Still, it can't hurt to practice having your horse get into a trailer every so often just to make sure she hasn't developed any strange attitudes about it.

The best advice when it comes to trailering your horse for a trail ride is to practice well in advance of the ride. Don't wait until the morning you are supposed to meet all your friends at the regional park before you try to load your horse for the first time. If your horse balks and won't get in, you'll find yourself incredibly rushed and frustrated—and probably very late. Instead, find a friend or trainer with a trailer who will let you practice loading your horse at least a couple of weeks before the ride.

Trailers come in a variety of different styles:

- *Two-horse straight load.* A trailer that holds two horses who travel with their heads pointing directly toward the front of the trailer.

- *Two-horse slant load.* A trailer that holds two horses who travel with their bodies at an angle to the trailer door.

- *Three-plus horse slant load.* A trailer that holds three or more horses who travel with their bodies at an angle to the trailer door.

- *Stock trailer.* A large, open trailer that does not usually have dividers between horses.

- *Ramp.* A trailer of any design that has a ramp leading from the ground into the trailer.

- *Step-up.* A trailer of any design that does not have a ramp for loading. Instead, the horse must step up into the trailer.

While a horse may be fine loading into a stock trailer, she may be afraid to load into a two-horse straight load, or vice versa. For this reason, it's prudent to practice with the same type of trailer you'll be traveling in.

When teaching a horse to load into a trailer, it helps to understand the equine mindset. Since horses are prey animals, they are genetically programmed always to be on the lookout for danger. The dark confines of a horse trailer spell danger for the uneducated horse, so resistance is common. A horse needs to learn that a trailer is a safe place to be, and the only way she will learn that is from experience.

Some horses have their first trailer ride as foals, at their mother's side. These horses learn at an impressionable age that trailers are not to be feared. After all, if Mom goes right in, what is there to worry about? Most horses don't have this experience, however, and must learn as adults to get into a trailer.

The first time you try to load your horse, have an experienced friend nearby to help you. Take an optimistic approach and assume your horse is going to load without a problem. If you act worried or nervous, you may jinx yourself. Horses are incredibly perceptive creatures and will pick up on your hesitation. That may give your horse a reason to refuse to load if she is already looking for one.

Open the horse trailer doors and put some hay inside the trailer. Lead your horse up to the trailer and let her take a good look at it. She will probably put her head down and sniff the floor, and you may notice her tense up. Then step into the trailer yourself and ask your horse to follow you.

If she does, lead her up to the hay and let her eat. If she seems relaxed, tie her inside the trailer and exit. Let her hang out in there and eat for about ten minutes and then ask her to back out. If she does all this quietly, you have a horse who loads well.

If your horse refuses to follow you forward into the trailer and plants her feet, continue to ask her to come forward. Have your help get behind her and cluck to her. This might be enough encouragement to get her to go in. If she flatly refuses, or starts to back up wildly, she needs trailer training.

Methods for teaching a horse to load into a trailer are almost as numerous as the trainers who teach them. If you are a novice horse person and have a horse who refuses to load, you need the help of someone who is experienced—such as a horse trainer. However, it's important to pick the right person to help you with this situation. Before you enlist the assistance of anyone, find out how they intend to get your horse into the trailer. If their methods include beating the horse relentlessly until the horse gets into the trailer just to escape the whip, say, "Thanks, but no thanks." This is not to say that a whip can't be useful in getting a horse into a trailer, but it should be used as a visual cue for a horse, not as a means of abuse.

When you find someone who is qualified to help you, do whatever you can to make the experience of being in the trailer pleasant for your horse. Put hay or chopped-up carrots in the manger so once the horse loads, she associates being in the trailer with something good to eat. With repeated practice at loading, your horse should eventually learn that the trailer is a safe place. Hopefully, by the time you are ready for your trail ride, your horse will be happily loading into the trailer. (See chapter 12, "Trailering to Trails," for more information.)

Tack Check

Last but not least, before you embark on a trail ride of any length, check your tack. Use the following list to make sure that everything is in good working order:

- *Bridle.* Make sure the screws on your bridle are tight. These are the screws that hold your reins and headstall to your bit. If one of these screws comes loose and gets lost on the trail, you won't have a workable bridle to use— or a means of controlling your horse from her back.

- *Saddle.* Take a look at the parts of your saddle that suffer the most stress during a ride. Make certain your stirrup leathers are securely fastened to your saddle. Check the girth or cinch for wear and make sure the leather is in good working order. Check screws and other connecting areas to be sure they are secure.

- *Saddle pad.* Examine the underside of your saddle pad for dirt, burrs, or anything that might irritate your horse's back on a long ride.

Don't forget to bring some important items along on your ride, as well:

- *Spare hoof pick.* You never know when a stone or other object might get lodged in your horse's hoof. A spare hoof pick can be a lifesaver in a situation when you need to pry something from the underside of your horse's hoof before it makes her lame.

- *Spare hoof boot.* If your horse wears shoes and you'll be going on a long ride, bring one of these valuable items along. If your horse loses a shoe far from home, a hoof boot placed over the foot can prevent the hoof from becoming damaged or bruised over rough terrain.

- *Water for yourself.* You wouldn't go on a long hike without water, and you shouldn't go on a long trail ride without it, either. Keep your water on a saddle pack designed to carry water bottles, or use a clip-on water bottle holder you can buy at a sporting goods store.

- *A snack.* If you'll be riding for many hours, bring along something to eat. Even though your horse is doing most of the work, you still need to keep your energy up. (See chapter 9, "Conditioning Yourself for Trail," for details on the best foods to bring along on trail rides.)

- *A saddlebag or pouch.* You'll need this to carry your spare hoof pick, hoof boot, and snacks, as well as personal items like lip balm, tissues, sunglasses, a camera, and anything else you might need (you'll find a full list in chapter 9).

- *Bug repellent.* If you'll be riding during fly and mosquito season, bring repellent for yourself and your horse.

Chapter 9

CONDITIONING YOURSELF FOR TRAIL

Even the most casual of trail riders can tell you that trail riding requires some energy. Although it seems to the casual observer that the horse is doing all the work, the truth is that it takes skill and energy to ride a horse hour after hour in hot sun, wind, rain, or cold.

If you are serious about trail riding and want to do a lot of it, it's important that you prepare yourself for the rigors of this sport, in addition to preparing your horse (covered in the previous chapter). Not only will you enjoy trail riding more if you are physically up to it, but your horse will like his work too. A fit rider is a lot easier to carry than one who tires easily and weighs a lot. If horses could talk, they'd be sure to tell us this.

Why Trail Riding Is Hard Work

If all you plan to do is walk along on a flat trail for an hour or so a couple of times a week, you won't need to be in great shape for this hobby. Aside from getting your muscles used to sitting in a saddle, your body won't be doing too much work. But if you plan to ride for a long period of time at a given stretch, whether it's on a pack trip vacation or on your own horse, your body will have some work ahead of it.

While the horse will be doing the majority of the work, carrying you up and down hills and covering many miles, it takes strength and energy to stay in the saddle for long periods of time. If you aren't used to it, a six- to eight-hour ride can really wipe you out. If you are going on a pack trip where you ride all day, stop and camp, and then ride again the next morning, repeating the same routine for the next several days, you'll soon be exhausted if you aren't in decent physical shape.

As anyone who has gone on even a short ride after not being in the saddle for a long time or even at all can attest, riding uses muscles that aren't used for much of anything else. If you aren't used to riding, the day after can be down-right painful, with sore, stiff leg muscles that hurt for days.

This is proof positive that riding takes muscle. While the inner thighs are the most obvious place muscles are taxed by riding, your back, arms, and abdomen are also put to the test when you are in the saddle. And the longer you ride, the more those muscles are put to use.

Most trail riding involves going up and down hills, and sitting in the saddle while your horse is scaling a hill requires working your muscles, especially if you do it right. When your horse is climbing uphill, you should be standing slightly out of the stirrups and leaning forward to get your weight off the horse's back. When he's going downhill, you should be leaning back to take your weight off his front end. Both of these positions require muscle strength, especially if you are encountering a lot of hills.

Keep in mind that when you ride, your body uses energy to keep you balanced and in position in the saddle. Riding is less tiring than walking, but don't be fooled—it's still hard work.

Getting in Shape

In order to be a good rider who is easy on his or her horse, light in the saddle, and effective in communicating with the horse through aids and cues, you need to be in reasonably good shape. If you are an athletic person who does rigorous exercise on an almost daily basis, then you are already fit. If you aren't used to riding, long trail rides may tax your muscles and leave you sore the next day, but your stamina is probably excellent.

This is not to say that everyone who trail rides has to have zero percent body fat and be built like a marathon runner. Many trail riders are of average weight. However, if you plan to trail ride a lot and want to keep both yourself and your horse feeling good, it's a great idea to be as lean as you possibly can be.

If you are serious about regular trail riding but don't exercise on a regular basis, it's a good idea to put yourself on a plan. After seeing your doctor for a checkup to make sure your body is able to handle an exercise regime, consider walking, jogging, or doing another type of aerobic exercise to strengthen your muscles and build your stamina. It's a good idea to start this new regimen at least a month before going on your first long trail ride, if not sooner.

Riding lessons can be a good way to combine improving your riding skills with building your strength and endurance, provided your lessons offer a good workout. Dressage and hunt seat lessons offer the greatest amount of aerobic exercise since they require a rising or posting trot, which is almost like jogging. Even cantering in a dressage or hunt seat saddle can make you work up a sweat, depending on the horse you are riding. (Some canters are harder to sit than others.) While Western riding is wonderful for trail riding, you won't get as much of a workout taking basic Western lessons since this discipline was designed to be slower and easier on the rider.

Even if you only go on long trail rides once every two months, it's a good idea to maintain your exercise routine to keep your wind up and your body in good shape. Your payoff will come when you spend a day of riding and still feel good afterward.

ANAEROBIC EXERCISE

While aerobic exercise is good for your stamina, anaerobic exercise is great for building muscle strength. Many equestrians regularly participate in yoga and Pilates classes, and also lift weights.

Let's take a look at how each of these forms of anaerobic exercise help to build fitness in riders:

- *Yoga.* One of the keys to avoiding soreness when riding is flexibility and limberness. Practicing yoga increases your flexibility. It also helps with balance and muscle strength, two tools you'll need when riding. Yoga also helps you learn to truly relax, something that can come in handy when dealing with a spooky horse who will take his cue from the tension in your body.

  Different types of yoga classes are available to the public; hatha yoga is among the most popular. Any type of yoga will help you get fit for riding, and will be an asset to you out on the trail. Some yoga schools are even starting to offer yoga for equestrians, with exercises specifically designed to help riders with their work in the saddle. If you are lucky enough to live near a yoga school that offers this class, by all means enroll. If not, consider ordering a videotape or DVD that teaches yoga for equestrians.

- *Pilates.* A type of strengthening exercise developed by Joseph H. Pilates, this is a popular workout with riders. Designed to improve flexibility and strength without building bulk, Pilates also includes mental conditioning that can help with coordinating your brain and your body—something infinitely useful when riding. Pilates classes are given around the country, and tapes and DVDs are also available for purchase at video stores, fitness centers, and over the Internet.

- *Weight lifting.* Another way to build strength, lifting with emphasis on repetition rather than heavy weights is appropriate for riders. You don't want to build bulk here, but rather long, sinewy muscles for riding. Whether working with free weights or a weight machine, keep the weights light and the repetitions many.

DIET

In addition to exercise, diet is an important element in keeping yourself fit for trail riding. By eating the right foods, you'll enable your body to withstand the rigors of being in the saddle and out in the elements for long periods of time on the trail.

The key to a healthy diet is eating a lot of protein and vegetables, with only a small number of carbohydrates per day. Refined sugar should be avoided because it causes your blood sugar to spike, resulting in "crashes" after your body finishes metabolizing it.

By eliminating preservatives, sugars, and processed foods from your diet whenever you can, and eating mostly whole grains and fresh foods, you'll help your body be strong and healthy for trail riding and any other sport you wish to undertake.

Ann Boroch, N.D., C.Ht, is a naturopathic practitioner based in Los Angeles who provides nutritional counseling to her patients. She recommends the following suggested meals as part of a healthy diet.

Breakfast ideas include:

- Eggs (scrambled, hard-boiled, fried, or poached)
- Omelette made with vegetables (avocado, spinach, tomato, onion, peppers)
- Hot cereal (oatmeal, brown rice, rye flakes, amaranth, quinoa) with nuts, splash of rice milk, cinnamon, and stevia (a natural sweetener)
- Turkey patties or chicken sausage (made without sugars/preservatives or pork casings)
- Potatoes or hash browns with onions/bell peppers
- Potato pancakes

Lunch and dinner ideas include:

- Salad (made with spinach, beets, peppers, onions, sprouts, carrots, corn, peas, jicama, nuts, apple, or the like)
- Brown rice and vegetables
- Buckwheat soba noodles in a stir-fry or sautéed with veggies, tofu, or chicken
- Turkey burger with chips (made with nonhydrogenated oils)
- Broiled/poached/sautéed fish (salmon, halibut, tuna, trout, and so on) and vegetables
- Baked potato topped with salsa or veggies
- Tuna or chicken salad on an avocado half
- Soups (nondairy and sugar free): lentil, three-bean, split pea, pumpkin, carrot/ginger puree, chicken, or vegetable
- Turkey chili
- Quinoa with vegetables
- Chicken/tofu/turkey tacos in corn tortilla with guacamole, salsa, and lettuce
- Chicken (broiled, roasted, baked, poached, or barbequed)
- Lamb/beef steak with onions

- Vegetable stir-fry with tofu (firm) or chicken, use cold-pressed sesame oil or olive oil
- Turkey hotdogs (no nitrates, sugar, or dairy) with oven-baked potatoes
- Spanish rice (brown rice); add tomato sauce with beans

By eating meals like these, your body will be healthier and your energy level greater. Keep in mind that if you are in the habit of eating a lot of sugar or junk foods, your body will need time to adjust to a healthy diet. Your energy level may be a little lower when you first begin the transition to eating right, but your body will bounce back in a short time.

Remember always to consult with your doctor before making any drastic changes to your diet.

Training for Trail

Being generally fit and eating right get your body ready for the next step in preparing for long trail rides: the riding. While having a healthy body is vital to being able to hold up to many hours in the saddle, your time spent training specifically for this activity will be well spent.

The following types of exercise will get you ready for that day-long ride, week-long horse packing trip, or new hobby of long trail riding:

- *Riding lessons.* As mentioned in chapter 2, "Getting Experience in the Saddle," riding lessons are imperative to learn how to control your horse. They are also important for long trail rides because you will learn how to balance yourself in the saddle, which is vital for staying on when the horse spooks or negotiates steep terrain. The proper seat and balance will make riding feel more effortless for you and keep you from becoming tired after the first hour or so of riding.

  Riding lessons will also help build your stamina and your muscles— two things you'll need to stay on a horse for hours at a time.

- *Trail rides.* When training for a particular long trail ride or a series of rides, you will need to gradually spend more and more time in the saddle, out on the trail. Trail riding is very different from arena riding, and you'll have to acclimate your body to this type of riding so you don't end up sore and exhausted when you participate in a particularly long ride.

  Just as you would build up a horse to trail riding when conditioning him (as discussed in chapter 8, "Preparing Your Horse for Trail,"), you'll need to do the same for yourself. Start out with hour-long rides and gradually work your way up to the point where you are going on a three- or four-hour ride once or twice before your big, all-day event. (If you don't have your own trail horse or one you can borrow, take as many lessons as you can per week to get yourself fit for an all-day or week-long ride.)

The Rigors of Trail Riding

People who don't ride can't imagine how much exercise riding can be. From the ground, it looks as if you are just sitting in the saddle being carried along. But it takes muscle strength to control a horse and stay balanced in the saddle. Trail riding in particular can be especially demanding for a number of reasons:

- You are riding for a long period of time, spending energy holding yourself in the saddle and commanding the horse.

- You are in the elements. Whether it's strong sun, heat and humidity, cold and dampness, or a steady wind, all these factors leech energy from your body.

- You are helping your horse negotiate difficult terrain. If you are riding in a mountainous area, you will use your body in different ways as your horse climbs up hills and picks his way back down them. Water crossings that require you to push your horse forward will also tax your energy over a period of time, as will repeated encounters with fallen trees and logs, crossing bridges, and dealing with any other obstacle that requires you to push your horse forward.

- You are taxing your mind. While trail riding is an incredibly relaxing activity, it's also an exciting one. You need to stay alert when you are trail riding and pay attention to your horse and how he is reacting to his surroundings. Most likely, you'll be seeing places you've never seen on a long trail ride, and having adventures you've never imagined. Even something as simple as coming across a herd of cattle scattered along the trail can be an exciting experience. As the bovines watch you pass, you'll get a close-up look at them in a way you probably haven't before. While loads of fun, all this leads to mental exhaustion at the end of the day.

For all these reasons, it's important that you prepare your body for the hard work ahead of you on long trail rides. You'll find it is well worth the effort.

If you plan to go on long trail rides on a regular basis, maintain your conditioning by doing at least a three-hour ride once or twice a month so an all-day ride won't completely wipe you out.

- *Cross-train.* Riding isn't the only way to get yourself in shape for a long trail ride. Build up your endurance by jogging or going on regular long hikes. Any activity that will help develop your stamina will help you when you are in the saddle for long periods of time.

Ride Day

You've gotten yourself in shape and the day of your first long ride or riding vacation is fast approaching. It's important to take good care of your body just before you embark on your ride so you'll feel fresh and full of energy throughout the entire ride.

The day before your ride, make a point of getting a lot of rest. Take it easy that day, and get plenty of quality sleep. Odds are, you'll be getting up early to get started, so go to bed at a reasonable hour so you'll feel refreshed when you get up.

GETTING STARTED

The morning of the ride, eat a healthy breakfast with plenty of protein and some wholesome carbs. Dr. Boroch recommends an omelette or eggs of some kind along with vegetables (or try some of the ideas listed earlier in the chapter). For your carbs, consider red potatoes or yams, or sprouted whole-grain toast.

After you eat your breakfast, take a multivitamin, preferably one that is food-based and without iron. Take a 1,000-mg tab of vitamin C as well, along with a B-complex tab. These nutrients will help your body cope with the rigors of the day, leaving you less tired and sore.

While you are thinking about food, prepare your snacks and a lunch if need be. If you'll be participating in an all-day ride, snacks will help keep your energy up during the day as you ride, and a nutritious lunch will keep you going until dinnertime.

Boroch suggests the following healthy snacks that you can tuck into your saddlebag and munch on along the way or during breaks from riding:

- Almond butter and brown rice cakes or whole-grain crackers
- Carrot sticks
- Celery sticks
- Trail mix with raw or dry roasted nuts and seeds—no chocolate chips or yogurt chips (these contain too much sugar)
- A banana and almonds

For a healthy lunch, consider proteins such as chicken, turkey, or beef, wrapped in a sprouted-grain tortilla (available at many health food stores). Make protein the main ingredient in your lunch, since this will provide you with more lasting energy than carbohydrates. If the weather is warm, store these in an insulated pouch in your saddlebag. Be careful not to weigh your horse down with ice packs, especially on a very long ride.

If you think you might need an afternoon pick-me-up, bring along some raw honey and place about a teaspoon of it underneath your tongue.

What to Pack: A Checklist

Here's a handy checklist of what items you might want to bring with you on the day of your ride (not including the items for your horse; see chapter 8):

❑ Facial tissues/toilet paper

❑ Lip balm

❑ Sunglasses

❑ Jacket, sweatshirt, or other clothing you can layer

❑ Any medication you normally take during the day

❑ Water

❑ Snacks/lunch

❑ Sunblock

❑ Insect repellent

❑ First-aid kit (see chapter 10, "Safety on the Trail")

❑ Cell phone

❑ Camera

❑ Identification and medical insurance card

❑ Cloth bandana (in case of windy conditions)

❑ Rain slicker (if rain is predicted on your ride)

❑ Compass

In addition to food, bring plenty of water. Begin hydrating yourself with water as soon as you get up in the morning. It's very easy to get dehydrated when you are trail riding, and drinking water during the ride will not be enough. Be prepared to consume half your weight in ounces of water for the day. (For example, if you weigh 150 pounds, you should drink 75 ounces that day.) Try to drink about a third of that before you start the ride.

Resist the temptation to hold off drinking so you won't have to go to the bathroom during the ride. If the ride is a larger, organized outing, bathroom breaks will likely be planned. If not, don't be shy; ask the group to stop so you can go to the bathroom.

Whether you are riding in an organized group, by yourself, or just with a couple of friends, be prepared to use Mother Nature as your restroom. This is something you'll have to get used to if you plan to be a trail rider, since portable bathrooms are few and far between in the backcountry!

STRETCH

Before you mount up the morning of your ride, do some stretching. This will warm up your muscles and make you less likely to be sore the following day. (In fact, stretching on a daily basis for several weeks before your ride will help your muscles bounce back even more.)

Spend about five minutes stretching before you get into the saddle. The following basic stretches are most important:

- *The quadriceps.* Stand up straight (do not arch your back) and bend your leg up behind you. Take hold of your ankle so your knee is bent and slowly pull your ankle so your knee points out behind you. Hold this stretch for ten seconds and switch to the other leg. Repeat this twice for each leg.

- *The hamstrings.* Stand up in front of a fence and use your hand to brace you forward as you reach your leg up onto the fence, as high as you can go. Bend forward and hold this position for ten seconds. Do this with the other leg too, and then repeat once more.

- *The inner thigh.* One of the sorest day-after spots for long-distance trail riders is the inner thighs. To stretch these out before you ride, sit on the ground with your knees bent out to the sides and the soles of your feet touching each other. Relax your hips and then push down gently on both knees. Do this twice for ten seconds each time.

- *The lower back.* This stretch is particularly important if you have lower back issues that cause your muscles to tighten up. Lay on your back with your knees to your chest. Wrap your arms around your legs just below your knees and pull your knees toward you.

- *The neck.* To prevent tension in your neck as you ride, stretch the muscles by tilting your head slowly first to the right (your ear toward your shoulder) and then to the left. You will feel a stretch in your neck muscles. Next, tuck your chin forward into your chest, and then back up toward the sky. Then, turn your head as far to the right as you can while keeping your shoulders straight. Do the same to the left. Follow this routine several times, holding each stretch for at least five seconds.

RIDE SMART

Long hours in the saddle can put a strain on your muscles and joints, especially if you aren't used to this type of activity. You can relieve that strain the following ways:

- *Dismount frequently.* To prevent your muscles and joints from stiffening by being in the same position for a long period of time, get off your horse whenever you can. If you are part of an organized group, you'll have to wait until the time is right for this, such as during a short break on the trail. If you are with friends or alone, get off every couple of hours to stretch your body and loosen your joints. Your horse will appreciate the break too.

If you take good care of your body, you can continue trail riding well into your senior years.

(Only do this if you are adept at getting back on your horse. Don't be afraid to use a rock or a log to mount up.)

- *Lead your horse.* It's not uncommon to see long-distance trail riders leading their horses over the trail. At times when the pace is slow, get off your horse and lead him. Your muscles and joints will have a chance to loosen up, your circulation will improve, and you'll get some aerobic activity to break up the day. The break from having a rider in the saddle will be good for your horse, too.

- *Change gaits.* If you travel the entire trail with your horse at a walk, you'll get tired more quickly than if you mix in trotting or cantering. Your body uses different muscles for each gait, and it will provide some relief for your tired body if you switch around. (If you aren't comfortable cantering on trail, even switching from a walk to an occasional trot will help.)

- *Drop your stirrups.* If you find that you can't dismount or change gaits for long periods of time, try taking your feet out of the stirrups and letting your legs hang. This will help loosen up your knee joints and stretch out some of the muscles of your legs. Do this only at the walk, and only if your horse is completely controllable on the trail.

- *Sustain your body.* Don't forget to drink plenty of water when you are riding, and to eat lunch and periodic snacks. Your body will function much better if you keep your energy up and avoid getting dehydrated.

AFTER THE RIDE

If you successfully completed your long-distance trail ride, congratulate your-self and give your horse a pat. Chances are you had a great time and are completely hooked on this activity.

Make sure you eat a good dinner after your ride, high in proteins and vegetables. You will probably want dessert as a reward for your hard work, so try to go for something healthy. Dr. Boroch recommends the types of dessert items you'd find in health food stores, such as cookies and soy ice cream made with natural sweeteners such as honey, barley malt, brown rice syrup, and fruit juice. These types of foods will keep your blood sugar from spiking and leaving you with a crash.

Expect to be tired after your ride. Long trail rides can be exhausting, and not just for your horse. After you eat, consider taking a long hot bath with Epsom salts to help relax your muscles. This will help reduce the amount of soreness you are bound to feel for the next couple of days.

If you are camping out and can't take a bath, do the stretching exercises you performed before you began your ride. This will help your muscles bounce back.

Either way, go to bed early. If you have more riding ahead of you the next day, you'll want to get as much rest as you can in anticipation of what comes next.

Chapter 10

SAFETY ON THE TRAIL

Trail riders tend to be adventurous types, people who love the outdoors and are always up for something exciting. And though brave and daring riders make for some of the most competitive and fun-loving trail partners, it's important to realize that safety is a big issue when riding on the trail.

Because of the many uncontrollable situations trail riders encounter when riding in the great wide open—and because horses can be both dangerous and fragile at the same time—your safety and that of your horse and other riders should be paramount in your mind.

Which isn't to say you can't be safe *and* have fun. In fact, the safer you are, the more fun you will undoubtedly have. After all, having a medevac helicopter come to pick you up in the middle of your trail ride can put a real damper on the day.

Safe Equipment

When you are out in the wilderness with your horse, you become extremely dependent on your equipment. You need your bridle to control your horse, and your saddle to stay properly mounted. If one of these items breaks when you are riding and you are far from home, you will never take them for granted again.

Likewise, certain items can prove to be invaluable to you when you are riding and get into a jam of one kind or another.

Consider the following before you leave on your trail ride:

- *Equipment inspection.* Start out with a safety check on your tack. Take a look at your horse's bridle to make certain everything is in working order and that no screws or buckles are loose. Examine your saddle to be certain the cinch or girth is secure. Be particularly alert for weak seams that could break when you are riding. Look at your stirrups in the same way. Remember, you will

Why Wear a Helmet?

In many Western riding circles, helmets are considered a nonessential. The original cowboys didn't wear them, and in keeping with tradition, most Western riders don't.

Most English riders, on the other hand, always wear helmets. Helmets are also a staple for competitive distance riders.

So should you wear a helmet when you trail ride?

The decision to wear a riding helmet is a personal one, with both pros and cons. The downside of helmets is that they can be mildly uncomfortable if you aren't used to wearing one (although newer models are very lightweight and well ventilated), and they can really mess up your hair. If you care about fitting in with the crowd and you are a Western rider, you will probably stand out like a sore thumb among your Western buddies.

The benefit to wearing a helmet is a powerful one: In the event of a fall from your horse, a helmet can save your life.

According to the Centers for Disease Control and Prevention (CDC), the rate of serious injury for horseback riders is greater than that for motorcyclists and automobile racers. State medical examiner records from twenty-seven states over an eleven-year period identified head injuries as the cause of 60 percent of horseback riding–related deaths.

Given the potential for serious head injury, the CDC suggests that all riders wear helmets approved by the Safety Equipment Institute (SEI) and American Society for Testing and Materials (ASTM) for equestrian use.

Although you might have an image of yourself on horseback with your hair blowing in the wind, stop and think about what could happen to you if you fall from your horse and hit your head. The possibilities are horrific, and hardly worth the risk. Do yourself and those who love you a favor and wear an ASTM/SEI-approved helmet when you trail ride.

have much of your weight in your stirrups when going up and down hills, and the leather needs to be in good shape to keep from breaking at just the wrong moment.

- *Halter and lead rope.* If you are going on a long ride, fit your horse with a halter underneath the bridle, and bring a lead rope along too, either looped to your saddle horn or coiled in your saddlebag. You never know when you might have to tie your horse up, and it's not safe to tie her by the reins of her bridle. Tying a horse by the reins can result in serious injury to the horse if she pulls back.

- *Hoof pick and Swiss Army Knife.* Another must for a long ride is a saddlebag equipped with a hoof pick and a Swiss Army Knife. The hoof pick will help you remove stones or other harmful objects from your horse's hooves along the trail. The Swiss Army Knife will be particularly valuable should your horse get hung up in wire or dense brush, or if a screw on your bridle becomes loose.

- *First-aid items.* A small first-aid kit can be a godsend if you or your horse become injured in some way. (See the "First-Aid Trail Kit" sidebar on page 141 for a list of items to include in your kit.)

- *A helmet.* Although many Western riders prefer to ride bareheaded or with a cowboy hat, the safest item to wear on your noggin during a trail ride is a helmet designed for equestrian use.

- *Proper footgear.* It's imperative that you ride with boots designed for equestrian use. Sneakers or other shoes without heels are not safe for riding because in the event of an acci-

On long rides, check your tack now and then to make sure everything is in good working order.

dent, your foot may slide through the stirrup and your leg could get hung up. If you fall from your horse and get your leg caught in the stirrup, you could be dragged and seriously injured. Also, footgear designed for equestrians will help protect your feet in the event that your horse steps on you.

- *Adequate clothing.* Check the weather report before you embark on your ride and bring the right clothing along with you. Unless you are riding in hot and humid weather, it's usually a good idea to layer so you can add and remove clothing as the weather dictates. If the weather will be cool, be sure to bring nonslip gloves along that you wear while you are riding, and warm socks to keep your toes from getting cold.

Trail Etiquette

Whether you are going on a short ride or a long one, alone or with a group, trail etiquette is something you should know and follow. When it comes to trail riding, good etiquette is not just for the sake of courtesy, but it's a matter of safety as well.

Riders who practice good trail etiquette are a pleasure to ride with and encounter along the trial because they are not only considerate of their fellow riders, but they are the purveyors of safe riding.

RIDING IN GROUPS

If you are riding with one or more other people, you need to follow some basic
rules to make your excursion fun and safe for everyone involved. Follow these
fundamental rules of trail etiquette:

- *Keep a safe distance.* The general rule when riding in a group is to keep
  your horse one body length's distance from the horse in front of her. This
  can be difficult to do at times since many horses prefer to travel with their
  noses just behind the tail of the horses in front of them. The problem is
  that if the horse in front of you stop shorts, your horse will crash into her.
  Another problem is that the horse in front of you might not appreciate
  your horse's nose in her rear and may kick out. You or your horse may be
  injured if that occurs.

- *Tie a red ribbon.* If you are riding in a group and have a horse who is a
  kicker, tie a red ribbon at the base of her tail. This is a universal signal to
  other riders that your horse kicks and that they need to stay back. Try to
  keep your horse at the rear of the group to avoid situations where she
  might kick.

- *Go slow.* Keep your horse at a walk unless you have a consensus from
  other riders to pick up the pace. Keep in mind that horses tend to get
  excited when the speed picks up in a group situation. The quiet lope you
  have in mind might turn into an out-of-control gallop if a number of horses
  are involved. Not all riders are equally skilled, and while you might be
  able to control your horse at a trot or lope, a less-skilled rider in the group
  might lose control of his or her mount when you start going fast.

- *Don't pass without permission.* If your horse wants to be at the front of the
  line, ask those in front of you for permission to pass and lead the group.
  Don't just let your horse barge ahead of everyone. This is not only rude,
  it's unsafe, especially on a narrow trail.

- *Stop to drink.* If you come across a water source along the trail, and the
  horses want to drink, be courteous and wait your turn, especially if the
  source is a small trough. It's important for horses to drink along the way,
  especially on a long trail ride, and you shouldn't do anything that will dis-
  courage a fellow rider's horse from drinking. Actions that can stop another
  horse from drinking include allowing your horse to aggressively barge in
  and threaten the other horse while she's trying to drink, allowing your
  horse to pin her ears at other horses while they are drinking, and pulling
  your horse away from the water source too fast when the horses still have
  their muzzles in the water. Keep your horse quiet and passive during the
  watering session. If you are having trouble getting her to behave, pull her
  aside and wait until the other horses are finished before you let her have
  her share. Also, don't ride off until all the horses are finished drinking;
  many horses will forego getting a drink if they feel they are being left
  behind.

- *Help calm a spooky horse.* If a rider up ahead of you in your group starts having trouble with a spooky horse, stop your horse if you can and wait for the rider to get the horse under control. Another option is to check with the rider to see if he or she would like you to pass so your horse can help calm the frightened one. Obviously, this will only work if you are sure your horse won't be spooked by whatever is scaring the other rider's horse. Since horses tend to take cues from one another, your horse may object to passing the object as well. In this case, hang back and wait for everyone to calm down before you proceed.

- *Be courteous of dismounted riders.* If one of the riders in your group must dismount, keep your horse standing still while he or she gets off. Continue to keep your horse quiet when the other rider mounts, and don't head off back down the trial until the other rider gives you a verbal signal that he or she is ready to move on.

- *Prepare your horse.* Before you take an inexperienced horse out on the trails, make sure she's safe. Expose her to some of the things horses regularly encounter on trails in your area. If your horse tends to be nervous and spooky, inform the other riders in your group of this so they can determine whether they want to ride with your horse. Some horses pick up on the nervous energy of another horse and can become unruly themselves. (See chapter 8, "Preparing Your Horse for Trail," for more information.)

- *Communicate with your fellow riders.* It's important always to keep in mind that people have different skills and confidence levels when it comes to riding. Trail riding can be the most challenging type of riding for timid or less-skilled riders. Check in with your fellow riders to make sure everyone is feeling okay and secure, and try to solve problems calmly as they come up.

RIDING ALONE

Although riding with another person is much safer, some people prefer to ride alone. When riding by yourself, you have much more autonomy, and can pick your own pace and route. However, you still need to honor the rules of trail etiquette should you encounter other riders or trail users, such as hikers, backpackers, or mountain bikers.

When encountering other riders on the trail, keep the following rules in mind:

- *Pass quietly.* If you see another rider on the trail ahead of you that you would like to pass, keep your horse at a walk. Many horses can become out of control when they hear or see a horse trotting or loping up behind them. Make sure the rider ahead of you knows you are about to pass and is okay with it, especially on narrow trails.

- *Approach slowly.* If you see a rider up ahead approaching you, keep your horse at a walk as you pass one another. If the trail is narrow, focus on your horse to make sure she doesn't kick or try to bite the other horse as she passes by.

- *Resist the urge to hot-rod.* A good gallop on the trail can be a lot of fun, but it's important to pick the right moment to let your horse go for it. Choose a trail that is flat; has good, even footing; and allows you plenty of visibility up ahead. Be sure to keep your speed to a walk when passing other riders or trail users.

- *Be careful of blind curves.* Narrow single-track trails in areas of high brush can harbor a lot of blind curves. Always negotiate blind curves at a walk. You never know if another horse—or a hiker or mountain biker—is coming in the opposite direction.

- *Control your dog.* If you like to trail ride with your dog in tow, keep the dog on a long leash (practice riding with your dog on a leash close to home until the dog and your horse get the hang of it) or have the dog under strict voice control at all times. Don't allow your dog to approach other horses on the trail. This is for the safety of both the horse and your dog.

SHARING THE TRAIL

Most if not all the trails accessible to equestrians these days are multi-use trails, meaning others also utilize them. Hikers and mountain bikers are the most common users of trails located near urban and suburban areas. Backpackers often use wilderness backcountry trails as well.

Because hikers and mountain bikers are more numerous than equestrians are, they often have more clout when it comes to trail use. Equestrian groups around the United States are continually fighting to keep the rights of trail riders intact. More than one trail has been made off limits to equestrians, while other special interest groups are permitted to continue their use.

For this reason, it is vital that trail riders be particularly courteous and considerate of nonequestrian trail users. It's also important to keep in mind that a horse has significant potential to seriously injure a trail user on foot, leaving riders with a great amount of responsibility in keeping trails safe.

The following guidelines can help keep trails safe for various users and create good feelings toward equestrian users:

- *Use your right of way.* Technically, equestrians have the right of way on narrow trails, and some parks and recreational areas are quick to point that out to all trail users. If you encounter a hiker or mountain biker who stops to give you the right of way, politely accept it. However, if the other user doesn't give you the right of way, take it in stride and pull your horse over so she is safely out of the way.

Help Your Horse

When negotiating hills and obstacles, you can do a lot to help your horse out.

When riding up a steep hill, lean forward and lift yourself slightly out of the stirrups to take your weight off your horse's back. If the hill is very steep, you may need to hold onto your horse's mane to keep your balance.

When going down a steep slope, lean back to take your weight off your horse's front end. Be careful not to pull back on the reins to do this. Your horse needs her head to keep herself balanced.

If your horse is stepping through water, over a log, or negotiating another obstacle on the trail, lift your weight slightly out of the saddle to help her carry herself over. Be sure to let her have her head so she can see where she is going.

Lean back in the saddle when your horse is going down a steep slope.

- *Take care around blind curves.* While you should go slow when walking through blind curves to avoid crashing into another rider, this is even more important when you are riding on multi-use trails. A mountain biker can come around a blind turn very quickly, and the slower you are going on your horse, the more time the biker will have to swerve and avoid hitting you. You can also avoid running down a hiker on your horse if you are walking around a blind corner instead of trotting or cantering through it.

- *Remove manure.* While horse people know that manure is innocuous and quickly degrades in the environment, many urban hikers and mountain bikers consider horse manure to be as noxious as dog excrement. If your horse relieves herself on a well-traveled trail, dismount and kick the manure off into the bushes. While this might sound like a needless and silly task, horses have been banned from a number of trails because of manure complaints.

- *Be understanding.* While it's hard for most horse people to fathom, some folks are terrified of horses. If you encounter a multi-trail user who seems afraid of your horse, go out of your way to avoid getting too close to him or her.

- *Be polite.* Whenever you pass a hiker or mountain biker, offer a smile and a hello. Thank the other trail user for giving you the right of way, and avoid getting angry and losing your temper if the other user doesn't seem to know the rules of etiquette. Keep in mind that at that moment, you represent all equestrian users to that hiker or mountain biker. It's your responsibility help create goodwill.

Safety in the Wilderness

When early pioneers like Lewis and Clark mounted up their horses and rode out into the wilderness more than a century ago, they faced harsh perils such as starvation, exposure, and disease. Today, trail riders traverse the wilderness on horseback for recreational purposes and don't have to worry about encountering the hardships suffered by those early adventurers.

This doesn't mean the wilderness is benign for recreational trail riders, however. Plenty of hazards still face those who choose to brave the same deserts, forests, and mountains traveled by those who came before us. Unlike our predecessors, however, we know what we are dealing with and, with common sense, can enjoy the wilderness with safety.

Consider the following when riding out on the trails, especially if you'll be riding alone. Keep in mind that even trails in urban areas can be hazardous to trail riders. You don't have to be in the backcountry to encounter a potentially dangerous situation.

- *Know where you are going.* If you are heading out on a trail that you've never ridden before, map out your route carefully. Make sure you have an idea of how long it will take you to do the ride, from start to finish. If the trail is long, bring a trail map with you. Keep in mind that if you do get lost, your horse may be able to find her way back. Horses have a strong sense of direction and are often motivated to get back home. If you are completely disoriented and don't know how to get back, give your horse her head—she might know the way.

- *Tell someone where you are going.* Just as if you were going on a solo hike, tell somewhere where you are going and when you expect to be back. That way, if you fail to return, someone will know you are missing and where to look.

- *Stay on the trail.* Although it can be fun to blaze new trails, stick to the beaten path if you are riding alone in unfamiliar territory. Most riders and hikers get lost when they stray from well-marked trails.

- *Bring appropriate food and water.* If you will be gone all day, bring enough food and water to keep yourself hydrated and nourished while you are gone. Water is especially important if you are riding in hot weather.

- *Identify yourself and your horse.* Carry ID on your person, and put a tag on your horse's halter or bridle with your name, phone number, and address. In the event you have a fall and are knocked unconscious, ID will help your rescuers. If you become separated from your horse, her ID tag will eventually get her back to you.

- *Carry a cell phone.* Bring a cell phone with you whenever you ride. In the event of an emergency on the trail, a cell phone can be your lifeline to help. Make sure you keep the phone on your person and not in your saddlebag. If you fall off your horse and need help, you want the phone to be within reach. (Keep in mind that your cell phone may not work if you are riding in a wilderness area.)

Make sure horses are tied safely to a secure object when you stop for breaks along the trail.

DEALING WITH THE ELEMENTS

If you are headed out on an all-day ride, keep in mind that your bright sunny day may end up miserably hot, incredibly windy, or unpleasantly chilly. Follow these guidelines to be safe in all kinds of situations:

- *Check the weather report.* Take a close look at the weather forecast the night before your ride so you can see what you will be up against. Bring the appropriate clothing for whatever Mother Nature is predicted to throw your way.

- *Bring plenty of water and sunblock.* Although the forecast may not be for extreme heat, riding in the sun all day no matter what the temperature can do a number on your skin. Wear sunblock and drink water throughout the day to keep from becoming dehydrated. You will know if you are dehydrated if you get dizzy, have a headache, and stop urinating. Drink more water if you start to feel this way. Don't assume you aren't dehydrated just because you aren't thirsty.

- *Be prepared for wind.* If the area where you are riding becomes windy at certain times of the day, or if a windstorm is forecast, be prepared. Bring along a bandana you can tie around your face to reduce the amount of dust you will inhale, and have a pair of sunglasses along to help shield your eyes. Strong winds may bring the temperature down as well, so bring extra clothing on your ride. If you'll be riding in a heavily forested area, be aware that wind can cause debris to fall from above, potentially spooking your horse and possibly striking you both. If the wind gets bad in an area with a lot of trees, consider returning home for your safety and that of your horse.

- *Be prepared for nightfall.* If you are headed out on a long ride and may not be home until after dark, bring along a flashlight. Keep in mind that turning the light on as you ride will cause your pupils to constrict, as well as those of your horse, ruining the night vision for both of you. Horses have excellent night vision, so it's best to avoid interfering with your horse's ability to see in the dark. To prevent this, attach a piece of red fabric across the glass of the flashlight with a rubber band. If you need to use the flashlight during your ride, the light you cast will have a red glow and will not disturb your or your horse's night vision.

ENCOUNTERING WILDLIFE

For many trail riders, the possibility of encountering wildlife on a ride is very exciting. As a rule, trail riders love nature and appreciate coming across animals in the wild.

Some animals can be dangerous to riders, however, for various reasons. By taking certain precautions, you can enjoy your ride in the wilderness and the wildlife you encounter while still keeping you and your horse safe.

Here is an overview of some of the animals you may run into on your rides that may cause a problem, and how you can best deal with them:

- *Deer.* One of the most beautiful animals you may encounter on a trail ride is the deer. Deer, which are most active during the hours of dawn and dusk, are harmless to horses and generally timid. However, problems may arise if your horse has never seen a deer before and suddenly encounters one along the trail. Some horses simply stop and look, while others panic and want to run the other way. Hopefully, you have learned how to handle your horse when she's spooking and can reassure her that the deer won't hurt her. In fact, it's a sure bet the deer will head off in the other direction once it sees you and your horse won't have to worry about this scary creature for very long. The next time out, your horse will be less concerned, and eventually, deer will be no big deal.

  Even a seasoned trail horse might react to a herd of deer bounding through the woods, however. If you've done your homework in the arena and have your horse under good control, you should be able to manage her as she spooks at a herd of fleeing deer across her path or in the adjacent woods.

- *Bears.* The black bear is the most common bear species in North America, and the one most often encountered by trail riders in the wilderness. Black bears are generally not aggressive, although a mother with cubs can be very protective if she feels threatened. If you see a bear in your path, turn your horse quietly around and go the opposite way. The bear will likely ignore you and wander off. The more difficult part will be convincing your horse that the bear won't eat her. Some horses are fine with the sight of a bear in the distance, while others come completely unglued. Repeated exposure to bears will help your horse learn that these animals are usually not to be feared.

  If you ride in Alaska, Canada, or another area where grizzly bears (a type of brown bear) are found, you have more to be concerned about the bear issue than those riders dealing only with black bears and some of the other more docile species. Grizzlies will avoid humans most of the time and attacks by grizzlies on humans are very rare, and practically unheard of on mounted horses. But some grizzlies (particularly if it's a mother with cubs nearby) will not turn and run if faced with a horse ridden by a human. If you come face to face with a grizzly, try to keep your horse calm. Do whatever you can to keep your horse from running off because this might incite the bear's chasing instinct. Keep in mind that a horse is much too big for the bear to consider prey. If the bear were to attack, it would likely be out of defensiveness.

  If your horse is acting up when in the proximity of a bear, resist the urge to dismount. You are safer on your horse than you would be on the ground. Try to get your horse to walk away from the bear as calmly as you can.

  Whether you are in black bear country or grizzly country, avoid encounters by being aware of your surroundings. Bears are most active during dawn, dusk, and at night. You can find out if a bear is in the area by being alert and looking for signs. Some of these include an animal carcass, which may belong to a bear in the area. Bear droppings on the trail are another bit of evidence that a bear is nearby, as are large holes the bear has dug in search of roots or grubs to eat. If you see a bear cub along the trail, avoid the urge to stop and admire it. Chances are the mother bear is nearby and feeling protective.

Bears will avoid an encounter with you and your horse whenever possible. If they hear you coming, they will hightail it out of the area before they run into you. When riding in bear country, consider putting a bell on your horse's bridle or saddle to warn bears that you are coming.

- *Wild cats.* Mountain lions are of concern to riders in areas where these large cats live, although a rider on a horse is very unlikely to be attacked by one of these predators. Mountain lions, who do most of their hunting at dawn and dusk, prefer smaller prey like rabbits and opossums, and a horse with a human on her back is less than appealing.

    Of course, your horse doesn't know that, and if she should get a whiff of a mountain lion on the trail, or actually see one, you will probably have your hands full. Try to reassure your horse that all is well and ask her to calmly leave the area. Avoid galloping down the trail to get away from the mountain lion, since there is a slight chance this could trigger the cat's chase instinct and encourage an attack (if this happens your horse may not be able to outrun the predator).

    Bobcats and lynxes are smaller wildcats sometimes encountered on the trail. Not much bigger than a large housecat, these animals are no threat to horses or humans, and don't usually frighten horses.

- *Snakes.* Most snakes found in the North American wilderness are harmless, although about twenty-five species are poisonous. The most common and well known of these reptiles is the pit viper, which includes the rattlesnake, cottonmouth or water moccasin, and copperhead species. These snakes can deliver a poisonous bite that can make a horse or human very sick.

    If you encounter a pit viper on the trail, give it a wide berth. Pit vipers will coil before they strike (rattlesnakes will give a warning rattle with their tails). If you see a viper in this position and you can't walk at least thirty feet around it, turn around and go the other way. The snake will probably leave the trail once you are gone, and you can go back several minutes later to see if the animal has returned to the brush.

    In the event that your horse accidentally steps on a pit viper or lowers her head to investigate the snake and is bitten, stay calm. After you move your horse away from the snake, keep your horse still, since making her move will speed up the venom's spread through the bloodstream, in the event the bite resulted in an injection of venom. (Not all pit viper bites result in a venom release.) If you are with another rider, send this person for help. If you are alone, use your cell phone to call for assistance. If you have neither a trail buddy nor a cell phone, tie your horse and go get help.

When traveling in areas where snakes are abundant and the weather is warm (reptiles need sun to get their bodies moving), it's a good idea to carry two five- to six-inch-long pieces of garden hose with you in your saddle pack. If your horse is bitten in the face, her nostrils are likely to swell up and cut off her breathing. Insert a piece of hose into each nostril as soon as the horse is bitten to keep her air supply clear.

Whatever you do, do not put a tourniquet above the bite, or cut the wound and try to suck out the venom. These methods are old wives' tales that will do more harm than good.

- *Coyotes.* It won't be long before coyotes inhabit all of North America, so odds are you will eventually encounter one on the trail. Despite a plethora of urban legends, coyotes pose no danger to horses and riders. Most coyotes, which travel alone, will run or walk in the opposite direction when they see a horse and rider coming. If the coyote is used to seeing horses, he may not run but simply sit by the side of the trail and watch you pass. You don't need to worry about the coyote attacking you or your horse; coyotes feed on rabbits and other small mammals, and don't consider horses as prey. Although coyotes will occasionally hunt deer in packs, mounted horses have little to fear from a group of coyotes.

- *Alligators.* Riders in certain parts of the South may encounter alligators when on trail rides near water. Most alligators are shy and have no interest in taking on a horse, let alone one with a person on its back. If you come across a gator, give it a wide berth so the animal doesn't feel threatened. If the gator is sunning itself in the middle of the trail, try to find a way to go around it. The gator will not bother you as long as you stay out of its space. If you come across an alligator when you are crossing water, don't panic. The gator will probably go out of its way to avoid you.

POISONOUS PLANTS

Unless you have done a great job of teaching your horse not to eat when she's out on the trail, chances are your equine companion will want to snack along the way. From the horse's perspective, a trail ride is like a stroll through a bakery for us. Everywhere your horse looks, she sees something yummy to eat.

Although the foliage you encounter may be beautiful, danger lurks in some of those handsome leaves. Vast arrays of poisonous plants grow alongside trails throughout North America. Although it is true that horses often avoid the plants that are not good for them, more often than not they are clueless as to the hazards.

Before you ride through an area, learn about some of the plants that are common alongside the trails. Following is a partial list of trees, shrubs, and other plants that are poisonous to horses:

- Red maple
- Black locust
- Oak
- Horse chestnut
- Black walnut
- Wild cherry
- Oleander
- Boxwood
- Azalea
- Mountain laurel
- Rhododendron
- Castor bean
- Mesquite

- Hydrangea
- Hemlock
- Lantana
- Fern palm
- Lupine
- Milkweed
- Aster
- Broomweed
- Snakewood
- Rape
- Clover
- Locoweed
- Fitweed

- Ground ivy
- Onions
- Mistletoe
- Cotton
- Buckwheat
- Buttercup
- Larkspur
- Indian paintbrush
- Tobacco
- Arrowgrass
- Fescue
- Squirreltail grass

Negotiating Difficult Terrain

One of the most enjoyable aspects of trail riding is challenging yourself and your horse with interesting terrain. Many trail riders get bored riding on solid, flat ground mile after mile, and crave a more diverse topography. Plus, the most beautiful places to ride are made up of varying terrain, like mountains, rivers, and cliffs.

In order to go out and ride tough terrain while keeping your horse safe and sound, you need to know what you are getting into. It's good to be brave, but bad to be reckless. More than one horse has had to be pulled from a bad spot by a rescue helicopter, or worse, euthanized on the trail because the rider took a foolish chance in rough terrain.

When dealing with the various types of landscape you may encounter out on the trail, keep the following points in mind:

- *Water crossings.* As discussed in chapter 8, you should know what you are getting into before you ask your horse to cross water. Stop and think about how deep the water is and what the bottom is likely to be like. Determine that the depth and footing are safe before you ask your horse to cross. If the water is deep enough so your horse must swim, be sure she's not over-loaded with tack and equipment before you send her into the water. If your

First-Aid Trail Kit

You never know what kinds of emergency situations you might encounter when riding on the trail. Create an emergency first-aid kit for you and your horse that will fit into your saddlebag. Include the following items, which are available in small containers that are easy to pack:

- *Antibiotic ointment.* In the event you or your horse becomes injured on the trail, a triple antibiotic ointment can be applied to the wound to help prevent infection.

- *Antiseptic wipes.* Packaged antiseptic wipes can be used to clean the wound if you or your horse is injured.

- *Elastic bandages.* Available in tack stores, elastic bandages can be wrapped around a wound without the need for tape or pins to keep them in place.

- *Gauze pads.* In the event of an injury, a gauze pad can be applied directly to the wound and held in place with an elastic bandage.

- *Tweezers.* If a cactus prong or other plant material becomes lodged in your horse's skin, a pair of tweezers can be used to remove it.

- *Small scissors.* You'll need a pair of small scissors to cut the bandage and gauze in the event of an injury to your horse. Blunt-nosed scissors are the safest type to carry.

- *Two pieces of garden hose.* Two five- or six-inch-long pieces of garden hose can be a lifesaver if your horse is bitten in the face by a poisonous snake. The sections of hose can be inserted into the horse's nostrils before the face swells and cuts off her breathing.

- *Pain medication (for you).* In the event you become injured on the ride, a pain reliever such as aspirin, ibuprofen, or acetaminophen can help you cope with the situation until you can get help.

- *Antihistamine (for you).* If you have allergies to bee stings or certain plants, consider packing an antihistamine in the event you have a severe allergic reaction.

- *Adhesive bandages (for you).* More commonly known by the brand name Band-Aid™ adhesive bandages can be used to cover cuts and other wounds after antiseptic wipes and antibiotic ointment have been applied.

- *Hydrocortisone cream (for you).* A cream with hydrocortisone can be applied to an area of the skin that is swollen as a result of an insect bite or encounter with poison ivy or poison oak.

horse is having trouble keeping her head above the water when she's swimming across, swim out of the saddle. Hold on to the saddle and let the horse pull you to shore. If you are able to stay aboard your horse, give her her head. When a horse swims, she needs to stretch her head out in front of her.

If the water you plan to cross has a strong current and is too deep for your horse to walk across, reconsider. Your horse can easily be swept away by rushing water if the bottom is too deep for her to stand.

Be very careful about the banks where you plan to cross the water. Quicksand is a huge problem at certain water crossings, particularly after a strong rain. If you aren't sure of the footing, get off your horse and walk the area yourself. Keep in mind that your horse weighs about ten times as much as you do. If you sink into the sand, your horse will do so even more, and may not be able to get out.

If your horse does get trapped in quicksand, get out of the saddle as fast as you can. Sometimes when the weight of the rider is removed, the horse can free herself. If not, keep your horse quiet and send for help. Try to keep your horse from struggling since this can make her situation worse.

- *Steep cliffs.* When riding on trails that are located along a steep cliff, be very careful. Keep your horse at a walk, and move her as close as you can away from the cliff. Horses have been known to fall down the sides of sheer cliffs and get trapped in the ravine below. Trotting or galloping on a trail located in this kind of terrain is taking a chance with your horse's life, as well as your own.

- *Rocky trails.* Some trails are strewn with large rocks, making them slippery and hard for horses to negotiate. Go slow on these types of trails. If your horse is slipping a lot, get off and lead her. She'll be more likely to maintain her balance without a rider on her back, and should she fall, you won't get hurt.

- *Snow and ice.* When riding through deep snow, keep in mind that this kind of terrain is exhausting for a horse to negotiate. Plowing through a foot or more of snow takes a lot of energy. Give your horse plenty of rest along the way. If the snow is light, avoid the urge to gallop. Unless the weather is warm enough for melting, you may encounter ice patches that could cause your horse to slip and fall. If you absolutely must cross a patch of ice, get off your horse and lead her over it.

Have Fun!

Despite all the precautions, it is possible to have a good time out on the trails! If you build safety and common sense into your regular routine, after a while, being cautious will become second nature.

Remember to ride with a buddy whenever you can, since just about any situation you encounter will be made a lot safer if you have a friend along to help. Plus, riding with a friend is always more fun than riding alone.

Chapter 11

Finding Good Trails

aving a good horse and knowing how to ride is three-fourths of the battle when it comes to the sport of trail riding. Another vital aspect is finding good trails to ride.

The ease or difficulty you encounter when trying to locate trails for riding depends a lot on where you live. If you are in an urban or suburban area, the number of trails with immediate access will probably be limited. But before you go green with envy over those who live out in the country, know that even rural residents can have trouble accessing decent trails.

If you own a horse trailer or have a trail buddy who has one, your options for trail riding are vastly increased. You'll no longer be limited to just the trails you can reach by horseback. The next chapter discusses trailering your horse; for now, let's take a look at what types of trails are available to you.

Trail Quality

Before you begin your quest for places to ride, it helps to know a good trail from a bad one. Trails suitable for hikers and mountain bikers are not always good for equestrians. When considering any trail for a ride, look for the following criteria:

- *Legal for equestrian use.* Before you can even consider a trail for riding, you need to make certain that horses are allowed. More and more trails are becoming off limits to trail riders for a variety of reasons. Don't assume equestrians are allowed on a trail. Check the rules to make certain you and your horse are welcome.

- *Well maintained.* In order to have a safe, enjoyable ride, it's important that you ride only on well-maintained trails, especially when you are first getting started in the sport. Poorly maintained trails can be a disaster, especially for a novice trail rider. Trails that are not cared for end up overgrown with plants and blocked by fallen trees and branches, often making them impassable. If you are confronted with a trail you can't pass, you'll be forced to head back or go off the beaten path, which might get you lost. Poorly maintained trails can also suffer from erosion damage, making them dangerous and sometimes even nonexistent in certain spots.

- *Well marked.* Only ride in areas where the trails are well marked with signposts. Unless you are an experienced trail rider and are good at reading trail maps, you could get lost if you ride in an area with unmarked trails.

- *Safe terrain.* Know the terrain of the trail before you set out on a long ride. A lot of steep hills with rocky trails are fine for riders and horses experienced in this type of trail riding, but novices do better in areas that have mostly even ground, with easy-to-navigate trails.

- *Good location.* Some trails are located in areas that are not conducive to safe and pleasant riding. If the trail you are considering has a large section that runs alongside a busy street, complete with large trucks barreling down the road, or is located in an industrial area void of nice scenery, think about an alternative trail choice.

- *Other trail users.* Equestrians often share the trails with other users, including hikers and mountain bikers. If the trail you are considering is widely used—some trails in urban areas are literally jammed on the weekends—consider an alternate trail or riding at a time of day when hikers and mountain bikers will be less numerous. While passing an occasional hiker or mountain biker is no big deal, facing large hordes of either one of these users along the trail can put a damper on your ride.

Types of Trails

When the United States was young, one kind of trail could be found: the wilderness trail. Horses either traveled through town on a dirt road, or they carried their riders across the deserts, through the woods, and over the mountains.

Things have obviously changed, and trails are quite different than they were even fifty years ago. Nowadays, equestrians are faced with a variety of different trail choices:

- *Urban trails.* A great many urban and suburban dwellers are limited to riding on urban trails. These types of trails are found in city areas and suburban neighborhoods. Urban trails usually share all or part of their boundaries with a city street, which means traffic and pedestrians, and everything that come with those two elements, are part of the mix.

   While most urban and suburban riders would rather be out in the wilderness, these trails are the only option for many riders. Urban trails can be a good substitute for a more rugged and untamed trail experience, and often offer opportunities to see wildlife and breathe relatively fresh air.

- *Local parks.* Many urban and suburban dwellers, as well as some rural residents, take advantage of trails in local parks. While small city parks are not conducive to trail riding, many regional parks have extensive trails that can provide an enjoyable wilderness experience. These types of parks are accessible from areas where horses are kept, or can be easily reached by horse trailer. Because local parks get a lot of use and are managed by local municipalities, they are often well marked and well maintained. Some even permit horse camping (see chapter 13, "Camping with Your Horse").

- *State parks.* Managed by state government parks departments, state parks are often wonderful places for trail riders. Beautiful and often pristine wilderness areas make up the state parks system throughout the United States. Many state park trail systems are open to equestrians, and generally feature well-maintained and well-marked trails.

- *National forests.* Managed by the United States Department of Agriculture Forest Service, the national forest system provides the greatest number of trails open to equestrians in the United States. National forests are found throughout the country and encompass all kinds of terrain, from shoreline to deserts to mountains. Because national forests are open to a wide variety of uses, equestrians are often welcome in these protected areas. Horse camping is usually permitted in national forests.

- *National parks.* The most beautiful and well-kept trails in the country are part of the national parks system, administered by the United States government's National Park Service. Areas such as Yosemite National Park, Bryce Canyon National Park, and the Great Smoky Mountains National Park, among others, all allow equestrian use. While not all national parks allow horses, the ones that do can provide you with some spectacular trail riding.

- *Designated wilderness areas.* Various other types of designated wilderness areas are open to equestrians, including some

Kings Canyon National Park in California is only one of many national parks that offer wonderful trail riding opportunities.

national monuments and conservation areas. Many designated wilderness areas have wonderful trails that are often little used.

Trail Preservation

Real estate values have gone up significantly just about everywhere in the United States over the last two decades, and as a result, land is at a premium. Areas that once offered glorious trail riding opportunities are now paved over and covered with houses and office buildings.

In addition to this reality of economics, a growing concern over native plant life, as well as worries about overuse of wilderness areas, has impacted equestrian trail users. The result is that trail riders are finding fewer and fewer areas where they can ride.

If you care about being able to ride your horse in the wilderness, it's important to do what you can to help preserve the rights of equestrians when it comes to trail usage:

- *Be a conscientious trail rider.* Follow the guidelines outlined in this chapter to minimize your horse's impact on the environment where you ride. Be polite to other trail users, and always follow the rules that have been established by the governing authority for the park or area where you ride.

- *Get involved.* Support local trail use groups that are trying to preserve the trails in your area. If these groups are made up of trail users other than equestrians, be a voice for trail riders in your area.

- *Write letters.* Keep abreast of local trail issues and contact your legislators to express your concerns over preserving equestrian trail use.

- *Join up.* Become a member of your local or state horsemen's association. These groups are often working to preserve trail usage for riders and need your support.

Responsible Riding

For equestrians, being able to use the nation's trails is a great privilege and one that can be easily revoked if not exerted with responsibility (see the above sidebar, "Trail Preservation"). As a trail rider, it's your job to become familiar with the rules—both written and implied—governing the trails you are using.

Before you embark on a trail ride in a local or state park, or a national park or national forest, educate yourself about the area where you are riding:

- *Is riding allowed?* Find out first if horses are even allowed. Don't take it for granted that every trail system is open to equestrian use. Not only will you be turned away when you show up with your horse, you will also give park officials the impression that equestrians are not responsible trail users.

- *Can I bring my own horse?* Some places permit horse rentals within their boundaries, but do not allow outside horses. If you plan to bring your own horse, make sure this is permitted.

- *Rules of the trail.* Learn the rules of the trail where you will be riding, such as who has right of way on the trail, details about whether you can bring hay into the area, how you are expected to manage your horse's manure, and where you can tie your horse along the way. If the area where you will be riding has a website, visit the page that details the rules. If you can't find this information, call the park offices and inquire.

- *Tread lightly.* Horses can make a big impact in the wilderness if they are not properly managed. Keep your horse on designated trails whenever possible, and avoid tying your horse to a tree where he may destroy bark or branches with his teeth. Don't stake or tie your horse in a meadow since grazing and moving hooves can damage fragile meadow flora. Don't harass the wildlife (don't chase deer or other animals), and always pack out whatever you bring in.

Trail Maps and Compasses

If you plan to be an adventurous trail rider, you'll need to learn to read trail maps and use a compass. A trail map—also called a topographical map—can keep you on track and can be a life-saver should you find yourself lost or disoriented while you are riding. A compass will help you read the map and keep you oriented in unfamiliar territory.

Unfortunately, reading a trail map is not as intuitive as you might think. Trail maps are a bit harder to read than street maps because you can't use highways and intersections to orient yourself. Trail maps have no such landmarks, and instead have an assortment of other elements, such as grid references, relief and vertical intervals, back bearings, and other alien components.

Trail maps also work best when used in conjunction with a compass. Reading a compass takes some skill too, and isn't as simple as just figuring out which way is north.

Amazing vistas are among the sites you'll see when you venture into the wilderness on horseback.

Organized Rides

A great way to enjoy trail riding is to be part of an organized ride. Organized trail rides are just that: group rides that have been planned by a club or association. Organized rides are mapped out ahead of time, and the route preplanned. These rides can have anywhere from ten participants to four hundred, depending on the ride and the club.

Organized rides can be a great way to learn the trails in your area or discover new trails. You can meet other trail riders in your area and make new friends, for both you and your horse. A well-run organized ride is a real joy and something you'll want to participate in time and again.

Before you sign up for an organized ride, make certain the ride is well run. As fun as a great organized ride can be, a bad one can be disastrous enough to make you wish you'd never gotten on your horse.

Here are some questions to ask the organizer of the ride to be sure the event you are considering will be a success:

- *How long is the ride?* Make certain your horse is up to the distance or the number of hours being planned for the ride. Don't take an out-of-shape horse on a five-day, fifty-miles-per-day ride. You need to be in shape for it, too. (See chapters 8, "Preparing Your Horse for Trail," and 9, "Conditioning Yourself for Trail," for tips on how to prepare for longer trail rides.)

- *How many horses will be on the ride?* Small group rides are usually less problematic than large ones. A ride with three hundred horses can be enjoyable if well managed, but the bigger the group, the more potential for problems.

Before you head out on a long trail ride in unexplored (by you) terrain, lessons on how to read a trail map and how to read a compass are a good idea. If you are lucky, you'll find a class in your area sponsored by a local wilderness appreciation group or learning center. Or you can learn to read topographical maps by purchasing a good book on the subject. (See appendix B, "Resources," for some book suggestions.)

Where to Look

Now that you know what to look for in a good trail, how do you know where to find them? An amazing array of resources for trails is at your disposal if you know where to look:

- *What is the pace of the ride and the skill level of the other riders?* Find out if the pace will be mostly walking with a bit of trotting, or if a lot of galloping is planned. If you are a novice rider and/or your horse isn't used to riding in groups, skip a ride with a fast pace filled with experienced riders. Horses tend to get very excited when they go fast in a group setting, and you may not be comfortable with your horse's reaction. Stick to rides that are slow and designed for novices.

- *How often has this ride been conducted?* If this is the first time the ride is being held, be aware that there may be kinks that haven't yet been worked out.

- *Will water be available?* Few things are as upsetting as finding yourself on a long ride in hot weather with no available water for your horse. Make certain the ride organizer has planned for water along the way.

- *What are the emergency provisions?* If the ride is being held in a wilderness area, find out what kind of arrangements have been made in advance in the event of a horse or rider emergency. If none have been made and you'll be riding far from civilization, think twice about participating.

- *Have any horses or riders been hurt on the ride?* For rides that have been held before, ask about prior injuries. If you find out injuries to horse and rider have been frequent, something is wrong with the situation, and you are well advised to stay away.

- *State or local horsemen's associations.* Many states and regions around the United States have horsemen's associations, made up of equestrians with various interests (see appendix B for several listings). Because trail riding is the most popular equestrian activity, most of these state and local groups have regular trail riding activities or programs. By joining your state or local horsemen's association, you'll be able to access the knowledge of fellow trail riders who know all the best trails in the region.

- *The Internet.* The Internet is an incredible source of information when it comes to sleuthing out good trails. Not only do local governments post trail information online, but other trail user groups, such as local hikers and mountain bikers, also post this kind of information on their group websites and in bulletin board and discussion forums. To find local trail information on the Internet, use one of the search engine sites such as

Be sure to carefully research any group ride before you commit to it.

Google.com or Yahoo.com and type the word "trail" in the search field, along with a plus sign (+) and the name of your state or county. You'll be amazed at what comes up.

- *Local horse publications.* If your area has a local horse publication, read it on a regular basis to learn about places to trail ride in your area. Although most local horse publications spend most of their space covering horse shows, trail activities are often listed in the calendar of events section. Miscellaneous articles on trail rides and trail riders can also give you a sense of the riding opportunities in your area.

- *Word of mouth.* Other trail riders can be a great source of information when it comes to good trails in your area. If you board your horse, talk to fellow boarders to find out which trails are the best and most accessible from your facility. If you keep your horse at your home, talk to your neighbors and other horse people you come across in the area, such as riding instructors and tack store owners. Ask them the best places to ride, and get details on how to get to them and what the trails are like.

Chapter 12

TRAILERING TO TRAILS

Once you get involved with the sport of trail riding, you're bound to get hooked on it. You will enjoy taking your horse out in the wilderness so much, you won't be able to get enough of it. Before long, your local trails will feel too familiar, and you will crave new adventures. You'll want to get out an explore trails that are beyond your front door.

At this point, you will come to realize that you need to add another component to your trail riding life: a horse trailer.

For trail riders, owning a horse trailer opens up a whole new world of exploration. If you have a trailer, you can ship your horse to variety of places. You can take her to trail heads five miles away or five hours away. You can go on weekend horse camping trips with your buddies, or weeklong riding vacations with your spouse. The possibilities for trail riding adventures are limitless if you have access to a horse trailer.

Anatomy of a Horse Trailer

Before you begin your quest for a horse trailer, it's important to know the major differences between the types of trailers that are out there. Some of this was covered in chapter 8, "Preparing Your Horse for Trail," since the style of trailer can affect your horse's willingness to load. But trailers have even greater relevant detail that you'll need to consider when shopping.

BUMPER-PULL VERSUS GOOSENECK

First, the basics. Horse trailers come in two basic exterior styles: *bumper-pull* and *gooseneck*.

Bumper-pulls (sometimes called *standards* or *bumper hitches*) are the most common type of small horse trailer. These types of trailers are so named because they attach to the bumper of a tow vehicle with a hitch.

Bumper-pulls have both pros and cons. The benefits to these trailers are that they are generally less expensive than their gooseneck counterparts. They can also be towed behind a variety of vehicles, including large SUVs and RVs, as well as pickup trucks. Tight turns are more easily negotiated with a bumper-pull trailer.

The downside of bumper-pulls is more potential for sway when you are driving. If you've ever felt a trailer sway behind you while driving down the road, you know how disconcerting this can be.

Gooseneck trailers, on the other hand, are so-called because of their shape. Unlike a bumper-pull, which is essentially a box-shaped container that is hauled behind a vehicle, goosenecks have a front section that fits over a truck bed. The trailer is hitched to the truck at the bed.

Many horse owners prefer gooseneck trailers because these trailers have less sway than bumper-pull trailers. They also offer overhead storage areas in the gooseneck section of the trailer. In the case of trailers with living quarters (which are always goosenecks), a sleeping area is located over the truck bed. Gooseneck trailers are more stable than bumper-pulls, and offer better control for the driver. Also, goosenecks designed for three or more horses have a better resale value than do bumper-pulls holding the same number of horses.

Sharp turns are harder to make with a gooseneck trailer. Greater tongue weight can tip the towing vehicle upward, making truck headlights shine higher. Goosenecks are also more expensive than bumper-pulls, and they weigh more, which means you need a stronger towing vehicle to pull one of these trailers.

Two-horse straight-load trailers are the most popular type of trailer among trail riders.

Gooseneck trailers provide more stability while driving and also offer storage over the truck bed.

SLANT, STRAIGHT, AND STOCK

The other significant design difference in trailers concerns the interior of the trailer. Horse trailers essentially come in three different loading styles: *slant, straight,* and *stock.*

Slant-load trailers feature partitions that position the equine occupants at an angle to the front of the trailer. Instead of facing the back of the towing vehicle, the horses stand at a nearly 45-degree angle to the front of the trailer. Slant-load trailers can hold anywhere from two to four horses, sometimes more, depending on the design.

Some horse owners prefer slant-load trailers because they believe the design makes it easier for horses to balance when the trailer is in motion. The horses can also face a window and see out, making the trailer feel less claustrophobic. Trailers with slant-load designs can accommodate more horses in a shorter trailer length. They are also reported to be easier to load. Some people believe that horses are not built to bear their weight from side to side, which is inevitable in a slant-load trailer. Slant-load trailers also tend to be wider than straight loads, so allow for decreased driver visibility.

The most commonly seen trailer type, the straight-load trailer, has partitions that separate the horses and make them stand facing the direction they are traveling. These are the most popular horse trailers around, and are usually seen in two-horse trailer designs. Straight-loads are usually less expensive than slant-load trailers, and, according to some people, easier on the traveling horse.

Manger/tack compartments and escape doors for each individual horse are also possible with straight-load designs. Driver visibility is good with straight-loads, as is maneuverability of the trailer. Towing weight is minimized because there is no excess space inside the trailer.

Some horse people believe that straight-load designs are harder on the horse because of the weight shifts from front legs to back during braking and acceleration. Horses that are difficult to load and are poor haulers can be especially troublesome in a straight-load.

Stock trailers are essentially open boxes without partitions that allow the horse to stand in just about any position. Most people tie their horses in a stock trailer, and position them so they are at a 90-degree angle from the front of the trailer. Others allow the horses to stand loose, which permits the horses to choose their own position while traveling.

Stock trailers can usually hold more horses than a slant- or straight-load trailer of comparable size. Stock trailers are also less expensive and provide more ventilation than other types of trailers. In hot weather, stock trailers stay cool because of the slatted upper portion.

Some horse people believe that stock trailers are not safe for use with horses, since they are designed primarily for cattle and smaller livestock. Wind and cold weather can be uncomfortable for horses since stock trailers offer little protection from the elements.

RAMP VERSUS STEP-UP

Another fundamental difference between trailer designs concerns the means of entrance. Two designs are typically seen: *ramp* and *step-up*.

Ramp trailers feature a door that opens down into a ramp. This allows the horses to walk gradually into the trailer as they load. This can be a good design for horses who are hesitant about stepping up into a trailer, either because they dislike going into a trailer or because they are short in stature and would have to jump up without a ramp. Some horses also find unloading to be less stressful with a ramp since they can gradually back out instead of having to make a big step down. The downside to ramp designs is that certain horses dislike the sound their hooves make when they walk on the ramp floor and so are reluctant to load.

Step-up trailers do not have a ramp door, and require that the horse step up and into the trailer, lifting her body up without a gradual descent. Shorter horses and those who are difficult to load sometimes balk at step-up trailers.

SIZE

Another crucial element in trailer design is size. Trailers come in a vast array of sizes, from the one-horse trailer to the huge commercial hauler that can accommodate as many as twenty horses or more. For most trail riders with a single horse, a two-horse trailer is ideal. Even though you may only have one horse, it's good to have a two-horse trailer so you can also haul a friend's horse on a trail ride. Also, you never know when you might decide to add another trail horse to your family.

Aside from the obvious differences between a trailer that is meant to hold two horses as opposed to six or more, each trailer features differences in size relating to headroom and width. Keep in mind that in a straight-load trailer, a horse needs floor room in front of and behind her in order to brace herself during braking and acceleration. Headroom should also be a concern. A horse should be able to comfortably hold her head in a normal position while in the trailer, with room to spare. You'll see three different trailer sizes available on the market: Quarter Horse, Thoroughbred, and Warmblood. Here's a look at each:

- *Quarter Horse.* The majority of two-horse, straight-load trailers are considered Quarter Horse trailers, and are designed for small to average-sized horses. Stalls in these types of trailers are normally six feet in height. Horses who are taller or longer than the average Quarter Horse or Arabian may be too big to be comfortable in a trailer of this size.
- *Thoroughbred.* Designed for horses who are somewhat taller than the average Quarter Horse yet have considerably longer bodies, Thoroughbred trailer stalls usually measure seven feet in height. Length varies from model to model.
- *Warmblood.* A relative newcomer to the American market, Warmblood trailers usually feature stalls that are seven and a half feet tall. The length of the stall is longer than even a Thoroughbred trailer to accommodate the overall size of most Warmblood breeds, which are on the large size. Smaller horses can also travel in this size trailer very comfortably.

Your Towing Vehicle

Before you learn any more about trailers, it's time to think about what you'll need to tow one. After all, if you don't have a vehicle that is capable of pulling a horse trailer, you'll either have to hold off adding a trailer to your horse equipment or start shopping for a new vehicle. Let's not put the cart before the horse, or in this case, the trailer before the truck. Learn what you need to pull a trailer before you embark on buying one.

It would be nice if you could just hook a two-horse trailer to your Honda Civic and drive off into the sunset, but unfortunately it's not that easy. These days, in order to haul a two-horse trailer with two horses in it, you need a full-sized truck or large SUV. The reason for this is the weight of the trailer. A passenger car, compact truck, or standard SUV just doesn't have the engine capacity to pull a large load. Try doing it and you will jeopardize the safety of your horses and yourself, since you will have a hard time stopping, making it up hills, and negotiating turns. (The rare exception to this would be certain trailers manufactured in Europe that are made of lightweight materials and designed to be hauled by a passenger car.)

Whatever you do, don't overload your towing vehicle. Overhauling is the number one cause of trailer accidents. The last thing you want to do is risk your horse's safety or your own on the road.

When shopping for a towing vehicle (or trying to determine if the truck or SUV you have is powerful enough to tow a horse trailer), first figure out the weight you'll be towing. Figure each horse weighs around a thousand pounds (more if you are hauling Warmbloods or draft horses). Add to that the weight of the trailer (available from the trailer's manufacturer) plus accessories you've added such as floor mats, and you have your load weight.

Next, look at the gross combination weight rating (GCWR) of the towing vehicle you are considering. The GCWR should be greater than your weight load. In other words, if you add the weight of your trailer (plus the horses, tack, feed, and so on) to the weight of the towing vehicle, you should get a number that is less than the gross combined weight of the towing vehicle (the GCW). (If you plan to add a camper to your truck bed and haul a bumper-pull trailer behind you, remember to add the weight of the camper to your tow vehicle weight.)

The more power you have in your towing vehicle, the better. Don't cut it too close when determining how much weight you'll be towing. Buy a vehicle that exceeds your needs by at least 10 to 20 percent.

Another element to consider when purchasing a towing vehicle is the amount of engine torque you'll be getting. The more torque the better, since you'll be pulling a heavy load behind you. Substantial torque will make it easier to pull the trailer.

As with trailers, buy the best towing vehicle your budget can afford. (Keep in mind that the best vehicle is not necessarily the one with the nicest stereo, but the one with the most hauling power.)

If you already own a truck or large SUV and hope to use that as your towing vehicle, be honest with yourself about how much that vehicle can really haul. If you want to get your horse safely to trail rides, you may need to upgrade to something more powerful.

Buying a Trailer

You can always borrow a trailer from a friend to go on trail rides, or even rent one from a trailer dealer, but the easiest approach is to buy your own. If you have your own trailer in your driveway, not only will you be able to use it whenever you want to (even on impulse if you wake up one morning and want to go on a ride ten miles from the barn), but you'll have peace of mind knowing that you have an emergency vehicle at the ready should your horse become ill and need transport to a hospital, or if you need to evacuate. It's also nice to have a trailer you can use to help friends and neighbors who may need to transport their horse in a hurry.

If you read the earlier section on horse trailer anatomy, you probably have an idea of what kind of trailer you would like to buy. In addition to the basic designs described there, you'll need to consider the following other elements when thinking about the kind of trailer you want.

MATERIALS

Most trailers are made from steel or aluminum. Each of these metals has pros and cons.

Steel has been the standard material in trailer production for decades. Most horse trailers are made exclusively of steel. Steel trailers are durable and long lasting, and are priced lower than aluminum models. The downside is that rust can be a big problem with galvanized steel. One manufacturer produces high-end stainless steel models, which are expensive but immune to rust.

Aluminum trailers have steel axles and chassis. They are lightweight, immune to rust, have a higher resale value, and are easier to maintain than steel trailers. However, they are generally more expensive than steel trailers and are more prone to wear and tear.

Some trailers combine aluminum wall construction with steel frames. Steel frames can provide strength while the aluminum provides protection from rust. Rubber must be placed between the steel and aluminum connections to prevent corrosion. (Most aluminum trailer manufacturers are now using reinforced aluminum for their frames, making steel unnecessary.)

While the majority of trailers are made from either steel or aluminum, other options such as fiberglass/Wisaform/steel combinations are available, each with its pros and cons.

OTHER FEATURES

One of the most enjoyable parts of trailer shopping is deciding which features you want included in your new rig. If you have the money to add these luxuries to your trailer, go for it. You will probably spend a lot of time driving your trailer, and will come to appreciate these extras:

- *Living quarters.* If you purchase a trailer with living quarters, you'll be the envy of all your horsey friends. Available in a number of gooseneck-style trailers, living quarters can make camping with your horse a real luxury. Akin to what you'll find in an RV, trailer living quarters usually feature a bathroom with shower, a small kitchen with sink, and a sleeping room for four. The more money you spend, the bigger your living quarters—and the bigger your trailer. Keep in mind that you'll need a serious towing vehicle to pull a horse trailer with living quarters.

- *Electronic braking system.* Electronic brakes are the most popular brakes offered as an option on horse trailers, especially on trailers accommodating two to four horses. Similar to the brake systems used on recreational vehicles such as camper-trailers, electronic brakes provide the most efficient and cost-effective system for trailers.

- *Floor mats.* A necessity with any trailer, floor mats provide traction for your horse while she's traveling. The mats will need to be taken out of the trailer and cleaned regularly, since urine can become trapped underneath and can contribute to rust. Depending on whether the horse paws or wears heavy shoes, floor mats may wear out and have to be replaced over time.

- *Wall pads.* An important option for every trailer, wall pads provide protection for the horse while in transit. Should your horse be thrown to one side of the trailer or kick the walls, wall pads can protect her from serious injury. While styles vary among manufacturers, all are designed to be soft yet durable. Most wall pads are made from rubber.

- *Ventilation windows.* Adequate ventilation is important for horses in transit, so ventilation windows are a must. They provide airflow, which is especially important when trailering in hot weather. Ventilation windows also allow moisture to escape from the trailer, making it a healthier environment for the horse. The ability to close the windows is equally important, since traveling horses need protection from blowing wind, rain, and cold weather. Opt for as many ventilation windows and air vents as you can afford.

- *Interior lights.* While it may not seem like much of a necessity, interior lighting is actually very important in a trailer. Horses tend to load easier into a lit trailer than a dark one, and good lighting will allow you to see what you are doing inside the trailer regardless of the time of day. There should be one inside light for each horse you intend to haul.

- *Tack compartment.* A tack compartment is a fun and important option for your trailer. Think about your needs before you shop for this accessory. As a trail rider, you'll need to think about how many horses you'll be hauling and what you plan to take with you when you take them to trails. You want room for at least two saddles (to accommodate a friend even if you have only one horse of your own), pads, buckets, feed, grooming products, and anything else you'd like to bring along. Plan ahead and determine how much space you need before deciding on this important feature.

- *Escape doors.* Escape doors are a necessary and important feature on any horse trailer, and are usually standard (although not always). In an emergency situation, escape doors can mean the difference between getting to your horse or feeling helpless outside, knowing your horse is in distress. Escape doors also keep you from becoming trapped inside the trailer should a problem arise during loading.

- *Outside tie rings.* A very convenient feature, outside tie rings give you a place to tether your horse when you are parked at your destination. Make sure the rings are not so low that the lead rope will dangle, but yet aren't so high that you or your children can't reach them. There should be at least one tie ring for each horse you intend to haul.

- *Removable partitions and butt-bars.* Trailers with removable partitions and butt-bars are more versatile since they will allow you to give more room to a horse who is a difficult traveler. Removable partitions can even allow you to convert your trailer to haul other items, such as motorcycles or equipment.

POINTS TO CONSIDER

There are a few other points to keep in mind when shopping for a trailer. These issues can make a big difference in the comfort and safety of your horse:

- *Cost.* New horse trailers cost anywhere from around $1,000 (for a single-horse trailer) to $50,000 or more (for multiple-horse trailers with living quarters). As you can see, there is a wide range of prices to fit just about any budget. The best rule regarding cost is to buy the best trailer you can afford. If your budget is small and you can't find what you want in a new trailer, consider buying used (see the "Buying Used" sidebar on page 160).

- *Size.* When it comes to interior size, the bigger the trailer, the better for your horse. Even if you have a small Arabian or Quarter Horse, consider buying a warmblood trailer to give your horse the most room possible for comfort's sake. Exterior size is another matter, however. The smaller your trailer, the easier it will be to maneuver, especially in remote destinations where you might be trying to turn around on trail heads or in campgrounds.

- *Color.* It's a good idea to select a light-colored trailer, both inside and out. A light outside color will keep the trailer cooler in hot weather and be more visible to other drivers. A light-colored interior will make the trailer more inviting to your horse. A more inviting trailer means a horse who is easier to load and is more comfortable during transit.

- *Weight.* If you plan to be traveling on dirt and gravel roads—and most trail riders do—a lighter rig will be easier to handle. This is especially true when roads are muddy or filled with deep sand.

MAINTAIN YOUR INVESTMENT

Once you've purchased your horse trailer, you'll want to carefully maintain it. The better care you take of your trailer, the longer it will last. You'll be able to haul horses in it for years to come, or sell it for a good price should you decide to do so.

Your best friend when it comes to trailer maintenance is the owner's manual that came with your rig. In it you'll find detailed instructions on how to care for your trailer to maximize its life span. (If you purchased a used trailer, the manufacturer may be able to sell you a manual for your model.)

Buying Used

If your budget doesn't allow for the purchase of a brand-new rig, consider purchasing a used trailer. Trailer dealers who sell new models are good sources for used trailers. Dealers often provide limited warranties on used rigs. The best deals usually come from individual sellers, however, and can be located in local equine publications or in the classified section of your local newspaper.

Before you begin looking for a used trailer, investigate brands and models. Go to trailer showrooms and trailer shows to take in as many trailers at one time as you can. (Local horse fairs are another great place to window-shop.) Study the different brands to learn their styles and features. Find out what kind of warranties the manufacturers offer on the new trailers, keeping in mind that brands with long-term warranties are more likely to hold up over time.

Consider all the points in a used trailer that you would consider in a new one, including color, size, style, and features. Determine which trailer you want based on what you know is best for your horse, along with your own wish list.

Once you find a used trailer that fits your budget and style preferences, perform a thorough inspection to make sure the trailer is in good working order. The following points will help you assess the condition of the rig:

- Take a look at the axles. You want to avoid bent axles since this will affect the safety and performance of the rig. Uneven tire wear can be a clue to axle problems.

- Have a mechanic check the condition of the brakes. If the brakes aren't working properly, find out the cost to fix or replace them, and factor this into the price of the trailer.

- Lift up the floor mats and look for rot or corrosion on the floor.

- If the trailer is steel, look for rust, especially underneath the trailer.

- Make sure all divider and door latches are working properly and that ramp springs are in good condition.

- Find out how often the trailer was used by the seller. Stay away from trailers that have endured a lot of hauling, since they are more likely to suffer from structural weakness.

- Consider the size of your horse when shopping for a used trailer. Make sure the stalls are tall enough, long enough, and wide enough for the horse to travel in comfort.

- Examine the roof of the trailer carefully for areas where there might be leaks. (Run a garden hose on the roof to find out if the trailer leaks.) If the trailer has a ramp, inspect it for rotted boards.

- Don't get caught up in the outside appearance of a trailer. Structural integrity is more important than a good paint job. You can always paint the trailer.

Hitting the Road

Hauling your horse to trail rides and for camping trips can be a lot of fun as long as you know what you are doing. Before you embark on your first trip with your horse in tow, practice learning to drive with your trailer. Your horse will thank you for it.

LEARN TO DRIVE IT

Driving a trailer takes special skill for several reasons. Simple driving maneuvers like backing up and parking are a whole new experience when you have a trailer hooked to your vehicle. Spend some time behind the wheel with an experienced trailer hauler in the passenger seat so you can get advice and hopefully acquire some skills before you add your precious cargo.

Another aspect of trailer driving that you'll need to learn is slow, gentle motion. Turning, accelerating, and braking should all be done slowly and carefully when horses are loaded in your trailer. If you aren't clear why, think back on times when you were on a bus or train. Remember how your body lurched and you nearly lost your balance every time the vehicle stopped, started, or turned? Although horses have two extra feet on which to balance, sudden moves can cause them to lose their balance—and quickly learn to hate riding in a trailer.

If you have an experienced hauler you can rely on for advice, you are in luck. Ask this person to take you on a ride around the neighborhood in your vehicle with the trailer hitched in back, explaining how he or she negotiates turns, backs up, parks, stops, and accelerates. This will give you a good idea of how to maneuver the truck and trailer before it's your turn to give it a try in a safe area where there are very few other vehicles to contend with.

When it comes to freeway or highway driving, you will be traveling mostly in the right lane with your horses in tow. This is because you will need to move at a relatively slow pace (perhaps just below the speed limit). Also, it's safest to travel to the right when hauling horses just in case you need to pull over quickly in the event of an emergency.

If you don't usually drive in the right lane with a large vehicle, start practicing. You will need to learn to deal with merging cars and trucks on a regular basis. It will take some doing to learn to judge when you can have time to brake to allow someone to get in front of you, and when you need to accelerate to allow someone to merge behind you. Remember, when horses are in the trailer, you shouldn't make any sudden moves, so all of this has to be done smoothly.

Practice driving with your trailer, without your horse, for as long as it takes for you to feel comfortable. Before you put your horse in the trailer and drive off, make sure handling the towing vehicle and trailer feels like second nature to you.

TEACH YOUR HORSE

Most adult horses have had some experience with trailering. Hopefully, for your horse, that experience has been good. If your horse has never had a bad experience in a trailer, or is simply an obedient soul, she should load into your new rig the first time you ask her. If she doesn't, you'll need to train her to go into your trailer. (Keep in mind that she may load in other trailers, but not yours. She must learn to get into *your* trailer since that is the one she'll be traveling in.)

Chapter 8 provides some advice on how to train your horse to load into a trailer. If you have a particularly difficult horse who is dead set against getting in, or you know absolutely nothing about loading and unloading a horse and tying her in a trailer, you'll need the help of an experienced horse person— preferably a reputable trainer. When it comes to trailer loading, it doesn't take long to figure out that a horse has to be willing to go in. You won't be able to force your horse into the trailer. Horses are simply too strong to be physically coerced. (Make sure your trailer is hitched to your tow vehicle before you begin loading or else the weight of your horse will tip the trailer forward and scare the heck out of both of you.)

Once your horse has reached the stage where she will go into your trailer willingly, practice often and reward her with food when she gets in. Leave some grain or her favorite hay at the front of the trailer and let her munch for a while before you unload her.

Eventually, take your horse for some short rides around the neighborhood just to give her the feel of being in the trailer while the rig is in motion.

It's wise to practice this many times before the day you actually plan to travel with your horse. More than one person has had the experience of trying to load their horse for the first time on travel day only to discover the horse wants nothing to do with the trailer.

TRAVEL DAY

When the day comes for you to hit the road with your trailer, be sure to inspect the trailer and towing vehicle first, before you load your horse. This is especially important if you'll be driving for a lengthy period of time. You want to make sure your trailer is safe before you begin your journey, for the sake of you, your passengers, and your horse.

Use the following safety checklist as a guide when you are inspecting your tow vehicle and trailer:

- Have someone sit in the driver's seat of your tow vehicle and put on your turn signals, and step on your brake. Stand behind the trailer to make sure the signals and brake light work on the trailer.

- Make sure the safety chains are properly adjusted.

- Go inside the trailer and check the floorboards to make certain they are in good condition and able to bear the weight of your horse.

- Make sure the rubber floor mats inside the trailer are clean and dry (no manure or wet bedding).

- Do a safety check on your towing vehicle to make sure that brake fluid, transmission fluid, coolant, and engine oil levels are where they should be.

Make sure your wiper fluid reservoir is full too, since you are bound to encounter splattered bugs and dust on your trip.

- Make certain the trailer is securely hitched to the tow vehicle and locked into place.

- Fill up your tow vehicle's gas tank before you hitch up the trailer. That will save you time and effort once the trailer is hitched and the horse loaded.

You should also check your trailer every six months for general repair. Examine tires for wear and air pressure, check electrical connections, and look for any sharp edges inside the trailer that could be dangerous to your horse. Be sure to lubricate latches and hinges, tighten any loose partitions, and verify that windows correctly open and close at this time as well.

What to Bring

In addition to your horse and trailer, you will need to bring a few more items. Whether you are just going away for a day's ride or plan to be away overnight or longer will determine how much food and other supplies you bring for yourself and your horse. Here are the basics:

- *Tack.* Bring any tack you might need on the ride, including your saddle, pad, and bridle. It doesn't hurt to have an extra halter on board in case the one your horse is wearing breaks. You'll also want to bring leg boots, a crop, and any other items you normally use. Some trail riders also bring along an extra headstall, girth, reins, and other backup items in case something breaks during the ride.

- *Grooming supplies.* You'll need to bring your horse's brushes, hoof pick, mane and tail comb, and any other grooming items you regularly use before and after a ride.

- *Feed and supplies.* Bring some of your horse's hay, along with a hay net or hay bag you can hang from the side of your trailer. (The amount of hay you bring depends on how long you plan to be away.) Also bring a water bucket and electrolytes or any other supplement you might need to give your horse before you return home.

- *A first-aid kit.* If your horse becomes sick or injured on the road or on the trail, you'll be grateful to have first-aid supplies on hand. See chapter 10, "Safety on the Trail," for details on what to put in your kit.

- *Travel documents.* If you are traveling out of state, you may need to have a copy of your horse's Coggins test (a blood test for equine infectious anemia) and other health certificates with you. Be sure to find out ahead of time what is required and keep this information with you in your towing vehicle so you can present it to authorities should you be asked.

- *Emergency road kit.* In case you run into mechanical trouble on the road, it's a good idea to have an emergency road kit in your rig. This should include a flashlight, a jack and crowbar, and emergency flashers and reflectors for the road, for you, and for your horse. A fire extinguisher is also a good idea, along with a tool kit. (A cell phone is also a valuable tool in the event of a roadside emergency, although cell phone reception is unreliable in many rural areas.)

- *A detailed itinerary.* When traveling with horses, it's always wise to know exactly where you are going. Have your route planned out, and bring detailed maps with you.

- *Spare tires.* Both your tow vehicle and your trailer should have spare tires on hand and in good repair.

Loading Your Horse

Follow these guidelines when loading your horse:

- Fit your horse with a halter and lead rope for travel.

- Put shipping boots and a head bumper on your horse to protect her during travel. (If she has never worn these items before, practice walking her around with them on a few times before travel day.)

- Put an inch or more of dust-free shavings or other dry bedding on the floor mats to help with traction and absorption of urine.

- Open the windows of your trailer to allow your horse the optimum amount of ventilation. (Don't open the windows so wide that your horse can stick her head out. It's dangerous for a horse to travel with her head sticking out the trailer window.)

- Provide your horse with some hay to munch on while on the road. Do not give her pellets since she may choke on these if she can't get her head down while traveling.

- If your horse is traveling alone in a two-horse trailer or larger, load her on the driver's side of the trailer. This will help balance the trailer on the road.

- Tie your horse to the inside of the trailer, using a safety knot. Be sure the lead rope is long enough to allow your horse to lower her head, but not long enough to step on the rope.

HORSE CARE ON THE ROAD

If you are hauling your horse for just a short trip to a local trail head (two hours or less), you don't need to worry about too much. Once you have securely loaded your horse, you won't need to check on her until you arrive at your destination.

If your trip is a longer one, however, you'll need to take some breaks, for both your own and your horse's sake.

The Automobile Association of America (AAA) recommends that drivers stop every two hours for a break to alleviate driving fatigue. You should also stop every four hours to give your horses a break too. Some experts believe horses should be unloaded every four hours to give them time to stretch their legs and relieve themselves (some horses won't urinate in a trailer). Others believe this is dangerous since if the horse gets loose near an open road, the results can be fatal. Also, if you have a horse who is difficult to load, you may not want to take the chance that you won't be able to get her back into the trailer.

At the very least, stop every few hours to give your horse a break from the rocking motion of the trailer. It takes physical effort for a horse to balance herself in a moving trailer, and when the trailer is at rest, the horse can take it easy too.

If you'll be traveling for more than twelve hours, consider stopping at a "horse motel" to let your horse have a good rest before continuing on the road the following day. Horse motels are located all across the country, many close to busy interstates. (Equine Travelers of America offers a book called *Nationwide Overnight Stabling Guide;* see appendix B, "Resources," for details.) Some provide quarters for horse owners too, although most simply provide a stall or paddock for your horse to bunk down while you spend the night in a nearby hotel.

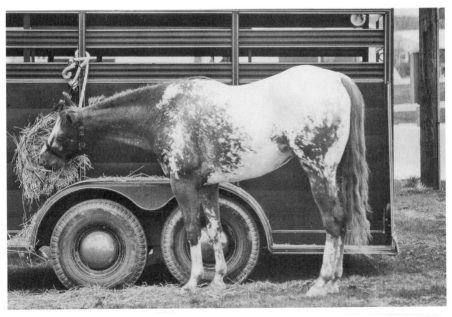

Giving your horse hay to munch on while tied to the trailer will help your horse relax at the new destination.

Whenever you stop for a break, make the following check on your rig and your horses:

- Open windows wide and lower the trailer door to allow fresh air to get into the trailer. (Make sure the butt-bars are secure so your horse doesn't back out.)

- Offer water to your horse. If you are traveling for a long period of time and your horse refuses to drink, remove her source of hay. If your horse eats a lot of hay without drinking water along the way, she can develop an intestinal impaction, causing colic.

- Take a look around the trailer to make sure everything is in working order. Check tire pressure, latches, and your fuel gauge. Fill up your tank whenever possible if you'll be traveling off the beaten path. The last thing you want is to run out of gas with a horse in your trailer.

EMERGENCIES ON THE ROAD

When traveling with a horse, things sometimes happen on the road. Whatever you do, try not to panic if something does happen. Your horse needs you to keep a calm head. Keep your cell phone handy to dial 911 in the event of an accident.

Try to keep these points in mind should something occur beyond your control:

- If you find you have a sick horse, call directory assistance and ask for an equine veterinarian in the area.

- Use your first-aid kit to deal with any injuries, but remember that a horse in pain can often be unpredictable. If you are traveling alone, avoid unloading your horse until help arrives.

- Use your voice to keep your horse calm in the event of an accident. Remember, she is counting on you to take care of the situation and make everything right. Assure her that help is on the way and that she will be okay.

Part IV
ADVANCED TRAIL RIDING

Chapter 13

CAMPING WITH YOUR HORSE

Trail riding is addictive, as you already know or will soon find out. Once you become hooked on it, you'll find that you want to do more and more of it. Eventually, you'll want to take your horse camping so you can spend more than one day trail riding out in the wilderness. This might be just for fun, or you might need to camp because you are participating in a distance event, such as competitive trail riding or endurance. Either way, it's important to know how to safely camp with horses before you embark on this next level of trail riding.

The best way to learn how to camp with horses is to go along with an experienced horse camper the first couple of times. Learning "on the job" is invaluable, and an experienced horse camper will be able to show you the ropes. This method of learning sure beats the "trial by fire" method.

Getting Started

Before you can start camping with your horse, you need to be prepared, both mentally and physically—and so does your horse.

At first thought, camping with your horse might not seem that different from camping with your dog or some friends. But in reality, it's very different. Taking a 1,000-pound animal on the road requires some thought and plenty of preparation.

PREPARING YOUR HORSE

First off, you need to make sure you have a horse who can handle the experience of being in a strange new environment and spending the night in an unusual place. For some horses, the sights, sounds, and smells of an unfamiliar place can be unnerving, especially if the horse is used to living in a stall and doesn't get out much. Before you take your horse camping for the first time,

169

trailer him out of his usual confines and ride him on the trails as much as you can. The camping experience alone will be new and exciting for him. You don't want to introduce him to trail riding at the same time.

If you have a horse who is comfortable being out in the trail, your next step is to make sure he's comfortable riding in a trailer. Review the information in chapter 12, "Trailering to Trails," and spend time hauling your horse to local trails so he gets used to the idea of riding in the trailer and seeing new places at the other end of the trip.

Before you take your horse on a camping trip that will consist of significant trail riding, make sure he's in proper condition. See chapter 8, "Preparing Your Horse for Trail," for details on conditioning your horse for trail riding. The last thing you want to do is ask your horse for work on a camping trip that is beyond his physical abilities. Should he colic, "tie up," or become lame, you'll be trying to deal with his problem in the middle of nowhere. (See also chapter 9, "Conditioning Yourself for Trail.")

Be sure to bring along an experienced horse the first few times you take your horse camping so your horse has a buddy. Most horses are more secure when in the company of other equines, and your horse will be calmer if he has another horse by his side who has done this kind of thing before.

PREPPING YOURSELF

Your horse isn't the only one who needs to get used to the idea of camping. If you aren't an experienced camper, you should get a few horseless camping trips under your belt before you try doing it with your horse. If you'll be roughing it by sleeping in a tent or under the stars, you'll find it takes some getting used to. Expect to toss and turn quite a bit your first time out. Cooking your food over an open fire also takes some skill. Be sure to bring an experienced camper along with you to teach you the skills you'll need.

Of course, the level of camping you'll be doing will be a big factor in the kinds of skills you'll need. If you are traveling in an RV that comes complete with a bathroom, kitchen, and sleeping areas, you won't need to learn too much other than how to use these familiar amenities in tight quarters.

If you'll be tent camping or just sleeping outdoors, you'll need to learn to set up a tent, start a fire, cook outdoors, wash yourself and your eating utensils in a spigot or with water you brought along, and other camping skills. Make sure you have all this down pat before you introduce a horse to the mix.

Before you embark on your trip, be sure you have scoped out the area where you'll be camping to determine the following information:

- *Whether horses are allowed at the campsites.* Only designated campgrounds allow horses, so be sure to check this first before planning your trip.

- *Whether you need reservations.* Some sites require reservations for horse campers. Again, be sure to find this out before you head out.

- *What kind of facilities are available for horses, if any.* Some campgrounds open to horses have corrals available for use, while others have no horse facilities. If the site you have chosen does not have a place to confine your horse, you'll have to consider tying your horse to the trailer, or bringing a set of portable corrals. (See the next section for more information on this.)

- *If water is available.* Not all campsites provide running water. If the site you are planning to visit doesn't have accessible, potable water, you'll have to bring water for both you and your horse.

- *If horses are allowed on the trails accessible from the campsite.* While horses might be permitted in the campsite, they might not be allowed on the

Camping in the snow can be a fun experience, especially with horses along.

trails. Find out if you can ride your horse out of camp. If not, you may need to trailer your horse to various trail heads.

- *What the weather will be like during the time you'll be camping.* Check the forecast to see if it will be raining, snowing, or very hot. Since your horse will be out in the elements the entire time, you need to be prepared for what nature has planned.

If the campsite you are considering can't provide you with the kind of facilities you need, choose a different area to camp. When you and your horse are first learning to camp, you may want to choose sites that offer the most amenities, including corrals and running water. This will allow you and your horse to ease into the camping experience. You can tackle the more rustic campgrounds once you've gotten a few camping trips under your belt.

What to Bring

When camping with your horse, you need to bring along everything he will need to get by for a couple of days, and then some. The following list can get you started with your packing:

- *Your trailer.* Of course you need your trailer in order to get your horse to the campgrounds, but make sure it is properly equipped for the job of horse camping. If you'll be tying your horse to the trailer overnight, double-check to make sure the tie rings are secure. If you are using overhead tie, make sure it is securely fastened to your trailer. Refer to chapter

12 for information on conducting a safety check on your trailer before you hit the road. (If you plan to sleep in your trailer, make sure you bring supplies to clean the floor before you lie down your sleeping bag.)

- *Feed.* Don't think your horse can live on grass while you are out camping with him. He will need to eat his regular feed while he's away from home. Bring at least half a bale of hay for each day you intend to be gone, along with whatever grain and supplements he normally gets. You can store your hay in the feed or tack compartment of your trailer, and you can use a bale cover to keep the bale contained once you cut the baling twine.

- *Water.* If the campground you'll be staying at does not have potable water, you will have to bring at least five gallons of water per day per horse for drinking—more if you plan to work your horse hard and/or if the weather will be particularly hot. You can buy large water containers designed for camping purposes at outdoor stores. Bring at least a gallon of drinking water per day for yourself—more if you'll need water for washing dishes, cooking, and the like.

- *Portable corrals.* If the campground does not provide corrals for horse campers and you don't want to tie your horse to the trailer, you'll need a set of portable corrals. Portable corrals come in different styles and materials, and should be purchased based on your horse's size and habits, as well as your budget. (Be sure to have a separate portable corral for every horse.)

- *Tack.* Don't forget to bring everything you'll need to ride your horse on the trail during your camping trip. Bring extra tack if you have it, too, especially an extra girth, reins, headstall, halter, and lead rope.

- *Hay bag.* If you'll be tying your horse to the trailer, you want to bring a hay bag or hay net along to attach to the side of the trailer. Your horse will pull the hay from the bag or net as needed.

- *Buckets.* You'll need a muck bucket for manure, a bucket for your horse's grain, and a bucket for water.

- *Manure fork.* It's important that you clean up after your horse before you leave your campsite. Leaving a manure-laden campsite only gives horse campers a bad name with authorities and other campers. Bring a manure fork along so you can scoop your horse's poop. Dump it in designated bins at the site, or carry it back with you.

- *Horse first-aid kit.* You should have one of these in your trailer at all times, but just in case you don't, be sure to bring it with you camping. See chapter 10, "Safety on the Trail," for details on what to keep in your kit.

- *Hoof boots.* These rubber shoe-replacers can be a lifesaver if your horse loses one or more shoes while you are camping. You'll still be able to ride him if you have one of these boots to replace a lost shoe.

- *Insect repellent.* The bugs can get nasty out in the wilderness, especially during the summer. Be sure to bring bug repellent for your horse, and consider bringing along a fly mask and fly sheet, too.

- *Horse blanket.* If you'll be camping in an area that is significantly colder than your home climate, or if it will be cold and rainy, you should bring a blanket along to cover your horse at night. (Make sure your horse is familiar with wearing a blanket before you go camping. Don't put it on him for the first time when he's tied to a trailer in unfamiliar surroundings.)

- *Emergency contact information.* Before you leave for your trip, find out the number of an emergency veterinarian in the area where you will be camping. If something happens and you need help fast, you'll be glad you have the number at hand.

If you are wondering what you should bring for yourself, see chapter 9 for a checklist on what to take along on rides. The food mentioned in that chapter is also good to bring on camping trips. Details on what to bring along for the humans on your camping trip can be also found in books about camping. Basically, you need supplies that will enable you to eat, drink, and sleep comfortably as you are tending to your horse.

Some campgrounds provide permanent corrals for horse campers.

Setting Up Camp

When you arrive at your campsite, your heart will probably leap with anticipation at the adventure that is about to unfold. Camping with horses is loads of fun, as you are about to discover.

But before you can jump on your horse and ride through new terrain, you need to attend to a few tasks.

FIND A GOOD SITE

If you reserved your campsite in advance, the official who received you at the campground will direct you to the site being held in your name. In this situation, your decision has already been made for you.

If you didn't need a reservation and are just looking for a good place to camp, keep the following criteria in mind as you cruise the campgrounds:

- *Space.* Look for a spot that will easily accommodate your trailer and tow vehicle. Remember that you will have to turn around and maneuver when you are parking and when you are pulling out at the end of your stay.

- *Proximity to trail heads.* If the campground is a large one, take note of where the trail heads are located and pick a spot that is relatively close. Of course, you don't want a spot that is so close that every rider and hiker in the campground will be parading through your camp. On the other hand, you don't want to be so far away that it will take you twenty minutes just to get to the trail once you've mounted your horse.

- *Proximity to water.* If the campground provides potable water, remember that you'll be filling up buckets and bringing them back to your site for your horse to drink and for you to use. Don't pick a site that is so far away from the water source that you'll be too exhausted from hauling water to even think about riding your horse.

- *Shade and shelter.* If you are camping during the hot summer months, choose a spot that will provide your horse with natural shade while he is tied to the trailer or secured in a permanent or portable corral. Likewise, if you are camping on a windy or rainy day, choose a site that will provide your horse with some shelter. (If the wind is fierce and/or lightning is present, keep your horse away from trees.)

- *Flat ground.* If you are tent camping, it's particularly important that you find a level spot on which to pitch your tent. Parking your towing vehicle and trailer on an incline and asking your horse to stand on a slant aren't ideal either, making a level camping spot the ideal place to set up.

The Joys of Horse Camping

If you love nature and camping in the wilderness, you will love it even more with a horse in your campsite.

Waking up in the dewy morning hearing the birds singing and breathing the fresh air of a mountain meadow or desert plain is amazing enough, but when you also wake up to the sound of your horse quietly munching on his hay or shuffling his hooves across the ground, it's hard not to feel like you are in heaven.

Horse camping is a lot of work, but the rewards are well worth it. Not only will you feel closer to your horse at the end of your camping trip, you will also feel closer to nature.

SETTLING THE HORSES

Once you've found a good place to set up camp, it's time to unload the horses and get them settled in their temporary home.

When you first unload, the horses will have high heads and be looking all around them as if to say, "Where the heck are we?" Experienced equine campers will soon relax, since they know the drill. If your horse is a first-timer, expect him to be pretty uptight for a while before he starts to settle down.

If your horse is calm enough, you can walk him a little bit after you unload him. This will help stretch his legs and let him get the lay of the land. If he's too worked up and is dragging you or being otherwise unruly, put him in one of the permanent corrals, or if none are available, tie him to the trailer. (Whatever you do, don't tie your horse to a tree with a regular lead rope around the trunk. Not only is this unsafe for your horse, but he is likely to do significant damage to the tree.)

Your next step is to set up portable corrals if you brought them. If not, this is one less step you'll have to take.

Offer your horse water right away, and give him some hay to help him relax. Leave him alone to get used to his new surroundings while you start setting up your tent, building your fire, or doing whatever chores need to be handled in camp. (Be sure to set up the tent and build your fire far from your horse for his safety.)

Spend some time horse-proofing your campsite once everything is set up, making sure your horse can't get into trouble in his temporary digs. If you are tying him to the trailer, make sure his lead rope can't get hung up on the trailer's wheel covers. Tie him long enough that he can lower his head somewhat, but not so long that he can get a leg caught in the rope or get his head underneath the rope.

Take a look at the entire area around where your horse will be corralled or tied with an eye for possible hazards. Remember that horses have an incredible knack for hurting themselves on seemingly innocuous objects!

Resist the urge to take your horse on a trail ride as soon as you arrive, especially if he hasn't had much, if any, camping experience. Wait at least a couple of hours for him to settle in before you saddle him up and hit the trail.

CREATE A ROUTINE

Although you may be far from home and from everything familiar, your horse will still appreciate a routine. This is especially true if you plan to camp for several days.

Feed your horse at approximately the same time you do at home, and take him out for rides around the same time. The exception to this would be if you plan to go on several all-day rides, which will start in the morning and end in the late afternoon or evening.

Remember that you should only ask your horse to do this kind of strenuous work if he has been properly conditioned and doing close to the same amount of riding at home. If not, give him plenty of breaks on an all-day ride, and give him a day off from long treks every other day.

Tethering trail mounts to a picket line is the good way to secure them without harming trees in the campground.

At the end of the day, give your horse a rubdown and his grain or a treat. Let him relax while you and your camping buddies relax around the fire. Avoid staying up late and making a lot of noise. Although you might feel like partying, the noise will keep your horses awake and prevent them from being able to get the sleep they need to be fresh for the following day. (Neighboring campers will appreciate the quiet, too.)

LEAVE NO TRACE

When it's time to pack up for home, remember to clean up after yourself and your horse. You want your campsite to look as if you were never there. That means picking up trash, loose hay, manure, and anything else that wasn't there when you arrived. Be sure to put out your campfire by covering it with dirt.

As a horse camper, you represent all equestrians in the eyes of the public, as well as the officials who determine who can and can't use our national and regional park systems. Do your best to leave no trace of you or your horses behind.

Chapter 14

JUDGING ON THE TRAIL

F or most riders, trail riding is a casual hobby, something to be done on the weekends when it's time to unwind. For others, trail riding is much more than that.

If you end up falling in love with trail riding like so many riders do, you may find yourself drawn to the competitive side of the sport. While horse shows can be fun and exciting, distance riding contests take competing on horseback to a whole new level.

Two distance sports that are great for beginning trail riders are competitive trail rides and trail trials. These events emphasize good horsemanship in a safe, educational environment that is also competitive.

Competitive Trail Rides

Competitive trail riding is a popular sport with participants all over the United States and Canada. A competitive trail ride is a timed event over a prescribed length of trail. Riders are judged along the trail for their riding and horsemanship skills, while their horses are evaluated for soundness and conditioning.

Competitive trail ride participants enjoy this sport because it enables them to spend a day out in the wilderness with their horses. Most competitive trail events involve camping out with horses and riding through beautiful country. All the while riders are enjoying exploring new trails, they are competing for awards.

A number of regional trail riding organizations hold competitive trail riding events, each with their own rules (see appendix B, "Resources," for contact information). Only one organization sanctions competitive trail rides throughout the United States, however: the North American Trail Ride Conference, or NATRC.

The North American Trail Ride Conference began in the 1960s with the idea of promoting safe and competitive trail events in the United States. Since that time, the organization has grown to encompass a total of six regions, representing all fifty states.

How It Works

The North American Trail Ride Conference has specific goals that are reflected in the organization's rules. NATRC events are designed to:

- Stimulate greater interest in the breeding and use of good horses possessed of stamina and hardiness, and qualified to make good mounts for trail use
- Demonstrate the value of type and soundness in the proper selection of horses for competitive riding
- Learn and demonstrate the proper methods of training and conditioning horses for competitive trail riding
- Encourage good horsemanship as related to trail riding
- Demonstrate the best methods of caring for horses during and after long rides without the aid of artificial methods or stimulants

NATRC puts much emphasis on the proper selection and care of trail horses, and NATRC awards are based on these priorities.

Separate awards are given to the rider and the horse at each NATRC event. Horses are rewarded for good behavior and proper conditioning, while riders are judged on their horsemanship skills.

Horses must be at least 4 years old to compete in a NATRC event. Younger horses are not permitted because they are not physically developed enough to safely compete in such extensive rides.

A Typical Ride

Riders participating in a NATRC ride show up at the ride headquarters the day before the ride is to begin. The

One of the most enjoyable aspects of competitive trail riding is being able to ride with your friends.

ride headquarters are typically a horse-friendly campground with access to the trail head that will be used for the ride.

The Night Before

At a prescribed check-in time the day before the ride, the competition officially begins. Because camping is part of the NATRC experience, riders are expected to set up a safe camp for their horses and are judged on the safety of that camp. Each rider shows his or her horse to a veterinary judge to determine if the horse is sound. Riders are judged on their presentation methods to the judge, and the quality of the horse's grooming. Riders are weighed with their tack to determine their weight division, with *lightweight* riders being 100 to 189 pounds, and *heavyweight* riders over 190 pounds. Juniors are children under the age of 17.

All riders are preregistered before ride day, at which point they declare a ride division. The *Novice* division is for any horse and adult rider combination that has not won more than four first-place awards in the horse category at a NATRC event. The pace of the Novice division rides is anywhere from 3.5 to 5 miles per hour, which means mostly walking with a little bit of trotting, over a preset 15- to 25-mile trail.

The *Competitive/Pleasure* division is for any horse and rider team, and is usually the division riders move to once they are no longer eligible to compete in Novice. The pace is similar to that of Novice, and the ride distance the same. No weight or age limitations apply. For many riders, Competitive/Pleasure serves as a bridge between Novice and Open because it increases the number and type of horse and rider combinations that each rider must compete with.

The *Open* division is the most difficult division in NATRC, and only horses 5 years or older are eligible. Open rides can be held in one of three distance types: 25 to 35 miles for a "B" ride, 50 to 60 miles for an "A" ride, and 80 to 90 miles for an "AA" ride. The pace is 4 to 6 miles per hour, faster than in Novice or Competitive/Pleasure. This means more trotting and some cantering to complete the ride in the time given.

After dinner, riders are given a briefing about the next day's ride, and are shown maps and given some idea of what the trails will be like.

Ride Day

On ride morning, riders groom and tack up their horses in anticipation of the ride start. Each ride division leaves at a different time and follows a different trail pattern. Ride organizers often stagger riders as they leave to avoid a mad rush of excited horses all starting out at once.

Riders follow a marked trail, which is usually designated with colored ribbons. Each rider has a trail map and is expected to follow the trail accurately. If you go off track, this will affect your timing; riders must complete the course within a prescribed time range. If you finish too fast and come in before the designated minimum time for the ride, you'll be disqualified. If you go too slow and don't make it to the finish line before the maximum time allowed, you are also disqualified. For this reason, it's important to keep your eye on your watch and pace your horse so you finish the ride within the prescribed time range.

Rides are set up to take all day, and breaks are factored into the pace. A lunch break is allowed, and does not count toward the time you are riding. Shorter breaks are up to you, if you feel you have the time to take them.

Along the way, you and your horse are being judged. You'll be riding along chatting with your friends when you spy a judge up ahead stationed at a water crossing, a hill, or another natural obstacle that is part of the landscape. After exchanging greetings and letting the judge see the number you have pinned to your back, you will negotiate the obstacle with the judge watching. The way you handle your horse over the obstacle will determine the score you're given by that judge. Judges are looking for balance and lightness, body and leg position, control, and hands, as well as the cues you give to your horse on ascending, descending, and level terrain.

Judges will stop you along the way to ask you to dismount and mount, and back up your horse. The judge will also check your tack for proper fit and safety. If you are following the horse in front of you too closely or doing anything unsafe on the trail and a judge sees you, you'll be marked down.

Horses and riders at competitive trail events are judged as they negotiate obstacles on the trail.

An important part of the judging consists of pulse and respiration checks, where horses are stopped at various intervals on the ride to have their conditioning evaluated. At the checkpoint, horses are given some time to recover before their pulse and respiration is checked by a veterinary judge. Horses are given higher scores for having lower pulse and respiration rates, which indicate they are in top physical condition.

The End of the Ride

After you have completed the day's ride, you'll be expected to groom your horse thoroughly before presenting her one more time to the veterinary judge. The judge will check the horse's physical condition, including soundness, and will give the horse a score based on this evaluation.

Once the judging is over, you can put your horse away and take a break before dinnertime. After the meal, the day's awards are given out to the successful horses and riders in each division. If another ride will be held the following day, riders are briefed on the route they will be taking.

Most riders who are only competing for the single day spend another night in camp and head out in the morning. Rides are usually held on Saturdays, which leaves Sunday as a travel day and a chance for horse and rider to recuperate.

NATRC and most other competitive trail riding organizations offer year-end awards in each division to recognize those riders who have achieved the most wins throughout the year. If you become a regular competitive trail ride participant, you have the chance to work toward earning ribbons, trophies, and other awards.

GETTING INVOLVED

If competitive trail riding sounds like fun to you, it's easy to get started in the sport. If you have a trail horse whom you have been riding regularly, all you need to do is condition her for your first ride (see chapter 8, "Preparing Your Horse for Trail"), condition yourself (see chapter 9, "Conditioning Yourself for Trail,") and start learning the rules of the sport.

Begin your quest for knowledge by obtaining a rule book and other helpful materials from NATRC (contact information can be found in appendix B). You don't have to be a member of NATRC to participate in competitive trail rides, which are held around the country mostly during the spring, summer, and fall. NATRC members get discounted entry fees, though, and receive the organization's publication in the mail, which contains helpful tips and ideas for competing. You'll become an automatic member of your local region as well, and will find out about judging clinics and other events designed to help you get to know fellow competitive trail riders in your area.

If you have another competitive trail riding organization in your area that you would like to try out, contact that group to learn their rules for the trail.

Competitive Trail Ride Skills

You and your horse will need to have the following basic skills and attributes to do well at a competitive trail ride:

- *Good control.* You must be able to control your horse out on the trail.

- *Good ground manners.* Your horse must be willing to be led quietly, stand without fussing, and stand still while you mount and dismount.

- *Good conditioning.* Your horse must be well conditioned for trail riding.

- *Good equitation.* As a rider, you need to have a good seat and hands, and sit in the correct position in the saddle.

Each competitive trail riding group has different regulations, and you'll do best if you learn about the particular organization you plan to ride with.

In addition to conditioning your horse and learning the rules, you'll want to make sure you have a way to get your horse to your first ride. If you have your own trailer, then you are all set. If not, you'll have to hitch a ride with another rider or consider renting a trailer (and towing vehicle, if yours isn't powerful enough to pull a horse trailer—see chapter 12, "Trailering to Trails," for details).

You'll be camping out at the competitive ride, so if you don't have an RV or camper at your disposal, you'll need to have a tent and other camping supplies on hand. Remember to practice camping with your horse a few times (see chapter 13, "Camping with Your Horse,") before you attempt your first competitive ride. You'll do better with the judging and the entire experience if you already know the basics of horse camping before you start competing.

Once you attend your first NATRC or other competitive trail ride, you are bound to get hooked on this wonderful sport. You'll make a lot of friends and find that a lot of people just like you love to ride competitively on the trail.

Trail Trials

Another less demanding form of trail competition is called trail trials. Designed to evaluate the skills of both horse and rider on the trail, these events consist of judging over obstacles and in various situations common to trail riding, usually over a course of 10 miles or less.

Trail trials are held by a variety of regional organizations around the United States, and each has its own specific rules. In general, trail trials are obstacle course competitions that test the trail skills of horse and rider over several miles. The trials are not conducted in an arena like trail classes at a horse show; the test takes place out on the trail.

Trail trial clinics are one of the best places to learn skills such as the log drag.

To participate in a trail trial, you need a good, well-trained trail horse. (You don't need to own the horse you ride, so a friend's horse will work too.) You also need the skills to handle that horse in different trail situations, such as crossing water and bridges, stepping over logs, walking through tunnels, and negotiating hills.

At trail trials, judges often ask riders to perform certain tasks with the help of their horse. Opening and closing a gate while mounted is often required, as is dragging a tire or a log. Horses must also be led from the ground, be willing to lift their feet when asked, and stand tied without fussing.

These are skills you'll need to practice with your horse well in advance of the event if you hope to do well. You can learn how to perform the mounted tasks by asking an experienced trail trailer to give you some pointers, or you can participate in a trail trial clinic. Many clubs that offer trail trials sponsor clinics that allow you to enroll your horse and spend a few hours learning how to perform the required tasks.

Riders are required to mount and dismount as well, and the judge will look at your tack to make sure it's safe and well maintained. Make certain you can get on and off your horse safely and efficiently, and that your equipment is in good working order.

Trail Trial Skills

You and your horse must know how to perform the following tasks in order to succeed at most trail trials:

- *Gates.* You must be able to open and close a gate without dismounting and without taking your hand off the gate.
- *Water crossings.* Your horse must be willing to step into and wade across water.
- *Drag.* You and your horse must know how to drag an obstacle behind you and from the front.
- *Mounting.* You must be able to mount your horse unassisted, and dismount as well.
- *Bridge.* Your horse must be willing to walk across a wooden or metal bridge.
- *Stepping over.* You must able to get your horse to step over obstacles such as logs without jumping over them.

ON THE DAY

Since most trail trials only last a few hours, it's not necessary to camp out the night before with your horse unless you have a long way to travel to get to the trial site. Since horse camping may not be permitted at the site of the trail trial, you may have to stay at a horse camp nearby.

On the morning of the trial, you'll need to check in with the trial trail officials. When you registered for the ride, you signed up for the appropriate division. For example, the California State Horseman's Association, an organization that sponsors trail trials, designates Novice, Intermediate, and Advanced divisions for trail trial riders.

Each division, whether it is for horses or riders, has different criteria, with horses and riders expected to complete different tasks on the trail, depending on the degree of difficulty.

The ride itself takes a few hours, with stops along the way to follow the directions of the judges. At the end of the ride, the scores are tabulated and participants are usually notified of their placements in the event.

Many trail trial clubs offer year-end awards for their most successful participants.

Chapter 15

RACING ON THE TRAIL

W alking along the trail at a relaxing pace definitely has its appeal, but if you have both a competitive nature and the need for speed, you'll fall in love with two popular trail riding sports: endurance and Ride-and-Tie.

Endurance and Ride-and-Tie are two activities that call for great athleticism in both horse and rider. They are also sports that put emphasis on speed. The faster you go, the more successful you will ultimately be.

Both endurance and Ride-and-Tie are sports to aim for if you are a beginning trail rider. You'll need to get a lot of trial miles under your belt before you pursue one of these activities. But if you have a good horse and are a decent rider, you will be amazed at how quickly you can take home awards in these exciting sports.

Endurance

The sport of endurance has been growing in leaps and bounds over the last several decades. What once was an occasional event held mostly in the western United States has become an international sport.

Endurance racing has been around for a long time in the United States, and was a favorite activity of horsemen who wanted to show off their horses' athleticism and stamina. Informal races with few rules were the order of the day in the 1800s, a situation that has changed significantly today.

While a number of regional organizations for endurance riding exist throughout the United States, only one group sanctions rides throughout the country: the American Endurance Ride Conference, or AERC. Established in 1972, the AERC defines endurance riding as "an athletic event with the same horse and rider covering a measured course within a specified maximum time." The AERC holds endurance races in all fifty states.

Endurance rides are races that are run in either 50- or 100-mile distances, covered in a single day. Extended endurance rides usually offer 50-mile-per-day rides, scheduled over a period of two or more days. Shorter rides, called Limited Distance rides, range between 25 and 35 miles in one day and are designed for novices. The terrain on these rides varies depending on the area where they are held. Endurance rides in California tend be very hilly, while rides in many of the Plains states are over flat ground.

The winning horse and rider team are determined by the fastest time. In order for a horse to qualify as the winning mount, he must be determined "fit to continue" by a ride veterinarian. Veterinarians check the horses throughout the ride at periodic "vet checks" to make certain the horses are physically able to continue. Horses who are not sound or are having a hard time coping with the distance are excused from the ride. Rides also have mandatory stops where riders must rest their horses for a period of time during the race. Many rides offer a prize for the horse who has the best conditioning of all the entrants.

Endurance rides are races, but many riders feel they have succeeded if they simply complete the ride successfully, with their horse sound and healthy at the end.

Because of the growing popularity of endurance riding around the world, the sport has been elevated to international levels. The United States Equestrian Team has endurance riders who travel around the world competing against endurance riders in other countries. Endurance riding is definitely the largest and most popular of all the trail riding sports.

How It Works

Endurance riders typically arrive at the campsite established as ride headquarters the night before the ride is to begin. The goal is to set up camp and rest their horses before the next day's event. Endurance rides start early in the morning, so you want your horse to be ready to go very early on start day.

You'll be camping out the night before the ride, and if you are far from home, the night after the ride as well. If you are participating in a two-day or longer endurance ride, you'll camp out for several days.

Most endurance riders stay in campers or RVs, although some sleep in tents. The more involved you get in endurance riding, the more you will want to invest in comfortable accommodations for camping. Endurance riding is hard work, and a good night's sleep before and after the ride goes a long way.

While you are camping with your horse at the ride, you'll need to feed yourself and your horse, as well as care for him in every other way. In most cases, headquarters camp has running water and other facilities to make this easier on the riders.

You'll need to pack your own water, lunch, snacks, and anything else you might need for the ride, and bring it along with you. Be careful not to overload your horse since that will make it harder for him to complete the ride.

If you can manage it, try to have at least one person work as your "crew" on your rides. In endurance, a rider's crew meets the rider at a designated spot along the ride (usually before a vet check), and helps him or her cool down and care for the horse. The crew person will hold the horse while the rider uses the bathroom, cool the horse by putting water on him, help feed the horse, provide the horse with drinking water, and the like.

A crew is not mandatory, but most riders find it helpful and comforting to have helpers along the way.

PREPARING YOUR HORSE

As you can imagine, endurance riding can be taxing on both the horse and rider, especially at the greater distances. As a newcomer to this sport, you'll need to carefully condition your horse and yourself before you can embark on your first endurance ride.

By following the advice in chapter 8, "Preparing Your Horse for Trail," you'll be able to eventually get your horse to the point where he can compete in a Limited Distance ride of 25 miles. You will need to learn to monitor his pulse and respiration, and become a student of your horse's physical well-being.

It's important to encourage your horse to drink whenever possible during an endurance ride.

If your horse is inexperienced at camping, you'll want to spend some time getting him used to this activity well before you embark on your first ride. Your horse should be relaxed with the idea of camping before you start doing endurance. Otherwise, your horse will expend a lot of his energy on nerves before you even mount up for the ride.

You should also make sure your horse is comfortable being ridden in groups as well as alone. When participating in an endurance ride, you'll find yourself with groups of riders at times, and then alone at other times. Your horse needs to be able to cope with both situations.

Try to attend your first endurance ride with a friend who has experience with this sport. Having someone to ride with you can be a huge help for your nerves, and will help ensure that you complete the ride. The trickiest part of endurance riding for a novice can be following the trail. Having an experienced endurance rider with you to help you read the trail markers can make a big difference.

If you don't know anyone who participates in endurance riding, contact the American Endurance Ride Conference (see appendix B, "Resources"). This organization has a mentor program designed to help novices in the sport hook up with experienced endurance riders in their area.

THE REWARDS

While endurance riding can be hard work for both horse and rider, the rewards are tremendous. The camaraderie in the sport is truly wonderful, and you'll be amazed at how many people are willing to help you get started. You will also build a tremendous bond with your horse, whom you will come to see as your partner rather than just your mount.

Endurance riders have the opportunity to ride trails that few others get to see. Even some national parks that are normally closed to horses will bend the rules to allow an occasional endurance ride.

AERC awards for endurance riders include patches to celebrate achievement of mileage plateaus, beginning at 250 miles. Horses receive medallions at 1,000-mile plateaus. The organization also gives out regional and national awards in various categories.

Overall, endurance riding is a fun and exciting sport that epitomizes the ideals of trail riders. The only caveat is that the sport is addictive. Once you go on your first endurance ride, you may never want to stop.

Ride-and-Tie

A truly exciting and unique sport is Ride-and-Tie, an activity that emphasizes teamwork between two humans and a horse.

Ride-and-Tie is essentially an endurance race, but unlike regular endurance riding, Ride-and-Tie requires that some of the race be run on foot by human team members. The races are typically 20 to 40 miles or more in length, and consist of anywhere from 10 to 50 teams. Mandatory vet checks are part of the course to help ensure the horses' well-being.

In Ride-and-Tie, the human team members alternate between riding the horse and running. The team that finishes the race first with a healthy and sound horse is the winning team.

Ride-and-Tie events are sanctioned by the Ride-and-Tie Association, which has established rules for these races and keeps track of winning teams around the country. The majority of races take place in California, although Ride-and-Tie events are held all over the country.

The Tevis Cup

For most endurance riders in the United States, the ultimate goal is to complete the Western States Trail Ride, or as it's more commonly known, the Tevis Cup. The oldest endurance ride still in existence, the Tevis Cup has taken place every year in northern California since 1955.

One of the most challenging endurance rides in the world, the one-day Tevis Cup covers 100 miles of rugged eastern Sierra mountain country, spanning from Lake Tahoe to Auburn. Riders who complete the course within the ride's 24-mile limit with a sound and healthy horse are given a silver Completion Award Buckle.

The winning rider of the race is the one who completes the 100 miles in the shortest amount of time with a sound and healthy horse. The Tevis Cup trophy goes to this rider. The most fit horse of the first ten finishers gets the Haggin Cup trophy, and junior riders who finish the race receive the Josephine Stedem Scripps Foundation Cup.

The Tevis Cup is sanctioned by the American Endurance Ride Conference and takes place every summer. Most of the greatest endurance horses in the country have completed this exciting ride.

The Tevis Cup ride in northern California is among the most challenging endurance rides in the world.

How It Works

Ride-and-Tie races are usually one-day events that begin early in the morning. Participants who bring their horses usually camp out the night before at the ride's starting point so they'll be fresh and ready to go the next morning. Some participants stay in nearby hotels if they don't have to tend to a horse.

The start of a Ride-and-Tie race is the most exciting part of the race, since both horses and humans are anxious and excited. All the teams take off at once at the sound of the official starter's shout or the wave of a flag. One of the human team members is mounted, while the other is on foot. The horses are stationed in front so when they take off at the start, they won't trample the runners. The runners charge from behind once the horses and riders have taken off.

Usually within about a mile from the start, riders tie their horses to trees and begin running ahead. The runner who began on foot catches up to the tied horse, mounts and speeds off to the next tie spot. Switches are usually made every mile or so, although runners and riders can switch off as often as they like, as long as they make at least six switches throughout the ride.

Along the way, horse and rider teams are stopped for vet checks. Horses who are not deemed to be sound and healthy are pulled from the race.

The three-member team that reaches the finish line first is the winning team. Both horse and rider and runner must cross the finish line before the team is considered finished.

A maximum time is set to complete the ride, and is usually ample enough for teams who prefer to walk rather than run. To win a race, you need to maintain a 10-mile-per-hour pace or more. At this speed, it will take you about 5 or 6 hours to finish a 25-mile race.

PREPARATION

The greatest challenge in Ride-and-Tie is definitely for the human components of the team. Unlike other competitive distance events, Ride-and-Tie requires the humans to do much of the legwork for this sport. That means your horse isn't the only one who needs to be in condition—you need to be in very good shape too.

Conditioning your horse for Ride-and-Tie is similar to conditioning him for other competitive distance events, and even just long trail rides. The primary difference with Ride-and-Tie is that your horse will be asked to start and stop often along the trail. He will also have to stand for mounting and dismounting, and will have to stand tied to a tree or other object along the trail while other horses and riders go galloping past him.

Beyond the usual conditioning for trail riding (see chapter 8 for details), your horse needs experience with group rides and various situations where other horses are present on the trail. You should also ask friends to help you train your horse to stand tied while other horses gallop past. Start by holding your horse from the ground yourself while other riders pass first at a walk and eventually at greater speeds. When your horse gets to the point where he doesn't freak out when other horses go past at a canter or gallop, he is ready for the "tying" part of the Ride-and-Tie experience.

You should also work on your horse to make sure he is easy to mount and dismount. Make certain he knows he must stand still when you get on. If you can't get him to stand still in a quiet setting as you mount, imagine what it will be like trying to get on when other horses are flying by. (Many veteran Ride-and-Tie riders do a "flying exchange," mounting while the horse is in motion. This isn't recommended for novices.)

Ride-and-Tie utilizes a three-member team: two humans and a horse.

Most horses are easy to dismount, although getting them to stop at a Ride-and-Tie event can be challenging if other horses are passing them at considerable speed. Make sure your horse stops when you ask him to before you attempt to take him to a Ride-and-Tie event.

Your horse is not the only one who needs preparation before one of the races. Both you and your human partner must be in good physical condition since you'll be running anywhere from 25 to 40 miles in one day. (Some novice events are only 10 miles, but that is still a substantial amount of trail to cover.) Some Ride-and-Tie teams are made up of one member who is a better runner than the other, and that person does most of the running. Some teams have one member who is a very good rider, while the other member barely knows how to ride at all. In those situations, the better rider spends most of the time on the horse's back while the other member does most of the footwork.

Because Ride-and-Tie races can be done at hiking speed and don't require you to actually run, you don't need to be ready for the New York City Marathon in order to participate. But you definitely need to be in good shape and be walking or jogging on a regular basis before you even attempt one of these competitions.

If Ride-and-Tie sounds like the sport for you and your horse, keep in mind you will need a human partner to compete alongside with you. If you don't know anyone to pair up with, the Ride-and-Tie Association can match you up with someone looking for a partner. If you are horseless, you can also participate in Ride-and-Tie since there are people who own a horse but don't have a partner to compete with.

The Ride-and-Tie Association also has a mentor program to help you get started in the sport. By contacting the association (see appendix B), you can find someone in your area who will guide you through your first few races.

THE REWARDS

Ride-and-Tie is an incredibly exciting sport that most competitors find exhilarating. Most horses seem to like the competition too, and build strong bonds with their human partners.

Winners at Ride-and-Tie events accumulate points toward a year-end championship. At the World Championship, everyone who completes the course gets a custom belt buckle. Winners also receive prizes like saddles and other goodies, many with considerable cash values. At local races, completion is usually recognized by a T-shirt.

Probably the greatest benefit of Ride-and-Tie is that you have fun while getting yourself in terrific shape. And since a fit rider is easier for a horse to carry, your equine buddy will appreciate you for all the work.

Happy trails!

Part V

APPENDIXES

Appendix A

GLOSSARY

abscess   A swollen pocket containing pus.

acre   A unit of land measuring 4,840 square yards.

action   The way a horse moves at the various gaits.

aged   A horse over the age of 9 years.

aids   Tools used by the rider to cue the horse.

azoturia   Painful cramping of the large muscle mass occurring after strenuous exercise.

bale   A measurement of hay.

balk   Refusal to move forward.

Banamine   Brand-name for the painkiller flunixin, used by veterinarians.

barn-sour   A horse who refuses to leave the stable or barn, or wants to return to the barn, when being ridden.

base narrow   Leg conformation where the top of the legs have a greater distance than the bottom.

behind the bit   An avoidance move where the horse places the head down to evade contact with the bit.

Betadine   A patented antiseptic scrub.

bombproof   A horse who rarely spooks.

bot fly   An insect that lays its eggs on the legs of horses, where they are ingested to begin a parasitic life cycle in the stomach.

brand   An identifying mark made on a horse either by burning the skin and removing the hair, or by using a freezing method that removes pigment from the coat.

bran mash   A mixture of wheat bran, molasses, and water.

breast collar   Piece of equipment that attaches to the front of the saddle and goes across the front of the horse's chest; designed to keep the saddle from slipping back when the horse goes uphill.

breeder   A person who breeds purebred horses as a hobby or for a living.

broken wind   A horse suffering from the respiratory condition known as heaves is sometimes said to have a broken wind.

broodmare   A female horse used strictly for breeding.

buck   When a horse jumps upward with an arched back, head down, forelegs stiffened, and hind legs, and sometimes forelegs, lifting off the ground.

bucked knee   Bending forward of the knee when the horse is standing still; conformational fault.

bute   See *phenylbutazone.*

by   Fathered by.

canter   English discipline term for a three-beat gait; same as a lope or slow gallop.

capped elbow   Scarring or swelling of the point of the elbow.

capped hock   Scarring or swelling of the point of the hock.

cast   When a horse rolls against a wall or fence and becomes lodged there, requiring assistance to get up.

cattle guard   A metal or painted grid on a road or gateway that stops cattle from crossing.

club foot   Abnormally upright hoof.

Coggins test   Blood test for equine infectious anemia.

cold-blooded   A heavy draft horse.

colt   An intact male horse under the age of 3 years.

conformation   The way a horse's body is put together.

cow hocked   Conformational fault where hocks are closer together than pasterns.

cribbing   Neurotic habit where the horse grasps an object with his teeth and sucks air into his belly.

crupper Piece of equipment that goes under the horse's tail and attaches to the back of the saddle; designed to keep the saddle from sliding forward when the horse goes downhill.

dam The mother of a horse.

dapples Round, self-colored markings on a horse's coat.

DMSO Dimethylsulfoxide; used in veterinary medicine as an anti-inflammatory agent.

D.V.M. Doctor of Veterinary Medicine.

easy keeper A horse who is easy to keep at the proper weight.

electrolytes Compounds that are essential for normal body functions; replaces essential elements lost during periods of heavy exercise.

enteroliths A stone formation in the intestine.

equitation The position of a rider's body, including hands, legs, back, and seat.

euthanasia Humane destruction of an animal with use of injected drugs.

filly A female horse under the age of 3 years.

fistulous withers Infection of the withers often caused by a poor-fitting saddle.

flake A measurement of hay; a bale of hay contains 10 flakes.

flexion test A test of soundness, performed by flexing the leg for one minute before trotting the horse.

foal A baby horse still at its mother's side.

founder Condition of the foot caused by rotation of coffin bone; also known as laminitis.

founder rings Rings in the hoof wall caused by laminitis.

gaited horse A horse who possesses a lateral gait, usually in lieu of the trot.

gallop A three-beat gait; the fastest speed a horse can go.

gelding A castrated male horse.

girth The strap that holds the saddle to the horse.

grain Any mixture of high-energy feed; usually consists of oats and other grains.

green   A horse who has little training and experience carrying a rider.

gut sounds   The noises that can be heard in a horse's abdomen.

hackamore   Bitless bridle that controls the horse through pressure on the nose, poll, and chin.

hand   A unit of measure used to measure the height of a horse.

hard keeper   A horse who is difficult to keep at the proper weight.

hay   General term for any grass or legume harvested and prepared as livestock feed.

head bumper   A pad placed on top of the horse's head to protect him during travel.

heat stroke   Collapse of the circulatory system caused by high temperature environment, often fatal.

hobbles   Cuffs that attach to the horse's front legs to minimize movement; used instead of tying or confining horse.

hoof tester   A device used to measure the sensitivity of a horse's hoof.

horseperson   Term for a man, woman, or child who has devoted considerable time and energy to learning about and being around horses.

horse trainer   One who trains horses to carry a rider.

hotwalker   A mechanical merry-go-round type of device where horses can be attached for exercise; most hotwalkers can accommodate four horses at a time.

in season   Term for a mare who is in estrus, or heat.

jog   A slow trot.

lead, left or right   Term for the foreleg that strikes the ground first at the canter.

legumes   Plants that have seed pods.

lipomas   Fat tumor, always benign.

lope   Western discipline term for a three-beat gait; same as canter or slow gallop.

mare   A female horse over the age of 3 years.

martingale   A leather device designed to control the position of the horse's head.

moonblindness   Equine recurrent uveitis (ERU), a disease affecting the eyes.

mule   The sterile offspring of a female horse and a male donkey.

nerve block   An injection given in the leg to numb an area.

pacing   A neurotic habit where a horse paces repeatedly back and forth in the stall.

paddock   A large enclosure.

pedigree   A written document detailing a horse's ancestry.

phenylbutazone   An aspirin-like veterinary medication use for pain relief and reduction of inflammation and swelling; also known as bute.

pony   A small horse, usually under 14.2 hands in height.

proud flesh   Excess, raw, granulation tissue emanating from a healing wound.

purebred   A breed of horse that produces consistent physical characteristics through generations of unmixed origin.

"put down"   See *euthanasia.*

riding instructor   One who teaches people how to ride.

ringbone   Degenerative joint disease of the leg; arthritis.

rogue   A poor-tempered horse.

rolling   When a horse lays down on his side and rocks to and fro on his back.

saddle rack   A stand designed to support a saddle when not in use.

saddle sore   An open wound on the horse's back caused by a poor-fitting saddle.

shipping fever   Respiratory illness that commonly arises when a horse spends considerable time in a trailer or shipping container.

shy   To walk past an object in a nervous manner.

sire   The father of a horse.

slicker   A waterproof coat worn when riding in the rain.

soundness   A horse's ability to move freely without pain.

splints   Bony enlargements on the cannon or splint bones, usually of the front legs; sometimes cause swelling, heat, and lameness.

spooky   A horse who is prone to fearful reactions.

stallion   An intact male horse over the age of 3 years.

stud book   A listing of breeding animals maintained by a registration organization.

tendon   Cord of dense material that attaches bone to muscle in the horse's leg.

thrush   Fungal disease of the foot.

tie-down   Western term for a standing martingale, a leather device used to control the position of the horse's head while riding.

trailhead   The point at which a trail starts; usually marked.

trot   A two-beat gait.

tying up   Another term for azoturia.

udder   The mare's mammary gland.

uveitis   Inflammation of the interior of the eye (see *moonblindness*).

V.M.D.   Veterinary Medical Doctor.

weanling   A male or female horse who has been weaned from the mother but has not yet reached 1 year of age.

weaving   A neurotic habit where the horse repeatedly shifts his weight from one front foot to the other.

wind sucking   A neurotic habit where the horse arches his neck and sucks air into his belly.

yearling   A male or female horse in its first year.

Appendix B

RESOURCES

Trail Riding Products

A&M Farms
www.madtack.net

Albette Saddles & Tack
www.buyabetta.com

Alternate Solutions Tack Store
www.vtc.net/~ags

Auburn Tack and Feed
www.saddleshop.net

Bit of Heaven Tack Shop
www.bohtack.com

Bits And Bridles
www.bitsandbridles.com

Canadian Trail House
www.biothanetack.com

Chicks Discount Saddlery
www.chicksaddlery.com

Cool Medics
www.coolmedics.com

Cool Tack
www.cooltack.com

Custom Iron Workers
www.ciwtrailers.com

Endurance Tack
www.hought.com/endthg.html

Equine Performance Products
www.equineperformanceproducts.com

Have Saddle Will Travel
www.havesaddlewilltravel.com

Jeffers Equine
www.jeffersequine.com

Long Riders Gear
www.longridersgear.com

Mahtowa Meadows
wwwarmbloods.com/meadows/page.php?page=crusader

Running Bear Farm
www.runningbear.com

Sportack
www.sportack.com

Stateline Tack
www.statelinetack.com

Valley Vet
www.valleyvet.com

Trail Riding Organizations and Programs

Note: Some of the following organizations list only a phone number; others can be contacted only through a website. Where a physical address exists, it has been included.

American Endurance Ride Conference (AERC)
P.O. Box 6027
Auburn, CA 95604
(866) 271-AERC
www.aerc.org

American Paint Horse Association Trail Rides
P.O. Box 961023
Fort Worth, TX 76161-0023
(817) 834-APHA
www.apha.com/trailrides

American Quarter Horse Association (AQHA) Trail Ride Program
P.O. Box 200
Amarillo, TX 79168
(806) 376-4811
www.aqha.com/recreation/ride

American Trail Horse Association
P.O. Box 293
Cortland, IL 60178
(877) 266-1678
www.trailhorse.com

American Trails
P.O. Box 491797
Redding, CA 96049-1797
(530) 547-2060
www.americantrails.org

Appaloosa Horse Club
720 West Pullman Road
Moscow, ID 83843
(208) 882-5578
www.appaloosa.com

Arabian Trail Riders Association
www.trailriders.org

Atlantic Canada Trail Riders Association
RR # 1 Box 11
Scotch Village, NS
Canada B0N 2G0
www.geocities.com/actrasite/trailride.htm

Backcountry Horsemen of America
P.O. Box 1367
Graham, WA 98338
www.backcountryhorse.com

Backcountry Horsemen of California, Inc.
P.O. Box 40007
Bakersfield, CA 93384-0007
(888) 302-BCHC
www.bchc.com/contact.html

British Columbia Trail Riders Association
(604) 557-9672

California State Horsemen's Association
264 Clovis Ave., #109
Clovis, CA 93612
(559) 325-1055
www.californiastatehorsemen.com/envirohorse.htm

Chattanooga (Tennessee) Trail Horse Association
P.O. Box 211
Dahlonega, GA 30533
www.ride-ctha.org/pages/960095/index.htm

Eastern Competitive Trail Ride Association
P.O. Box 76
Clarksville, NY 12041
www.ectra.org

Equestrian Land Conservation Resource
126B N. Main Street
P.O. Box 423
Elizabeth, IL 61028-0423
(815) 858-3501
www.elcr.org

Equestrian Trails, Inc.
13741 Foothill Blvd., #100
Sylmar, CA 91342
(818) 362-6819
www.etinational.com

Indiana Trail Riders Association
P.O. Box 185
Farmland, IN 47340
www.intrailriders.org

The Long Riders Guild
www.thelongridersguild.com

Mesa Verde Back Country Horsemen
P.O. Box 812
Cortez, CO 81321
www.mesaverdehorsemen.com

Minnesota Trail Riders
P.O. Box 984
Burnsville, MN 55337-0984
www.mntrailriders.com

National Trail Ride Association
P.O. Box 379
Big Sandy, TN 38221
(731) 593-5139
www.nationaltrailride.com

North American Trail Ride Conference (NATRC)
P.O. Box 224
Sedalia, CO 80135
(303) 688-1677
www.natrc.org

Ontario (Canada) Competitive Trail Riding Association
www.octra.on.ca

Riverside (California) Recreational Trails
P.O. Box 8022
Riverside, CA 92515
www.rrtrails.coms

Southeastern Association of Trail Riders (SEAT)
P.O. Box 15042
Chesapeake, VA 23320
www.seat-va.org

Texas Equestrian Trail Riders Association
P.O. Box 236
Placedo,TX 77977
www.tetratrails.com

Western States Trail Federation
1216-C High Street
Auburn, CA 95603
(530) 823-7282
www.foothill.net/tevis

Competitive Distance Riding Organizations

Appaloosa Distance Ride Association (ApDRA)
916 S. Madison Street, Lot 11
Waupun, WI 53963
dabf.itgo.com

Arabian Horse Distance Riding Association (AHDRA)
16128 2500 E. Street
Princeton, IL 61356
(815) 875-4776
www.ahdra.org

Backcountry Horsemen of Washington
110 W. 6th Avenue, PMB 393
Ellensburg, WA 98926
www.bchw.org

British Columbia Competitive Trail Riders Association
www.bcctra.ca

Distance Appaloosa Breeders Futurity
4228 S. 1100 W.
Modoc, IN 47358
(765) 853-6113
dabf.itgo.com

Eastern Competitive Trail Ride Association
www.ectra.org

Florida Trail Riders
www.flahorse.com

Gold Country Endurance Riders
P.O. Box 3412
Auburn, CA 95604
(916) 885-2552
www.gcer.org

Great Lakes Distance Riding Association
5130 Okemos Road
East Lansing, MI 48823
(517) 349-5344
www.geocities.com/RodeoDrive/5143

National Association of Competitive Mounted Orienteering
503 171st Avenue, SE
Tenino, WA 98589
(206) 847-8046
www.nhdid.com/nacmo

Nevada All State Trail Riders
c/o Connie Creech
P.O. Box 18757
Reno, NV 89511
(702) 882-6591
www.nastr.org

New Jersey Trail Ride Association
www.members.tripod.com/njtra2

Ohio Arabian and All-Breed Trail Society
6288 Eagles Lake Drive
Cincinnati, OH 45248
(513) 574-4898
www.oaats.org

Old Dominion Endurance Rides, Inc.
140 Spring Street
Herndon VA 20170
(703) 435-1935
www.olddominionrides.org

Ontario Competitive Trail Riding Association
www.octra.on.ca

Pacific Northwest Endurance Rides, Inc.
P.O. Box 1245
Oregon City, OR 97045
www.endurance.net/organizations/PNER

Quicksilver Endurance Riders, Inc.
P.O. Box 71
New Almaden, CA 95042
www.homestead.com/qsendurance/files

The Ride and Tie Association
987 Crows Nest Lane
El Cajon, CA 92019
(619) 445-4485
www.rideandtie.org

South Eastern Distance Riders Association
www.distanceriding.com/sedra.htm

Southern Oregon Horse Activities
P.O. Box 1414
Grants Pass, OR 97528
www.sohahorses.org

Southwest Idaho Trail & Distance Riders
P. O. Box 726
Eagle, Idaho 83616
(208) 938-5490
home.att.net/~switdr/

Texas Arabian Distance Riders Association
P.O. Box 532
Wortham, TX 76693
www.tadra.org (USA)

Upper Midwest Endurance & Competitive Riders Association
455 Moore Heights
Dubuque, IA 52001
(319) 583-0194
www.umecra.com

Books of Interest to Trail Riders

Barnett, Carellen. *Trial Riding Western Montana*. Guilford, CT: Falcon Press Publishing, 2001.

Burger, Sandra. *Horse Owner's Field Guide to Toxic Plants*. Emmaus, PA: Breakthrough, 1996.

Davis, Frances W. *Horse Packing in Pictures* (Howell equestrian library). New York: Howell Book House, 1991.

Ehringer, Gavin. *Truckin' & Trailerin'*. Colorado Springs: Western Horseman, 2004.

Equine Research. *Horse Conformation*. Guilford, CT: Lyons Press, 1999.

Equine Travelers of America, Nationwide Overnight Stabling Guide. Arkansas City, KS: Equine Travelers of America, 2004.

Frank, Curtis. *Re-Riding History: Horseback Over the Sante Fe Trail*. Santa Fe: Sunstone Press, 1997.

Fuller, Margaret. *Trails of Western Idaho from Sun Valley to Hell's Canyon*. Edmonds, WA: Signpost Books, 1992.

Goldman, Mary Elizabeth Sue, and Remy Renfrow. *A Trail Rider's Guide to Texas*. Blue Ridge Summit, PA: Republic of Texas Press, 1992.

Hancock, Jan. *Horse Trails in Arizona*. Phoenix: Golden West Publishers, 1998.

Hatley, George. *Horse Camping*. Moscow, ID: Appaloosa Museum, 1992.

Holden, Martha. *Horseback Riding Trails of North Carolina*. Winston-Salem: John F. Blair, Publisher, 1999.

Hollander, Lewis E., and Patricia Ingram. *Endurance Riding—From Beginning to Winning*. Redmond, OR: Green Mansions, 1989.

Kals, W. S. *Land Navigation Handbook: The Sierra Club Guide to Map and Compass*. San Francisco: Sierra Club Books, 1983.

Loving, Nancy S., DVM. *Go the Distance*. North Pomfret, VT: Trafalgar Square Publishing, 1997.

Mouchet, Paulette. *Horseback Riding Trails of Southern California*, Vols. I & II. Fremont, CA: Two Horse Enterprises, 2003.

Pavia, Audrey. *Horses for Dummies*. New York: John Wiley & Sons, Inc., 1999.

Pelicano, Rich. *Bombproof Your Horse*. North Pomfret, VT: Trafalgar Square Publishing, 2004.

Rails-to-Trails Conservancy. *1,000 Great Rail-Trails: A Comprehensive Directory*. Guilford, CT: Globe Pequot Press, 2001.

Vanderhoof, Ruth. *Trail Riding Oregon*. Tualatin, OR: Horsin Around Oregon, 1988.

Wolcott, John. *The Backcountry Horseman's Guide to Washington*. Guilford, CT: Falcon Press Publishing, 1995.

Trail Riding Magazines

Trail Blazer
4241 North Covina Circle
Prescott Valley, AZ 86314
(866) 818-4146
www.horsetrails.com/about.html

Trail Rider Magazine
730 Front Street
Louisville, CO 80027
(303) 661-9282
www.trailridermagazine.com

Appendix C

TRAIL RIDING OPPORTUNITIES

Vacation Ranches

The following horseback riding companies offer vacation ranch experiences that include formal riding instruction:

Cross Country International Equestrian Vacations
P.O. Box 1170
Millbrook, NY 12545
(800) 828-8768
www.equestrianvacations.com

Worldwide Horseback Riding Adventures
P.O. Box 807
10 Stalnaker Street
Dubois, WY 82513
(800) 545-0019
www.ridingtours.com

Exotic Rides

The following horseback riding companies offer trail riding experiences in exotic locales:

Boojum Expeditions
14543 Kelly Canyon
Bozeman, MT 59715
(800) 287-0125
www.boojum.com

Cross Country International Equestrian Vacations
P.O. Box 1170
Millbrook, NY 12545
(800) 828-8768
www.equestrianvacations.com

Worldwide Horseback Riding Adventures
P.O. Box 807
10 Stalnaker Street
Dubois, WY 82513
(800) 545-0019
www.ridingtours.com

Trail Riding Trainers

The following organizations certify horseback riding trainers, including those who provide lessons on the trail:

American Association for Horsemanship Safety
P.O. Box 39
Fentress, TX 78622
(512) 488-2220
www.horsemanshipsafety.com

American Riding Instructors Association
28801 Trenton Court
Bonita Springs, FL 34134-3337
(239) 948-3232
www.riding-instructor.com

Certified Horsemanship Association (CHA)
5318 Old Bullard Road
Tyler, TX 75703
(800) 399-0138
www.cha-ahse.org

ILLUSTRATION CREDITS

Photo by Karen Keb Acevedo: 129

Charles Barieau/Courtesy of the AERC: 190

Photo by Cathy Blakesley: 18

Joni Burns: 43 (bottom)

Photo by Candace Brown: 102

Photo by Cristy Cumberworth: 176, 181

Photo by Carrie Garufis: 179

Shawn Hamilton/CLIX: 188

Photo by Cynthia Hunter/Courtesy of Featherlite Trailers: 152

Photo by Audrey Pavia: 10, 22, 24, 27, 46, 50, 58, 59, 60, 67, 74, 80, 86, 96, 104, 125, 133, 135, 145, 147, 150, 153, 165, 184

Photo by Corey Rich: 192

Photo by Kirk Schlea: 71

Photo by Paula da Silva: 171

Pam Tanzey: 6, 8, 16, 34, 43 (top left, top right)

Photo by Janine Wilder: 173

INDEX

personality traits
  horses, 9–11
  trail horses, 27–28
Pilates, rider conditioning, 118
poisonous plants, wilderness riding, 139–140
politeness, multi-use trail etiquette, 134
portable corrals
  horse camping, 172
  purchasing, 48
portable water tanks, purchasing considerations, 48
posting, described, 17
pouches, checking before embarking on a trail ride, 115
prepurchase exam, horse buying element, 29, 35–37
preventative care. *See also* health
  deworming, 68, 69–70
  equine encephalomyelitis, 69, 71
  exercise importance, 73–74
  floating, 73
  hoof care, 68
  infectious diseases, 68–69
  influenza, 69
  inoculations, 68
  intestinal parasites, 69–70
  locating a veterinarian, 66–68
  parasites, 69–71
  rhinopneumonitis, 69
  shoeing, 71–72
  tetanus, 69
  tooth care, 68, 73
  vaccines, 68–69
  West Nile disease, 68–69, 71
prey animal, personality trait, 9–10
private boarding stables, selection guidelines, 56–58
probiotics, dietary supplement, 62
professionalism, boarding stable consideration, 57
professionals, spooked horse handling, 101
proximity to trails, camp site consideration, 174

publications
  instructor resource, 20
  trail resource, 150
pulse rate, trail conditioning measurement, 110–111
puncture wounds, first aid treatment, 88

Quarter Horse, trailer size, 155
questions
  horse buying process, 30–31
  instructor evaluation, 21

ramp trailers
  pros/cons, 113
  versus step-up trailers, 154
red ribbon, group riding etiquette, 130
reins, trail riding considerations, 44–45
relaxed attitude, spooked horse handling, 99
removable partitions, trailer, 159
rentals, advantages/disadvantages, 13–14
reservations, horse camp element, 170
resources
  books of interest, 211–212
  competitive distance riding organizations, 208–210
  magazines, 212
  trail riding organizations/programs, 204–208
  trail riding products, 203–204
  trails, 148–150
respiration, trail conditioning measurement, 110–111
respiratory system, heaves (chronic obstructive pulmonary disease), 82–83
responsiveness, trail horses quality, 28
rewards, spooked horse handling, 100
rhinopneumonitis, preventative care element, 69
Ride-and-Tie Association, 189–193
Ride-and-Tie, horse/rider competition, 189–193